WORLD WAR II
TRIVIA BOOK

Peter Darman

**BARNES
&NOBLE**

NEW YORK

Editorial and Design
The Brown Reference Group plc
8 Chapel Place
Rivington Street
London
EC2A 3DQ

Editor: Alan Marshall
Designer: Colin Woodman
Production Director: Alastair Gourlay

Picture credits
Robert Hunt Library: front cover

ISBN-13: 978-0-7607-9397-8
ISBN-10: 0-7607-9397-2

Printed and bound in the United Kingdom

1 3 5 7 9 10 8 6 4 2

Front cover photograph: (from left to right) Winston Churchill, Franklin
D. Roosevelt, and Joseph Stalin at the Yalta Conference in February 1945.

CONTENTS

ABOUT THIS BOOK

The *World War II Trivia Book* presents a wealth of information about mankind's most destructive conflict in the form of hundreds of questions and answers, revealing quotations, and fascinating "did-you-know?" boxes. Question topics cover strategy, tactics, battles, uniforms, weapons, espionage, equipment, and the individuals who led armies and nations between 1939 and 1945, such as Hitler, Roosevelt, Stalin, Patton, and Eisenhower. This book is a whole new way to learn about World War II—or to test what you already know about the conflict.

ROAD
TO
WAR

In the 1920s and 1930s, economic depressions in Europe created the conditions in which extremist politics could flourish. The people of Germany elected Adolf Hitler and the Nazi Party. while, in the Far East, Imperial Japan's territorial ambitions brought it into conflict with the United States.

Q What effect did the 1919 Treaty of Versailles have on Germany?

A At the end of World War I Germany was in dire straits: her population was near starvation and devoid of hope, and her army and navy were in disarray. The Treaty of Versailles of June 1919 added to Germany's woes as it removed her overseas possessions, implemented the occupation of part of the Rhineland (to ensure she complied with provisions of the treaty), and imposed huge reparations for the damage inflicted on France and other countries.

Q Was Germany in a position to pay reparations?

A No. Germany was almost bankrupt, which meant it was extremely unlikely that she would be able to pay—even less so when the world slump of 1921 added to her woes.

> **"** THE GODDESS OF THE ETERNAL TRIBUNAL
> OF HISTORY WILL TEAR APART
> THE SENTENCE OF THE COURT
> ADOLF HITLER AT HIS TRIAL
> FOLLOWING THE MUNICH PUTSCH **"**

Q Why did France occupy the Ruhr in 1923?

A In 1922 Germany defaulted on reparations payments for the second year running. In retaliation, France, showing amazing short-sightedness, occupied the Ruhr Valley, the center of German industry. This not only reduced the already slim chances of Germany paying any reparations, but also increased hostility between the two countries. The stoppage of the Ruhr industry had a calamitous effect on the mark, which plummeted in value. Overnight savings were wiped out, leaving millions penniless and destitute; their careers, hopes, and finances totally destroyed.

DID YOU KNOW

AT THE AGE OF NINE ADOLF HITLER BECAME A CHOIRBOY IN THE CATHOLIC CHURCH AT LAMBACH, AND CLAIMED IN LATER YEARS THAT HIS GREAT VOCAL POWER HAD DEVELOPED WHILE SINGING HYMNS. HE WAS AN AVERAGE, LAZY, AND REBELLIOUS STUDENT, WITH A TALENT FOR DRAWING. THIS TALENT DECIDED HIM ON A CAREER IN ART. HIS ORATORICAL REHEARSALS WERE NOT OVERLOOKED, THOUGH. AUGUST KUBIZEK, HIS CLOSE BOYHOOD FRIEND, RECALLED YOUNG ADOLF PRACTISING ELOCUTION IN AN OPEN FIELD. FROM HIS SCHOOL DAYS HITLER WAS A FANATICAL GERMAN NATIONALIST WITH A RANCOROUS HATRED OF OTHERS, MOSTLY SLAVIC RACES WHICH MADE UP THE AUSTRO-HUNGARIAN EMPIRE.

Q What were *Freikorps*?

A The *Freikorps* were groups of right-wing ex-soldiers that sprang up all over Germany following the end of World War I. Essentially, gangs of brutalized men whose allegiance was to their commanders only, the *Freikorps* fought for the elimination of all "traitors to the Fatherland."

7

Q What was the NSDAP?

A *National Sozialistische Deutsche Arbeiter Partei* (National Socialist German Workers' Party—NSDAP), the Nazi Party led by Adolf Hitler.

Q Why was the city of Danzig a potential flashpoint between Germany and Poland in the interwar years?

A Danzig was in theory a "free city" administered by the League of Nations organization, but in reality the Nazis had gained control of the city in 1934 and did largely what they liked. Hitler ranted that it and the strip of land that divided Germany and East Prussia should be returned to the Reich.

Q What was the "Polish Corridor"?

A Recreated after World War I, Poland had been given access to the sea via a corridor of land which reached the Baltic at Danzig. It had been formerly German territory, and Hitler was determined it would be again. Hitler ranted that Danzig and the strip of land that divided Germany and East Prussia should be returned to the Reich. Few people in the West knew or cared what the "Polish Corridor" was, but in March 1939 Britain and France took the fateful step of pledging themselves to the defense of Poland, which neither of them was in a military position to do.

Q What river flowed into the sea at Danzig?

A The Vistula.

> " TODAY WE ARE 600 STRONG, BUT IN SIX
> YEARS' TIME THERE WILL BE
> 600,000 OF US "
> JOSEF GOEBBELS, SPEAKING TO NAZIS IN BERLIN, 1927

Q On which side did Japan fight in World War I?

A Japan had fought on the side of the Allies against Germany's Pacific colonies during the war, and after 1918 was rewarded with territorial acquisitions throughout the Pacific.

Q Why was Japan aggrieved after World War I?

A Although Japan had gained some Pacific colonies, she was forced to relinquish Chinese regions conquered during the 1904–05 Russo-Japanese War. Worse, insult was added to injury in 1922 when the Washington Naval Treaty limited the size of the Japanese Navy to below that of the U.S. and British fleets.

DID YOU KNOW

IN JAPAN BEFORE WORLD WAR II ALMOST EVERY VITAL DOMESTIC AND
INDUSTRIAL PRODUCT, INCLUDING FOOD, RUBBER, AND MOST METALS, HAD
TO BE IMPORTED, AND THE UNITED STATES SUPPLIED AROUND 60 PERCENT
OF JAPANESE OIL. THE DEPENDENCE ON THE OUTSIDE WORLD RUBBED SALT
INTO THE JAPANESE WOUND, AND MANY FELT THAT JAPAN HAD BEEN
RELEGATED TO A SECOND-CLASS NATION WITHIN A GEOGRAPHICAL AREA IN
WHICH IT SHOULD HAVE BEEN DOMINANT. THE JAPANESE WERE PARTICU-
LARLY AGGRIEVED BY THE FACT THAT WHAT THEY FELT WAS THEIR NATURAL
SPHERE OF INFLUENCE FROM WHICH THEY COULD OBTAIN THE RAW
MATERIALS TO RUN A MODERN ECONOMY WAS LARGELY OCCUPIED BY
COLONIAL POWERS: THE BRITISH IN MALAYA, THE FRENCH IN INDOCHINA,
THE U.S. IN THE PHILIPPINES, AND ABOVE ALL THE DUTCH IN THE OIL-
RICH REGION OF THE DUTCH EAST INDIES—WHAT IS NOW INDONESIA.

Q Why did Japan invade China in 1931?

A First, China was the one big area where there was no colonial
power on the Asian mainland. Second, Manchuria, a northern
province semi-independent of China, occupied in 1931, was rich in
mineral resources.

Q Who were the Brownshirts?

A Their proper title was *Sturmabteilung* (Storm Detachment), or SA.
They were tough, unemployed ex-soldiers who frequented Munich
beer halls such as the Torbräukeller near the Isar Gate. They were
recruited by Ernst Röhm to protect Nazi speakers at public meetings. The
Brownshirts, as they became known, were party uniformed supporters
who wore brown shirts (hence their nickname) and who acted as body-
guards. They were to grow in number during the 1920s and early 1930s,
acting under Röhm's orders rather than Hitler's.

Q **In Germany, who were the "November Criminals"?**

A A term used by the Nazis and others on the right in the interwar years for those individuals who had signed the Treaty of Versailles, plus the communists, Jews, profiteers, and social democrats who had betrayed the army during World War I—the "stab-in-the-back" theory— and who still worked for Germany's downfall. These ideas were very popular with ex-soldiers, serving soldiers and the vast reservoir of anti-Semitism and antidemocratic resentment that existed in Germany during the interwar period.

Q **What was the Reichswehr?**

A The 100,000-man German Army of the Weimar Republic.

" MANKIND HAS GROWN STRONG THROUGH STRUGGLES AND WILL ONLY PERISH THROUGH PEACE "
ADOLF HITLER, *MEIN KAMPF*

Q **Why did Japanese expansion and tales of her atrocities infuri-ate many in the West in the 1930s?**

A The United States was particularly aggrieved by Japan's actions. It had long-standing missionary and trade connections with China, and close associations with the Nationalist leader Chiang Kai-shek. China was also militarily important to the U.S. and European powers, as "extra-territoriality" agreements permitted the Western nations to establish sovereign commercial settlements on Chinese territory with the accompanying ability to station military units.

DID YOU KNOW

Appeasement has, since the end of World War II, been equated with cowardice and is held in contempt. In the 1930s, however, appeasement as practised by British Prime Minister Neville Chamberlain and French leaders such as Edouard Daladier encapsulated reasonable steps that might be taken to prevent Hitler taking the law into his own hands. It was also the manifestation of a very real desire to avoid another general European war. Appeasement had its roots in the growing feeling in the early 1930s in Britain and France that the terms of the Versailles Treaty had been harsh on Germany. Seen in this light, Hitler's demands for a rearmed Germany and the restoration of "German" territories appeared reasonable. Thus, by assenting to these essentially "just" demands, Chamberlain believed he could lay the foundations for a lasting European peace. Unfortunately, appeasement relied on the goodwill of both parties to be a success. Thus, after the Munich Conference in September 1938, Chamberlain and Daladier agreed to Hitler's demands for the incorporation into the Third Reich of the German-speaking Czech Sudetenland. For his part, Hitler had expected a confrontation over the issue, and Britain and France's failure to stand up to him encouraged more brinkmanship. He occupied the rest of Czechoslovakia in March 1939, signaling de facto the end of appeasement as a workable policy.

11

Q Who became the Japanese prime minister in 1940?

A Prince Konoye.

Q Who were his minister of war and foreign minister?

A Hideki Tojo and Yosuke Matsuoka, respectively.

Q The book originally titled *Four and a Half years of Struggle against Lies, Stupidity, and Cowardice* was later called what?

A *Mein Kampf—My Struggle*, the autobiography written by Adolf Hitler while in prison in the 1920s.

Q *Deutschland Erwache* (Germany Awake) was a popular Nazi phrase. What was its origin?

A Hitler borrowed the phrase from one of Richard Wagner's works.

Q Who was the Nazi Party's head of propaganda?

A Josef Goebbels.

> **" IT IS THE LAST TERRITORIAL CLAIM WHICH I HAVE TO MAKE IN EUROPE "**
> ADOLF HITLER, ON THE SUDETENLAND AND CZECHOSLOVAKIA

Q What was *Lebensraum*?

A *Lebensraum* was an integral part of Nazi ideology, which linked the twin concepts of space and race. Hitler believed that Germany needed more farmland to support itself—the need to be self-sufficient. Given the Nazi theory of race, it was only natural that she should take lands from the "inferior" Slav peoples of Poland and the Soviet Union.

Q What was *Weltanschauung*?

A World View, i.e. the Nazi view of the world and its peoples, such as seeing the Aryan-Nordic race as the founder and maintainer of civilization, whereas the Jews were destroyers.

DID YOU KNOW

A FORECASTER IN 1928 WOULD HAVE PREDICTED NOTHING BUT DOOM AND GLOOM FOR THE NSDAP. IN FACT, THE NAZI PARTY WAS IN STEEP DECLINE; IT WAS GOING TO "HELL ON A HANDCART." IT SUFFERED A SIGNIFICANT HUMILIATION IN THE POLLS THAT YEAR. THE POLITICAL SITUATION WAS DIRE, THERE WAS LITTLE TO CELEBRATE, AND HENCE THERE WAS NO PARTY DAY IN 1928 (AT TIMES THE NAZIS GAVE THE APPEARANCE OF BEING SULKY CHILDREN). THE WEIMAR REPUBLIC, WHICH HITLER HAD SO BITTERLY CRITICIZED, WAS DEFEATING THE NAZIS RESOUNDINGLY IN ONE POLITICAL SKIRMISH AFTER ANOTHER. HITLER HAD RAVED ABOUT THE OCCUPATION OF THE RUHR, WHICH HAD BEEN OCCUPIED BY THE FRENCH AND BELGIANS IN JANUARY 1923 FOLLOWING GERMAN FAILURE TO MAKE TIMELY REPARATIONS PAYMENTS; WHEN THE FRENCH WITHDREW, THE WEIMAR GOVERNMENT REAPED THE REWARD. HITLER RANTED ABOUT INFLATION; AGAIN, THE WEIMAR GOVERNMENT STABILIZED THE SITUATION. HITLER'S PROTESTATIONS ON LAW AND ORDER WERE OVERLOOKED; WHEN IT WAS TEMPORARILY RESTORED AGAIN THE WEIMAR GOVERNMENT RECEIVED THE APPLAUSE. POLITICALLY, THE NAZIS WERE FADING FAST. THE WORLD ECONOMIC DEPRESSION OF 1929, HOWEVER, WOULD SEE THEM BECOME A FORCE AGAIN IN GERMAN POLITICS, AS HITLER BLAMED JEWS AND COMMUNISTS FOR GERMANY'S ECONOMIC TROUBLES.

13

Q **What was the Night of the Long Knives?**

A The liquidation of Ernst Röhm and the SA leadership by the SS in June 1934.

Q **Why did German troops occupy the Rhineland in March 1936?**

A The Treaty of Versailles had turned the Rhineland into an unoccupied buffer zone between Germany and France. Hitler had been burning to send troops marching back into the Rhineland, both in order to assert that it was an indivisible part of his new Germany and to show his contempt for the Treaty of Versailles.

Q What was the *Anschluss*?

A The Union between Nazi Germany and Austria in March 1938.

Q Why did Hitler wish to invade Czechoslovakia in 1938?

A After his success in absorbing Austria into Germany in March 1938, Adolf Hitler looked covetously at Czechoslovakia, where about three million people in the Sudeten area were of German origin. It became known in May 1938 that Hitler and his generals were drawing up a plan for the occupation of Czechoslovakia.

> **" A QUARREL IN A FARAWAY COUNTRY BETWEEN PEOPLE OF WHOM WE KNOW NOTHING "**
> NEVILLE CHAMBERLAIN, ON THE CZECH CRISIS, 1938

Q What was the Munich Agreement?

A A four-power conference in September 1938 to settle the dispute between Germany and Czechoslovakia over the Sudetenland.

Q What was the result of the Munich Agreement?

A The German Army was to complete the occupation of the Sudetenland by October 10, 1938, and an international commission would decide the future of other disputed areas. Czechoslovakia was informed by Britain and France that it could either resist Germany alone or submit to the prescribed annexations. The Czechs capitulated.

1939

War broke out when Germany invaded Poland at the beginning of September. The German Blitzkrieg defeated the Poles in three weeks, which stunned the British and French general staffs. No fighting took place in the West, though conflict did erupt between Finland and the USSR.

Q Which German battleship was launched in February 1939?

A The *Bismarck*. The launching ceremony on February 14 was attended by thousands of people, military personalities, government officials, and yard workers. Adolf Hitler delivered the prelaunch speech and the hull was then christened by Frau Dorothea von Loewenfeld, granddaughter of the German chancellor Otto von Bismarck, after whom the ship was named. Moments afterwards, at 13:30 hours, *Bismarck*'s hull slipped into the water.

Q Which firm built this ship?

A Blohm & Voss. The keel was laid down on July 1, 1936, at the Blohm & Voss shipyard facilities in Hamburg.

" THE AIM WILL BE
TO DESTROY POLISH
MILITARY STRENGTH
ADOLF HITLER, APRIL 1939 **"**

Q Which German battleship was launched in April 1939?

A The *Tirpitz*.

Q Which treaty did Adolf Hitler repudiate in April 1939?

A The Anglo-German Naval Treaty, signed in June 1935. This allowed Germany to have one-third of the tonnage of the Royal Navy's surface fleet (the largest in the world at this time) and an equal tonnage of submarines.

DID YOU KNOW

ADOLF HITLER (1889–1945), THE FOUNDER OF NAZI GERMANY, WAS BORN IN AUSTRIA. HIS EXPERIENCES AS A FAILED ARTIST IN VIENNA AND DECORATED SOLDIER IN WORLD WAR I HELPED SHAPE HIS EXTREMIST POLITICAL AMBITIONS, WHICH LED TO THE NAZI PARTY'S FOUNDATION. HE EXPLOITED WEIMAR GERMANY'S POLITICAL TURBULENCE AND SOCIAL UNREST TO MANEUVER HIMSELF INTO POWER IN 1933. VIOLENCE AND INTIMIDATION SECURED HIS POSITION AS DICTATOR. HIS NAZISM FUSED NATIONALISM WITH RACISM AND FORMED POWERFUL EXPANSIONIST AMBITIONS. HITLER ARTICULATED THE DREAM OF CREATING AN EMPIRE BY DESTROYING GERMANY'S SUPPOSED RACIAL AND IDEOLOGICAL ENEMIES. HITLER'S DESIRE TO REALIZE HIS TERRITORIAL AMBITIONS PLUNGED EUROPE INTO DIPLOMATIC CHAOS AND, ULTIMATELY, WAR.

Q Which two territories were occupied by Germany in March 1939?

A Bohemia and Moravia were occupied as "Protectorates," and as a result Czechoslovakia disappeared from the map of Europe.

Q What was the Anti-Comintern Pact?

A An agreement concluded first between Germany and Japan and then between Italy, Germany, and Japan before the war. Ostensibly it was directed against the Communist International (Comintern) but, by implication, specifically against the Bolshevik Soviet Union. The treaties were sought by Adolf Hitler, who at the time was publicly inveighing against Bolshevism and who was interested in Japan's successes in the opening war against China. The Japanese were angered by a Soviet-Chinese nonaggression treaty of August 1936 and by the subsequent sale of Soviet military aircraft and munitions to China. For propaganda purposes, Hitler and Benito Mussolini, Italy's dictator, were able to present themselves as defenders of Western values against the threat of Soviet communism.

THIS MEANS THE
END OF GERMANY
WILHELM CANARIS, ON THE GERMAN ATTACK ON POLAND

Q Who was head of the German SS organization?

A Heinrich Himmler.

Q What was *Blitzkrieg*?

A Lightning War. A term used by the Nazis to describe a military strategy that aimed to inflict a total defeat upon an enemy through a "lightning" offensive. This was achieved by speed, firepower, and mobility. General Heinz Guderian's book *Achtung! Panzer!* (1933) articulated the strategy that aimed to avoid the protracted, costly, and indecisive trench warfare of 1914–1918.

Q What did *Blitzkrieg* rely on for success?

A Tanks, mobile artillery, and aircraft. In the first *Blitzkrieg* against Poland in 1939, German attacks always avoided strong resistance in order to sustain the momentum of an assault, which concentrated upon rear areas to break lines of supply and communication. Once this was achieved, less-mobile forces could annihilate isolated pockets of resistance. The *Blitzkrieg* doctrine not only required new technology, it also needed commanders with the tactical vision and flexibility to fully exploit opportunities and overcome obstacles in order to sustain an attack's momentum.

Q What was Gestapo short for?

A *Geheime Staats Polizei*—Secret State Police. The Gestapo became the political police of Nazi Germany. The Gestapo ruthlessly eliminated opposition to the Nazis within Germany and its occupied territories, and in the war was responsible for the roundup of Jews throughout Europe for deportation to extermination camps.

Q Were there any checks on the Gestapo?

A No. The Gestapo operated without restraints. It had the authority of "preventative arrest," and its actions were not subject to judicial appeal. Thousands of leftists, intellectuals, Jews, trade unionists, political clergy, and homosexuals simply disappeared into concentration camps after being arrested by the Gestapo.

19

DID YOU KNOW

IT IS A LITTLE-KNOWN FACT THAT JOSEF GOEBBELS, GERMAN MINISTER OF PROPAGANDA, WAS OPPOSED TO A EUROPEAN WAR. HE REALIZED THAT GERMANY WOULD BE TAKING UNNECESSARY RISKS AND THAT HER POSITION OF POWER WOULD BE WEAKENED. DESPITE THE VICTORIES OF 1940 GOEBBELS SAID: "WE MUST NOT FOOL OURSELVES. IT WILL BE A LONG AND DIFFICULT WAR. ITS OUTCOME WILL NOT DEPEND ON BOISTEROUS VICTORY PARTIES BUT ON A DETERMINATION TO DO ONE'S DAILY DUTY." HE WAS PROBABLY THE ONLY NAZI LEADER TO CORRECTLY JUDGE THE LENGTH AND GRAVITY OF THE WAR. AS THE WAR TURNED AGAINST GERMANY, GOEBBELS SAW HIMSELF AS A GENERAL, HIS MINISTRY AS A GENERAL STAFF, AND THE PROPAGANDA WAR AS IMPORTANT AS THAT AT THE FRONT. IN BERLIN IN MAY 1945, IN THE BUNKER WITH HITLER, GOEBBELS AND HIS WIFE MAGDA COMMITTED SUICIDE. HE SHOT HIMSELF WHILE SHE TOOK POISON, THEN AN SS ORDERLY GAVE THEM THE COUP DE GRÂCE TO ENSURE THAT THE COUPLE WERE INDEED DEAD.

Q **What were the Nuremberg Laws?**

A Introduced in 1935, the Reich Citizen's Law, and Law for the Protection of German Blood and German Honor, were known thereafter as the Nuremberg laws. The laws defined two degrees of humanity: the *Reichbürger*, the Citizen of Pure German Blood, and the *Staatsangehörige*, the subject of the state, i.e. Jews. Intermarriage between the two groups was strictly forbidden. The lot of Jews living in Germany was getting progressively worse, and many were leaving the country. Some 250 decrees followed these laws, which excluded Jews from economic life.

Q **In Nazi Germany what was a *Gauleiter*?**

A A senior Nazi Party administrative figure in a *Gau* (District). In 1938 there were 32 Nazi Party districts; by 1942 there were 40.

DID YOU KNOW

THE *SS VERFÜGUNGSTRUPPE* (MILITARIZED SS) WAS ORIGINALLY AN ARMED FORCE AT HITLER'S PERSONAL DISPOSAL AND NOT A PART OF THE ARMED FORCES OR OF THE POLICE FORCES ALREADY IN EXISTENCE. THEREFORE, IT WAS ABLE TO BE LEGITIMATELY TRAINED BY THE *REICHSFÜHRER-SS* IN NAZI THEORIES OF RACE AND ALSO TO BE MANNED BY VOLUNTEERS WHO HAD COMPLETED THEIR COMMITMENT IN THE *REICHSARBEITSDIENST*, THE REICH LABOUR SERVICE. IN TIME OF WAR, ELEMENTS OF THE *TOTENKOPFVERBÄNDE* (DEATH'S HEAD UNITS) WOULD REINFORCE THE *SS-VERFÜGUNGSTRUPPE*. IF MOBILIZED, IT WOULD BE USED FIRSTLY BY THE COMMANDER-IN-CHIEF OF THE ARMY UNDER THE JURISDICTION OF THE ARMY, MAKING IT SUBJECT ONLY TO MILITARY LAW AND ORDER, BUT STILL REMAINING A BRANCH OF THE NAZI PARTY AND OWING ITS ALLEGIANCE ULTIMATELY TO THAT ORGANIZATION. SECONDLY, IN THE EVENT OF AN EMERGENCY WITHIN GERMANY, THE *SS-VERFÜGUNGSTRUPPE* WOULD BE UNDER HITLER'S CONTROL THROUGH HIMMLER.

"

HOW CAN A COUNTRY GO TO WAR WITH A POPULATION SO DEAD AGAINST IT?

WILLIAM SHIRER, U.S. JOURNALIST IN GERMANY

"

Q **What was the *Reichstag*?**

A The home of the German parliament in Berlin. After it was burnt down in February 1933, the parliament met in Berlin's Kroll Opera House.

Q **Why was the German Army suspicious of the armed SS?**

A The army had always been suspicious of the SS. As the supposed sole arms bearers of the state, it regarded the creation of armed units within the SS as a betrayal by Hitler. It had been hypothesized that Hitler was playing a double game and allowing the expansion of the *SS-Verfügungstruppe* as a counter to any possible coup by the army. In the early stages of his regime this was extremely unlikely, and Hitler bent over backwards in his efforts to appease the army.

21

Q **What was the Aryan race?**

A A term first used by the linguistic scholar Friedrich Max Müller to describe a group of people who migrated into Europe in ancient history; as used by the Nazis, it applied to the "Nordic" peoples of Europe, who formed the so-called "Aryan race."

Q **What was the treaty signed between Germany and the Soviet Union in August 1939?**

A The Russo-German Nonaggression Treaty.

Q **What was at the heart of the treaty?**

A Neither party would attack the other and mutual spheres of influence were agreed regarding the Baltic states and Poland.

Q **Why was the treaty so important to Hitler?**

A It meant Germany could attack and defeat Poland quickly, thus avoiding a two-front war if Britain and France came to Poland's aid.

" I KNOW I SUDDENLY REALIZED THAT BOTH MY HUSBAND AND BROTHER WOULD BE IN DANGER "
HEIDI BRENDLER, GERMAN HOUSEWIFE, SEPTEMBER 1939

Q **Why was the treaty disastrous for Poland?**

A Notwithstanding the many assurances she received, speedy assistance from the West was most improbable. Powerful enemies (Nazi Germany and the Soviet Union), who had just become reconciled to each other and were hungry to devour her, now hounded her on both sides.

Q **Who was the British ambassador in Berlin in August 1939?**

A Sir Neville Henderson.

DID YOU KNOW

HITLER'S FIRST DIPLOMATIC OVERTURES TO MOSCOW IN AUGUST 1939
WERE NOT SUCCESSFUL. THE SOVIETS WERE STALLING FOR TIME AS THEY
WERE ALREADY NEGOTIATING WITH GREAT BRITAIN AND FRANCE. HITLER,
DESPERATE TO CONCLUDE AN AGREEMENT, DECIDED TO INTERVENE
PERSONALLY AND ON AUGUST 20 SENT A TELEGRAM TO STALIN ASKING HIM
TO RECEIVE HIS FOREIGN MINISTER IMMEDIATELY. ON THE EVENING OF
AUGUST 21, HITLER WAS HANDED A TELEGRAM FROM STALIN. THE
FÜHRER WAS OVERCOME WITH UNCONTROLLABLE EXCITEMENT. "TO THE
CHANCELLOR OF THE GERMAN REICH, A. HITLER. I THANK YOU FOR YOUR
LETTER. I HOPE THAT THE GERMAN-SOVIET NONAGGRESSION PACT WILL
BRING ABOUT AN IMPORTANT IMPROVEMENT IN THE POLITICAL RELATIONS
BETWEEN OUR COUNTRIES. THE PEOPLE OF OUR COUNTRIES NEED TO LIVE
IN PEACE WITH EACH OTHER. THE SOVIET GOVERNMENT HAVE INSTRUCT-
ED ME TO INFORM YOU THAT THEY AGREE TO RECEIVING YOUR HERR VON
RIBBENTROP ON AUGUST 23 IN MOSCOW."

Q Did Hitler believe Britain and France would go to war over Poland?

A No. He believed there would be a Western renunciation of military intervention similar to those that had taken place in 1936, 1938, and again in the spring of 1939.

Q Name the date when Nazi Germany attacked Poland.

A September 1, 1939.

Q What was the Gleiwitz incident?

A A feigned attack on a German radio station on the Polish border by the SS on August 30, which left dead concentration camp inmates dressed in Polish uniforms at the site.

Q What was the German attack plan against Poland?

A Plan White, directed by General Walther von Brauchitsch, aimed to paralyze Poland's 24 divisions by swift encirclement to cut their lines of supply and communication. Poland's ill-prepared forces, lacking both air power and armor, were largely placed well forward on the border to meet the invaders. They were quickly overrun as reinforcements often arrived too late to halt German offensives.

Q Did Nazi Germany declare war on Britain and France?

A No. On September 2 ultimatums were delivered by Britain and France to Germany demanding her immediate withdrawal from Poland. The next day Britain and France declared war on Nazi Germany after their ultimatums expired.

" YOU'VE GOT YOUR DAMNED WAR!
IT'S ALL YOUR DOING
HERMANN GÖRING TO JOACHIM VON RIBBENTROP "

Q Which other countries declared war on Nazi Germany in September 1939?

A Australia, New Zealand, South Africa, and Canada.

Q Who was the prime minister of South Africa in 1939?

A Jan Christian Smuts.

Q Which was the first German army to reach Warsaw?

A The Tenth Army under General Walter von Reichenau, which reached the outskirts of the city on September 8.

Q Which British aircraft carrier was sunk on September 17, 1939?

A HMS *Courageous* was sunk by *U-29*, commanded by *Kapitänleutnant* Otto Schuhart. The aircraft carrier *Ark Royal* managed to escape a similar attack just three days beforehand. The Royal Navy acted quickly and withdrew its carriers to preserve these valuable vessels.

DID YOU KNOW

IN 1939 BEGAN THE SUBJUGATION OF NONGERMAN-SPEAKING NATIONALITIES TO THE TOTALITARIAN NAZI POLICE STATE. WHEN GERMANY STARTED WORLD WAR II, IT CAME AS THE LOGICAL OUTCOME OF HITLER'S PLANS. THUS, HIS FIRST YEARS WERE SPENT IN PREPARING THE GERMANS FOR THE APPROACHING STRUGGLE FOR WORLD CONTROL AND IN FORGING THE INSTRUMENT THAT WOULD ENABLE GERMANY TO ESTABLISH HER MILITARY AND INDUSTRIAL SUPERIORITY AND THEREBY FULFIL HER AMBITIONS. WITH MOUNTING DIPLOMATIC AND MILITARY SUCCESSES, THE AIMS GREW IN QUICK SUCCESSION. THE FIRST AIM WAS TO UNITE ALL PEOPLE OF GERMAN DESCENT WITHIN THEIR HISTORIC HOMELAND ON THE BASIS OF "SELF-DETERMINATION." THE NEXT STEP FORESAW THE CREATION OF A *GROSSWIRTSCHAFTSRAUM* (LARGE ECONOMIC UNIFIED SPACE) OR A *LEBENSRAUM* (LIVING SPACE) THROUGH THE MILITARY CONQUEST OF POLAND AND OTHER SLAVIC NATIONS TO THE EAST. THEREBY THE GERMANS WOULD ACQUIRE SUFFICIENT SOIL TO BECOME ECONOMICALLY SELF-SUFFICIENT AND MILITARILY IMPREGNABLE. THERE, THE GERMAN MASTER RACE (*HERRENVOLK*) WOULD RULE OVER A HIERARCHY OF SUBORDINATE PEOPLES AND ORGANIZE AND EXPLOIT THEM WITH RUTHLESSNESS AND EFFICIENCY.

DID YOU KNOW

IN GERMAN MILITARY CIRCLES IN AUGUST 1939 THERE WAS LITTLE
ENTHUSIASM FOR WAR, LEADING TO RUMBLINGS OF DISQUIET. MOST OF
THE OFFICERS WERE WELL AWARE OF THE POSSIBLE MILITARY AND POLITICAL
DIFFICULTIES THAT ITS ARMED FORCES MIGHT ENCOUNTER. THESE
OBJECTIONS, WHICH HE REGARDED AS DEFEATIST, HITLER OVERRODE,
BELIEVING IN HIS OWN INTUITION. THE POLISH MOBILIZATION ON MARCH
25, 1939, CAUSED HITLER TO DECIDE THAT THE GERMAN-POLISH
QUESTION COULD NOW BE RESOLVED ONLY BY FORCE, EVEN AT THE RISK
OF A PROBABLE OUTBREAK OF WAR. HITLER WAS CONFIDENT HE COULD
LOCALIZE ANY SUCH CONFLICT, GROSSLY UNDERESTIMATING BOTH HIS
OPPONENTS AND HIS INFLUENCE ON WORLD OPINION. WAR ON TWO
FRONTS WAS HITLER'S GREAT FEAR, STEMMING FROM THE BITTER
EXPERIENCE GAINED BY GERMANY IN WORLD WAR I—ONE THAT, AS YET,
HE WAS NOT READY TO RISK.

Q Did the Soviet Union invade Poland in 1939?

A Yes. In accordance with a secret clause in the 1939 Nazi–Soviet
Pact, the Red Army invaded Poland on September 17. Little
resistance was encountered on Poland's eastern border as the Polish
Army was already fighting in the west.

Q Did Britain and France declare war on the Soviet Union?

A Surprisingly, no. Both London and Paris made no threats as the
Soviets occupied eastern Poland.

Q Who was the commander of the British Expeditionary Force that landed in France in September 1939?

A General Lord Gort. Some 160,000 men and 24,000 vehicles arrived
throughout the course of September.

Q What was the most effective and largest Polish offensive of the 1939 campaign?

A A counterattack by 10 divisions, under General Tadeuz Kutrzeba, over the Bzura River against Germany's Eighth Army. It achieved only a limited success, however.

" THE POLES FOUGHT HARD,
EVEN THOUGH WE HAD GREAT
SUPERIORITY IN ARMS **"**
PAUL STRESEMAN, GERMAN SOLDIER IN POLAND

Q Who assassinated Romanian Prime Minister Armand Calinescu in September 1939?

27

A A fascist Romanian group, the Iron Guard.

Q Estimate German and Polish losses in the 1939 campaign.

A Germany lost 10,572 troops and the Soviet Union had 734 troops killed in the campaign. Around 50,000 Poles were killed and 750,000 captured.

Q What was the dividing line between the German and Soviet occupation zones in Poland?

A The River Bug.

Q What three Baltic states were forced to sign "mutual assistance" agreements with the Soviet Union in 1939?

A Lithuania, Latvia, and Estonia.

Q What was the Winter War?

A The war between Finland and the USSR that began in 1940. Finland, refusing to concede to the Soviet Union's territorial demands, mobilized her armed forces in October. On November 30 a Soviet force of over 600,000 men, supported by air and naval power, attacked Finland.

> **"** POLISH TROOPS OF THE REGULAR ARMY
> **HAVE BEEN ON OUR TERRITORY**
> **DURING THE NIGHT "**
> ADOLF HITLER, SEPTEMBER 1, 1939

Q Who led Finland's armed forces in 1939?

A Field Marshal Karl von Mannerheim.

Q What was the Mannerheim Line?

A A 1914–1918 system of fortifications on the Karelian Isthmus which ran through rugged terrain and dense forest.

DID YOU KNOW

WHEN WORLD WAR II BROKE OUT, NORWAY, TOGETHER WITH SWEDEN, DENMARK, AND FINLAND, ANNOUNCED HER NEUTRALITY. IN SEPTEMBER 1939, GERMANY ASSURED NORWAY THAT SHE WOULD RESPECT HER TERRITORIAL INTEGRITY, BUT WARNED HER THAT THE THIRD REICH WOULD NOT TOLERATE AN INFRINGEMENT OF THAT NEUTRALITY BY A THIRD POWER. GERMANY AT THIS TIME WAS SINCERE ABOUT RESPECTING NORWEGIAN NEUTRALITY, BUT ADMIRAL RAEDER KEPT REMINDING HITLER THAT NAVAL BASES IN NORWAY WOULD BE VERY USEFUL IN CARRYING THE WAR TO GREAT BRITAIN. IN ADDITION, RAEDER REMINDED THE FÜHRER THAT A BRITISH OCCUPATION OF NORWAY WOULD BE DISASTROUS FOR GERMANY, BECAUSE SWEDEN WOULD THEN COME ENTIRELY UNDER BRITISH INFLUENCE. THIS WOULD INTERFERE WITH IRON-ORE SUPPLIES AND OPERATIONS IN THE BALTIC. IN ADDITION, ALLIED AID THAT WAS BEING SENT TO THE FINNS MIGHT LEAD TO AN OCCUPATION OF NORWEGIAN PORTS. HITLER THUS BEGAN TO CONSIDER AN INVASION OF NORWAY.

Q What was the German ship involved in the Battle of the River Plate?

A The pocket battleship *Admiral Graf Spee.*

Q Who was her captain?

A Captain Hans Langsdorff.

Q What was the result of the battle?

A After engaging the British cruisers HMS *Exeter, Ajax,* and *Achilles* on December 13, the *Admiral Graf Spee* made for Montevideo, Uruguay, for repairs. On December 17, Langsdorff, believing that a superior force awaited him outside the port, scuttled his ship.

Q How was the British battleship HMS *Royal Oak* sunk?

A The *Royal Oak* was sunk, with 786 lives lost, after *U-47* passed through antisubmarine defenses at Scapa Flow, where the Home Fleet was anchored. Defenses were improved at the main fleet base after this dramatic attack.

Q What happened at the Battle of Suomussali in December 1939?

A The Soviet 163rd Division approached Suomussali village in eastern Finland. Halted by freezing conditions, its troops were targeted by the Finnish 9th Division, which severed its supply lines. The Soviet 44th Division, sent as a relief force, was blocked by Finnish attacks and both forces were forced to capitulate. Total Soviet losses in this defeat were 27,500 men.

" I CANNOT FORECAST TO YOU THE ACTION OF RUSSIA. IT IS A RIDDLE WRAPPED IN A MYSTERY INSIDE AN ENIGMA "
WINSTON CHURCHILL

Q Where was the location of the attempt on Hitler's life in November 1939?

A The Bürgerbräukeller in Munich. A bomb exploded shortly after Hitler left the hall on the 16th anniversary of the Munich *Putsch*.

Q What was the German OKW?

A *Oberkommando der Wehrmacht* (OKW), High Command of the Armed Forces.

1940

Repeating its success in Poland, the Wehrmacht defeated Allied armies in Scandinavia, France, and the Low Countries. Italy launched an abortive offensive in North Africa, while the Royal Air Force won the Battle of Britain and thus saved the country from a Nazi invasion.

Q Why did a plane crash in Belgium in January 1940 lead Hitler to say: "It's things like this that can lose us the war"?

A On January 10, a German military plane crash-landed near the Belgian town of Mechelen-sur-Meuse. The aircraft, on a flight from Münster to Cologne, became lost in thick cloud. After it came down, one of the passengers jumped out and raced for a clump of bushes, where he set fire to papers he had taken from his briefcase. Belgian soldiers closed in and retrieved the partly burnt papers. The man was Major Helmut Reinberger, a Luftwaffe staff officer, and the papers were operational plans, complete with maps, for a German airborne attack on the West, to begin on January 14 with saturation bombing attacks on French airfields.

> **" IN THREE WEEKS ENGLAND WILL HAVE**
> # HER NECK WRUNG LIKE
> # A CHICKEN'S
> GENERAL WEYGAND, APRIL 1940 **"**

32

Q Why did Hitler order an unlimited U-boat war in February 1940?

A To stop essential supplies of food and war materials reaching Great Britain from the United States.

Q What did this order allow U-boat captains to do?

A Torpedo without warning any ship that was under British control. The policy was already in effect, as was made evident by the sinking of Danish, Dutch, Norwegian, and Swedish ships in the days that preceded the order. Danish newspapers protested loudly at the sinking of one of their ships, the *5177*, by a U-boat.

DID YOU KNOW

THE *DEUTSCHE ARBEITSFRONT* (DAF)—GERMAN LABOR FRONT—WAS THE ORGANIZATION OF ALL GERMAN PROFESSIONAL AND MANUAL WORKERS. IT INCLUDED, IN PARTICULAR, THE MEMBERS OF THE FORMER LABOR UNIONS, OF THE UNIONS OF EMPLOYEES, AND OF THE FORMER ASSOCIATIONS OF EMPLOYERS, WHICH WERE UNITED IN THE LABOR FRONT ON A FOOTING OF COMPLETE EQUALITY. THE AIM OF THE LABOR FRONT WAS THE FORMATION OF A REAL NATIONAL COMMUNITY OF ALL GERMANS. THE LABOR FRONT HAD THE DUTY OF ADJUSTING THE LEGITIMATE INTEREST OF ALL PARTIES IN A MANNER CONFORMING WITH NATIONAL SOCIALIST PRINCIPLES. ATTACHED TO THE LABOR FRONT WAS THE "STRENGTH THROUGH JOY" LEISURE ORGANIZATION. THE LABOR FRONT HAD THE FURTHER DUTY OF LOOKING AFTER THE "PROFESSIONAL EDUCATION" OF ITS ADHERENTS.

Q Who took over as commander of Soviet forces in the war against Finland in early 1940?

33

A Semyon Timoshenko.

Q Which treaty ended the Winter War?

A The Treaty of Moscow between Finland and the Soviet Union in March 1940. Battered but not defeated, Finland retained its independence but had to surrender the Karelian Isthmus and Hangö (10 percent of Finnish territory). Campaign losses were: 200,000 Soviets and 25,000 Finns.

Q Who resigned as France's prime minister in March 1940?

A Edouard Daladier.

Q What was the *Altmark* incident?

A In February 1940 the British destroyer *Cossack* violated Norway's neutrality to rescue 299 British merchant seamen aboard the German transport *Altmark*.

Q What was Berlin's response to this incident?

A Germany accelerated its invasion preparations, believing that Britain was planning more military actions in Norway.

34

DID YOU KNOW

HEINRICH HIMMLER WAS APPOINTED DEPUTY SS LEADER AND THEN NATIONAL LEADER IN JANUARY 1929 WHEN HE COMMANDED APPROXIMATELY 1,000 MEN, WHEN THE SS WAS STILL PART OF THE SA. HE GRADUALLY ASSERTED THE SEPARATION OF THE SS FROM THE SA. HIMMLER BECAME *POLIZEIPRÄSIDENT* OF MUNICH AFTER HITLER BECAME CHANCELLOR IN JANUARY 1933. THIS MODEST POST ENABLED HIM GRADUALLY TO GAIN CONTROL OF THE GERMAN POLICE NETWORK EXCEPT IN PRUSSIA, WHERE GÖRING WAS MINISTER OF THE INTERIOR. BUT HE FINALLY ACHIEVED COMPLETE CONTROL IN 1936. HIMMLER DEVOTED HIS LIFE TO THE EXPANSION OF THE SS, GIVING IT MANY FACETS. THESE INCLUDED THE SS-FINANCED RESEARCH ORGANIZATION, THE *AHNENERBE*. FROM THE SECURITY POINT OF VIEW HE TOOK OVER THE GESTAPO AND MADE IT A EUROPE-WIDE ORGANIZATION. HE CONTROLLED THE CONCENTRATION CAMP SYSTEM, AND IN 1943 BECAME MINISTER OF THE INTERIOR AS WELL. HIMMLER WAS APPOINTED CHIEF OF THE HOME ARMY IN 1944, AND A WEEK BEFORE HITLER'S SUICIDE HE MADE AN EFFORT TO NEGOTIATE THE SURRENDER OF GERMANY. HITLER, HAVING HEARD OF HIMMLER'S TREACHERY, DISMISSED HIM FROM ALL POSTS. CAPTURED BY THE BRITISH IN MAY 1945, HIMMLER BIT ON A CYANIDE PHIAL AND WAS DEAD WITHIN SECONDS.

Q Why was Norway of interest to both Germany and the Western Allies?

A Swedish iron ore supplies passed through the ice-free port of Narvik in Norway to Germany.

" I HAVE TOLD YOU ONCE AND I WILL TELL YOU AGAIN—YOU BOYS WILL
NOT BE SENT INTO ANY FOREIGN WARS
FRANKLIN D. ROOSEVELT, CAMPAIGN SPEECH, 1940 **"**

Q What happened to the British destroyer HMS *Glowworm* in April 1940?

A She intercepted part of the German invasion fleet bound for Norway. *Glowworm* was sunk after ramming the heavy cruiser *Admiral Hipper*.

35

Q Why did the Allies want to mine Norwegian waters?

A To force Nazi ships carrying Swedish iron ore into the open seas and expose them to naval attack.

Q What was the German OKH?

A *Oberkommando des Heeres*—Army High Command.

Q What was the codename of the German invasion of Denmark and Norway?

A *Fall Weserübung* or Operation Weser Exercise.

Q What was notable about the German invasion of Denmark in April 1940?

A It was the first example in any war of a successful airborne operation.

Q Was the German invasion of Denmark costly in terms of casualties?

A No. Two German aircraft were shot down and a few armoured cars damaged. Thirteen Danish soldiers were killed and another 23 wounded. It was nothing more than a skirmish.

> **FRANCE HAS LOST THE BATTLE**
> **BUT SHE HAS NOT LOST**
> **THE WAR**
> CHARLES DE GAULLE, 1940

Q Name at least two German ships sunk during the invasion of Norway.

A German naval losses were heavy, with three cruisers, *Karlsruhe*, *Königsberg*, and *Blücher*, being sunk and a battleship damaged.

Q What was the British naval operation codenamed Wilfred?

A The laying of mines off the Norwegian coast in April 1940.

DID YOU KNOW

THE GERMAN NORWEGIAN INVASION FORCE INCLUDED SIX GROUPS. THE NORTHERNMOST FORCE—GROUP 1—CONSISTED OF THE 139TH REGIMENT OF THE ÉLITE 3RD MOUNTAIN DIVISION, EMBARKED IN 10 DESTROYERS WITH ONLY MINIMAL SUPPLIES AND EQUIPMENT. IN COMMAND WAS MAJOR-GENERAL EDUARD DIETL, A FOX-FACED AUSTRIAN IN WHOM HITLER PLACED CONSIDERABLE CONFIDENCE. DIETL'S MISSION WAS RISKY AT BEST: TO SEIZE AND HOLD NARVIK UNTIL RELIEVED BY FRIENDLY FORCES ADVANCING FROM SOUTHERN NORWAY. THIS LINK-UP WOULD DEPEND ON THE SUCCESS OF GROUP 2, CONSISTING OF THE 3RD MOUNTAIN DIVISION'S OTHER REGIMENT, THE 138TH, WHICH HAD TO SEIZE AND HOLD TRONDHEIM. FARTHER SOUTH, GROUP 3 CONSISTED OF TWO BATTALIONS OF THE 69TH INFANTRY DIVISION, WITH BERGEN AS THEIR OBJECTIVE. A COMPANY OF THE LUFTWAFFE'S 1ST PARACHUTE REGIMENT, MEANWHILE, WOULD SEIZE THE VITAL SOLA AIRFIELD NEAR STAVANGER. GROUPS 4 AND 6, WHOSE MISSION WAS TO SECURE THE PORTS OF KRISTIANSAND, ARENDAL, AND EGERSUND ON NORWAY'S SOUTH COAST, CONSISTED OF SEVERAL SMALL DETACHMENTS OF THE 163RD INFANTRY DIVISION. FINALLY, THE HIGH COMMAND ALLOCATED TO GROUP 5 THE MOST IMPORTANT OBJECTIVE: THE CAPTURE OF OSLO, THE NORWEGIAN CAPITAL. THE ASSAULT WAVE WOULD CONSIST OF TWO BATTALIONS OF THE 163RD INFANTRY DIVISION ABOARD THE POCKET BATTLESHIP *LÜTZOW*, THE HEAVY CRUISER *BLÜCHER*, A LIGHT CRUISER, AND VARIOUS SMALLER CRAFT. THE GERMANS ALSO ASSIGNED TWO PARACHUTE COMPANIES TO SEIZE FORNEBU AIRPORT SLIGHTLY WEST OF THE CITY. FOLLOW-ON WAVES WOULD THEN REINFORCE OSLO AND ADVANCE NORTH AND WEST TO LINK UP WITH THE OTHER GROUPS. IN A SUBSIDIARY OPERATION, *WESER* EXERCISE SOUTH, TWO GERMAN INFANTRY DIVISIONS AND A MOTORIZED RIFLE BRIGADE WOULD SIMULTANEOUSLY OCCUPY DENMARK.

37

Q Who was the Norwegian commander-in-chief in April 1940?

A Major General Carl Otto Ruge.

Q Why did the geography of Norway both aid the attacker and defender?

A Norway is an elongated, rugged country, whose major population centers are located on its coastline. This ruggedness favors the defense, but only if it is speedily and properly organized. Conversely, as the Norwegians discovered to their cost, the same feature lays the defense open to defeat in detail because of the scarcity of communications between the separated and exposed centers of population. This disadvantage is compounded if, as happened in April 1940, an attacker achieves surprise.

Q What were Norwegian tactics after the Germans had invaded?

A Based on the assumption that Anglo-French forces would arrive soon, they concentrated on delaying the German advance north of Oslo.

38

DID YOU KNOW

A TYPICAL GERMAN MOUNTAIN DIVISION COMPRISED A HEADQUARTERS, TWO RIFLE OR GEBIRGSJÄGER REGIMENTS, AN ARTILLERY REGIMENT, AND SUPPORT UNITS, INCLUDING A BATTALION OF SIGNALERS, RECONNAISSANCE TROOPS, ANTITANK GUNNERS, AND ENGINEERS—AROUND 13,000 MEN IN ALL. AS THE TROOPS WERE TRAINED FOR COMBAT IN INHOSPITABLE TERRAIN, THERE WAS A HIGH PROPORTION OF MULES AND HORSES, AND SUPPORT WEAPONS WERE LIGHTER THAN NORMAL FOR EASY BREAKDOWN INTO MAN-PORTABLE LOADS. THE MEDIUM ARTILLERY BATTALION, FOR EXAMPLE, HAD 105MM GUNS IN PLACE OF 150MM PIECES. THE GERMANS FOUND THAT A PERSONAL LOAD OF 40 LB (18.1 KG) WAS THE MAXIMUM THAT COULD BE CARRIED—HEAVIER LOADS IMPAIRED INDIVIDUAL SPEED AND MOBILITY.

Q Did the Germans use tanks in Norway in 1940?

A Yes. The first detachment of German light tanks in Norway went into action on April 16 and proved devastating against the Norwegians, who possessed no antitank guns.

> YOU ASK: "WHAT IS OUR AIM?"
> # I CAN ANSWER IN ONE WORD: "VICTORY!"
> WINSTON CHURCHILL, HOUSE OF COMMONS,
> MAY 13 ,1940

Q Why was air power decisive against the Allied navies during the Norwegian Campaign?

A German air power largely nullified Anglo-French naval superiority. The occupation of Denmark had proved an unqualified success, and with Danish as well as Norwegian bases the Luftwaffe was able to dominate southern and central Norway. Consequently, on April 9 German bombers successfully engaged the British Home Fleet west of Bergen, inflicting little physical damage but scoring an important psychological victory by demonstrating the threat to warships operating near the coast. Henceforth, the British Admiralty exercised great caution and risked only submarines to interdict German shipping en route to Oslo, with little success.

Q Why did the conquest of Norway cause long-term problems for Nazi Germany?

A Norwegian bases would prove useful against the Soviet Union beginning in 1941, but Norway became a drain on German resources as Hitler continually reinforced the garrison against a British invasion that never materialized. In addition, the failure to capture the Norwegian government on April 9 contributed to German problems in the long term, as the government-in-exile established in London fostered patriotic resistance and subversion.

39

Q Who replaced Neville Chamberlain as British prime minister in May 1940?

A Chamberlain was severely criticized over the Norwegian campaign during a House of Commons debate. He resigned after a significant fall in government support in a vote of confidence and the opposition Labour Party's refusal to serve under him in a coalition government. Winston Churchill replaced him and immediately formed a coalition government.

Q Who became Soviet commissar for defence in May 1940?

A General Semyon Timoshenko, who replaced Marshal Kliment Voroshilov.

Q What was the German plan codenamed Case Yellow?

A The attack on Belgium, Holland, and France.

❝ WE WOULD RATHER SEE LONDON LAID IN
RUINS THAN IT SHOULD BE
TAMELY ENSLAVED
WINSTON CHURCHILL, JULY 14, 1940
❞

Q What was the original German plan in Case Yellow?

A The German Army would outflank the French forces deployed along the fortified Maginot Line by a sweep into neutral Belgium and Holland. In truth, this plan remained an unimaginative one with little to recommend it. After a successful push into central Belgium, for example, the planners intended simply to leave it to the field commanders on the spot to recognize a tactical opportunity that they could exploit.

DID YOU KNOW

AT THE BEGINNING OF MAY 1940 IN THE WEST, IN TERMS OF NUMBERS OF DIVISIONS, BOTH SIDES WERE EVENLY MATCHED. THE FRENCH DEPLOYED NEARLY 50 DIVISIONS HELD IN OR IMMEDIATELY BEHIND THE MAGINOT LINE ALONG THE FRANCO-GERMAN BORDER. TO KEEP THESE FRENCH DIVISIONS FIXED IN THE SOUTH LONG INTO THE CAMPAIGN, THE GERMANS UNDERTOOK A DECEPTION SCHEME THAT FEIGNED AN INTENDED ATTACK BY ARMY GROUP C AGAINST THE LINE. IN A CLEVER *RUSE DE GUERRE*, THE GERMANS LEAKED FALSE INFORMATION THROUGH DOUBLE AGENTS THAT SUGGESTED THAT THE GERMANS WOULD LAUNCH AN OUTFLANKING ATTACK ON THE MAGINOT LINE BY VIOLATING THE NEUTRALITY OF NORTHWESTERN SWITZERLAND. AGAIN, THIS CONSTITUTED A CLEVER DECEPTION: BY APPEARING TO THREATEN THE OBVIOUS ACHILLES' HEEL OF THIS SUPPOSEDLY IMPREGNABLE DEFENSIVE BARRIER, THE GERMANS CLEVERLY TAPPED INTO THE SENSITIVITIES OF A MILITARY COMMAND THAT HAD NEARLY BANKRUPTED THE FRENCH ECONOMY CONSTRUCTING THE LINE IN THE FIRST PLACE.

41

Q Who was the French commander-in-chief in May 1940?

A General Maurice Gamelin.

Q What was the French plan called the Breda Variant?

A In response to a German attack in the West, French forces were to advance 102 miles (164 km) to reach the town of Breda in southern Holland to reinforce the Dutch Army. To achieve this new mission, Gamelin increased the forces committed to the maneuver from 20 to 32 divisions, largely by stripping the French strategic reserve of its mobile divisions and allocating them to General Giraud's Seventh Army in its coastal dash to Breda.

Q What was the codename of the final German plan for the attack in the West?

A *Sichelschnitt* (Cut of the Scythe).

Q Who devised it?

A Major General Erich von Manstein.

Q What did Cut of the Scythe entail?

A A swift surprise advance by concentrated mechanized formations through the Ardennes.

" HAD THE BRITISH HELD ON FOR ANOTHER
TWO HOURS I WOULD
HAVE WITHDRAWN "
EDUARD DIETL, GERMAN COMMANDER AT NARVIK

Q Why was Cut of the Scythe risky?

A The terrain of the Ardennes was very restrictive for large mechanized forces. The narrow, winding roads with steep banks on each side, the heavily forested and hilly ground, and the numerous fast-flowing rivers severely hampered movement. To move seven panzer divisions with 1,900 tanks, 41,000 motor vehicles, and 175,000 men through these communication routes—often only on a single vehicle frontage—would involve march columns that were 100 miles (160 km) long!

DID YOU KNOW

THE FINAL GERMAN PLAN FOR THE ATTACK IN THE WEST IN MAY 1940 ADVOCATED A CONCENTRATED MECHANIZED STRIKE THROUGH THE WEAK FRENCH CENTER, WHICH DISPOSED JUST 14 DIVISIONS FOR ITS DEFENSE. IF THE FRENCH SENT LARGE FORCES INTO BELGIUM AND HOLLAND TO IMPLEMENT THE BREDA VARIANT, AS GERMAN INTELLIGENCE BELIEVED THEY WOULD, THIS REDEPLOYMENT WOULD AID THE MANSTEIN PLAN BY SUCKING BRITISH AND FRENCH FORCES TO THE NORTH AWAY FROM THE CENTER. TO BE ABLE TO INFILTRATE THE WEAK FRENCH CENTER, THE GERMANS NEEDED TO ENCOURAGE THE EXISTING FRENCH MALDEPLOY-MENT. HENCE, THEY PLANNED TO LAUNCH A POWERFUL SECONDARY EFFORT INTO NORTHERN BELGIUM AND SOUTHERN HOLLAND. THE GERMAN ARMY HIGH COMMAND ASSUMED THAT THE FRENCH WOULD REGARD THIS AS THE MAIN GERMAN EFFORT. THE GERMANS THEREFORE EXPECTED THAT SUBSTANTIAL FRENCH AND BRITISH FORCES WOULD BE DRAWN AWAY FROM THE CENTER BY THIS DECEPTION ATTACK IN THE NORTH. ONCE THESE FORCES HAD REDEPLOYED NORTH, THIS POWERFUL GERMAN SECONDARY ATTACK COULD FIX THESE FORCES THERE IN A CONTACT BATTLE, WHILE THE MAIN GERMAN OFFENSIVE LANCED THROUGH THEIR REAR.

43

Q Did the Germans have more tanks than the Allies in May 1940?

A No. The attacking German forces fielded some 2,574 tanks out of their total arsenal of 3,380 machines, many of the uncommitted vehicles being the scarcely combat-worthy Panzer I light tank. The Allies had a total of 4,296 armored vehicles in the northeastern theater. The idea that the Germans had an overwhelming superiority in tanks is a myth: they just used their vehicles more imaginatively than did the British and French.

Q What was "Fortress Holland"?

A The Dutch main defensive position in the west of Holland.

Q Following the German attack on May 10, 32 divisions of General Billotte's First French Army Group, plus the British Expeditionary Force (BEF), crossed into Belgium and moved to their designated positions around Breda and thence south along the River Dyle in Belgium down to Sedan. The Luftwaffe did not impede these movements. Why?

A The Luftwaffe did not undertake major efforts to hinder this movement since it actually played into German hands by removing powerful enemy forces from the decisive central sector of the front.

Q Where did the Germans pierce the Allied line in the Ardennes?

A At Sedan.

Q Who commanded the German forces at Sedan?

A General Heinz Guderian.

DID YOU KNOW

DESPITE THE ADVERSE TERRAIN, THE GERMANS NEEDED TO ADVANCE SWIFTLY THROUGH THE ARDENNES IN MAY 1940, OTHERWISE THE FRENCH WOULD BE ABLE TO REDEPLOY FORCES TO BLOCK ANY GERMAN EGRESS ON TO THE PLAINS BEYOND. TO ENSURE MOMENTUM, THE GERMANS UTILIZED EFFECTIVE ALL-ARMS COOPERATION. A KEY COMPONENT OF THIS WAS THE PRACTICE OF UTILIZING MISSION ANALYSIS (*AUFTRAGSTAKTIK*). THIS FLEXIBLE ETHOS GAVE CONSIDERABLE LEEWAY TO SUBORDINATE COMMANDERS AND OBVIATED THE NEED TO PAUSE DURING OPERATIONS TO AWAIT FURTHER ORDERS FROM ABOVE. ON SEVERAL OCCASIONS THE COMMAND VEHICLE USED BY DIVISIONAL COMMANDERS WAS THE LEAD VEHICLE IN THEIR DIVISION—ALLOWING THEM TO MAKE RAPID AND WELL-INFORMED TACTICAL DECISIONS.

Q What units did he command?

A XIX Panzer Corps, comprising the 1st, 2nd, and 10th Panzer Divisions as well as the élite motorized *Grossdeutschland* Regiment.

> " I WONDERED WHAT HE WAS LIKE,
> THIS MAN I WOULD KILL. WOULD HE
> # DIE WITH THE FÜHRER'S
> # NAME ON HIS LIPS? "
> RICHARD HILLARY, RAF PILOT, BATTLE OF BRITAIN

Q Why did the German breakthrough at Sedan in May 1940 spell disaster for the Allies?

A It threatened to turn the southern flank of the still-cohesive British, French, and Belgian forces deployed on the Dyle River and in the Gembloux Gap down to the Meuse at Dinant.

Q What was the "Panzer Corridor"?

A The advance of the German panzer divisions from the River Meuse in the Ardennes to the English Channel in May 1940, which isolated Allied armies to the north from the forces in the south.

Q What was the "Miracle of Dunkirk"?

A Between May 27, and June 4, 1940, British, French, and Belgian forces resolutely defended the shrinking defensive perimeter they held around Dunkirk to permit the evacuation of a large part of these isolated forces. In this nine-day period, some 861 small boats transported 226,000 British and 112,000 French and Belgian soldiers to safety.

Q Why did the French put so much faith in the Maginot Line?

A World War I had devastated northeastern France, and from this the French military concluded that in the next major war the defensive firepower of artillery and the machine gun would dominate the tactical battlefield. Consequently, France based her interwar military strategy on a defensive posture, an orientation encapsulated by the construction of the Maginot Line during 1930–1935. This orientation also reflected French reaction to the huge casualties they had suffered during World War I, which had significantly reduced the country's adult male population.

Q Why wasn't the Maginot Line extended from Luxembourg along the Franco-Belgian border to the North Sea?

A French strategy prior to 1936 planned to send forces into central Belgium to help the latter resist any German onslaught. The construction of the world's most powerful defensive barrier along the Franco-Belgian border would hardly have sent the right message to the Belgian government. The fact that the construction of the existing 225 miles (362 km) of the Maginot Line had already virtually bankrupted France also influenced this decision not to extend the line to the coast.

Q Which supposedly impregnable Belgian fort dominated the German route of advance into central Belgium.

A Eben Emael.

> **" THE BATTLEFIELD WAS STREWN WITH BROKEN AND ABANDONED EQUIPMENT**
> CYRIL JOLY, BRITISH TANK COMMANDER IN NORTH AFRICA, 1940 **"**

Q How did the Germans intend to capture the fort?

A German planners had concluded that this powerful Belgian fortress remained vulnerable due to its lack of antiaircraft defenses. Consequently, they formulated a daring plan to land by surprise a glider-borne force on to the roof of the fort—the first time such a tactic had ever been attempted. Once on the roof, the German troops would use a novel lightweight weapon—hollow-charged rounds—to blast through the thick concrete walls of the fort.

Q Were these tactics successful?

A Yes. The German paratroopers, using explosive charges, had soon neutralized the fort's guns and forced the surrender of the garrison.

DID YOU KNOW

47

GERMANY'S SENSATIONAL SEIZURE OF FRANCE AND THE LOW COUNTRIES WAS THE PINNACLE OF BLITZKRIEG STRATEGY AND SECURED ADOLF HITLER'S MASTERY OF WESTERN EUROPE. THE INVASION THAT BEGAN ON MAY 10 FIRST STRUCK THE LOW COUNTRIES, WHICH HAD RELIED UPON THEIR NEUTRALITY TO SAVE THEM, AND WERE IN NO CONDITION TO RESIST THE WEHRMACHT. AS BRITISH AND FRENCH FORCES RUSHED INTO BELGIUM IN RESPONSE TO GERMANY'S DIVERSIONARY ATTACK, THE NAZIS LAUNCHED THEIR MAIN ASSAULT BY ADVANCING THROUGH THE ARDENNES FOREST. THE ALLIES HAD DISMISSED THIS AREA AS BEING UNSUITABLE FOR ANY TANK ADVANCES, WHICH ALLOWED THE GERMAN UNITS TO MOVE STRAIGHT THROUGH AGAINST MINIMAL OPPOSITION. THIS GATEWAY INTO FRANCE ENABLED THE FAST-MOVING ARMORED COLUMNS TO ADVANCE INTO THE ALLIED REAR AND DISABLE COMMUNICATIONS. AS THE PANZERS RACED WESTWARD TO THE SEA, THE ALLIED ARMIES IN THE NORTH WERE EFFECTIVELY ISOLATED FROM POTENTIAL REINFORCEMENTS IN THE SOUTH. THE ALLIES WERE UNABLE TO MATCH GERMANY'S EFFECTIVE EXPLOITATION OF ARMOR AND AIRPOWER OR DEVELOP A CREDIBLE STRATEGY TO COUNTERATTACK THE INVADERS.

DID YOU KNOW

48

Q In German military thinking, what was the concept of the integral battle of annihilation (*Vernichtungsschlacht*)?

A This military strategy was based, in part, on the Prussian/German High Command's interpretation—or, rather, distortion—of Clausewitz's ideas on the climactic, decisive, individual battle, an event that was prominent during the Napoleonic period. This military strategy centered on the intent to defeat an opponent swiftly through one single, continuous offensive action.

Q Who replaced the French premier, Paul Reynaud, in June 1940?

A Marshal Henri-Philippe Pétain.

Q What was the role of the Luftwaffe during the campaign in France in 1940?

A As the ground forces commenced their attacks on the border defenses, massed formations of German bombers and fighter-bombers began attacking enemy air bases. These attacks proved particularly successful in Belgium and Holland, where dozens of aircraft were caught on the ground and destroyed. These aerial operations represented a classic attritional counter-air campaign designed to achieve local air superiority over the theater. Once this had been accomplished, the Germans could then employ their air power to facilitate the ground advance through undertaking the missions of aerial reconnaissance, battlefield air interdiction (BAI), and close air support (CAS).

> **FOR SEVERAL DAYS AFTER THE OCCUPATION THE GERMAN ARMY IGNORED THE POPULATION OF PARIS**
> DEMAREE BESS, AMERICAN IN PARIS, JUNE 1940

49

Q What was Operation Dynamo?

A The evacuation of Allied troops from Dunkirk.

Q What was Operation Red?

A The codename for the German conquest of France in June 1940.

Q Where was the Weygand Line?

A The French Weygand Line stretched along the Somme and Aisne Rivers and aimed to protect Paris and the interior.

Q Why was Paris declared an "open city" by the French in June 1940?

A To save it from destruction at the hands of the Germans (all French forces had withdrawn to the south of the capital).

Q Was any British territory under German control in the war?

A Yes. The Channel Islands, which were invaded in June 1940.

Q What was the Special Operations Executive?

A A British organization to give support secretly to resistance groups across Nazi-occupied Europe.

Q What was Führer Directive No. 16?

A Preparation for the German invasion of Britain.

❝ THE ENGINE EXPLODED AND THE MACHINE
LURCHED VIOLENTLY FOR
A SECOND
ROGER HALL, RAF PILOT, BATTLE OF BRITAIN, 1940 **❞**

Q Upon what did it rely for success?

A Control of the sea for transporting the invasion force and the destruction of Britain's fighter capability to ensure a safe crossing for the army.

DID YOU KNOW

THE BATTLE OF BRITAIN WAS GERMANY'S ATTEMPT TO ACHIEVE AIR
SUPERIORITY OVER THE SKIES OF SOUTHERN ENGLAND. WITH THIS
ACHIEVED, SHE COULD THEN CONTROL THE ENGLISH CHANNEL FOR THE
CROSSING OF THE INVASION FORCE, WHICH WAS BEING PREPARED ON THE
CONTINENT. GERMANY'S AIR FORCE COMMANDER, HERMANN GOERING,
ASSEMBLED 2,800 AIRCRAFT AGAINST BRITAIN'S 700 FIGHTERS.
WIDESPREAD GERMAN ATTACKS ON PORTS, SHIPPING, AND AIRFIELDS
LURED BRITISH FIGHTERS INTO ACTION AND INFLICTED HEAVY LOSSES.
BRITAIN'S FATE RESTED UPON THE BRAVERY, DETERMINATION, AND SKILL OF
ITS FIGHTER PILOTS. THESE MEN WERE DRAWN FROM THE BRITISH EMPIRE,
NORTH AMERICA, CZECHOSLOVAKIA, POLAND, AND OTHER ALLIED
NATIONS. THE PERFORMANCE OF THE HURRICANE AND SPITFIRE FIGHTERS
THEY FLEW ALSO PLAYED A KEY ROLE.

Q Why was the French surrender of 1940 signed in a railway carriage?

A The French surrender was signed at Compiègne, in the same railway carriage where the Germans surrendered in November 1918. It was a deliberate insult to the French.

Q What was the German Operation Otto of August 1940?

A Hitler secretly ordered his staff to prepare a plan for the invasion of the Soviet Union, to be codenamed "Otto."

Q What happened at the Battle of Punta Stilo in July 1940?

A The British Mediterranean Fleet tried to separate the Italian Fleet from its Taranto base. An Italian battleship and cruiser were damaged, and Italian aircraft hit a British cruiser. The Australian cruiser HMAS *Sydney* and four destroyers engaged two Italian light cruisers. The Italians lost a cruiser and the *Sydney* was damaged.

51

Q Why did the Royal Navy attack French ships in Algerian ports in July 1940?

A Britain, fearing that France's navy would be seized by Germany, sent two battleships, a battlecruiser, and a carrier (Force H) to neutralize French vessels at Oran and Mers-el-Kebir, Algeria.

Q What was the result of the attack?

A After negotiations failed, the British sank one battleship and damaged two more. In Britain, two French battleships, nine destroyers, and other craft were acquired with minimal force. French naval forces in Alexandria, Egypt, were disarmed without a struggle.

> **"** ALONG THE PROMENADE, IN PARTIES OF 50, THE REMNANTS OF ALL THE **LAST REGIMENTS WERE WEARILY TRUDGING ALONG "**
> CAPTAIN RICHARD AUSTIN, DUNKIRK, MAY 1940

Q What was the Burma Road?

A A road linking Burma with China. When it was built, Burma was a British colony.

Q Why did the British close the Burma Road in July 1940?

A British Prime Minister Winston Churchill agreed to close the Burma Road to disrupt supplies to the Chinese in order to avoid a confrontation with the Japanese. The onset of the monsoon season meant that supply lines were disrupted anyway.

Q In the first phase of the Battle of Britain, what were the targets of German aircraft?

A In July 1940 Hermann Goering, the Nazi air force chief, ordered attacks on shipping and ports in the English Channel. The movement of Allied vessels in the Channel was soon restricted as a result of British naval and aircraft losses.

Q In July 1940 America restricted the export of oil and metal products outside the Americas. Who was this directed at?

A This measure was particularly directed towards Japan, which was heavily dependent upon imports of these resources.

Q What was the consequence of America's action?

A As a consequence, Japanese strategic planning devoted greater attention to the resources of the Dutch East Indies and Malaysia to relieve their raw material shortages.

53

DID YOU KNOW

WINSTON SPENCER CHURCHILL (1874–1965), SOLDIER, JOURNALIST, AND STATESMAN, HAD HELD MINISTERIAL OFFICES BUT WAS RELEGATED TO THE MARGINS OF POLITICAL LIFE IN BRITAIN DURING THE 1930S FOR HIS ANTI-APPEASEMENT STANCE. HE WAS PROPELLED INTO POWER, HOWEVER, AS PRIME MINISTER IN 1940 AS THE NAZIS APPEARED CLOSE TO TOTAL VICTORY. CHURCHILL REVERSED THE FORTUNES OF THE NATION BY DISMISSING ANY SIGN OF DEFEATISM. THE BOLD BUT OFTEN IMPATIENT PRIME MINISTER CONSTANTLY URGED HIS MILITARY COMMANDERS TO TAKE OFFENSIVE ACTION. CHURCHILL FORGED A COALITION OF ALLIED NATIONS, BUT IT WAS THE SOLID SUPPORT HE SECURED FROM THE UNITED STATES THAT WAS CRITICAL TO BRITAIN'S SURVIVAL.

Q What factors aided the British in the Battle of Britain?

A A centralized command-and-control structure and radar network enabled fighters to be effectively concentrated to meet enemy attacks. The RAF also benefitted from longer flying time as it operated over its own territory. In addition, crews that baled out were able to resume fighting, unlike their opponents who parachuted into captivity.

Q In the Battle of Britain, what was "Eagle Day"?

A A four-day German air offensive designed to destroy Britain's Fighter Command with raids on military airfields and industrial targets.

Q Who led the RAF in the Battle of Britain?

A Air Chief Marshal Sir Hugh Dowding.

Q What change in German strategy in September 1940 resulted in the RAF winning the Battle of Britain?

A Germany's gravest strategical error was the decision, from September 7 onward, to concentrate on bombing British cities, despite eroding the capability of Fighter Command by widespread and incessant raids across southern England. This change in strategy enabled the RAF to concentrate its fighters and inflict heavier losses on the Luftwaffe.

> **THE HOUSE ABOUT 30 YARDS FROM OURS**
> **STRUCK BY A BOMB.**
> **COMPLETELY RUINED**
> VIRGINIA WOOLF, LONDON, SEPTEMBER 1940

DID YOU KNOW

HITLER DID NOT WANT A CONFLICT ON HIS SOUTHERN FLANK IN THE BALKANS, AND HAD RESTRAINED HIS AXIS PARTNER MUSSOLINI ON SEVERAL OCCASIONS DURING THE SPRING AND SUMMER OF 1940 FROM INITIATING PLANS FOR AN ITALIAN INVASION OF YUGOSLAVIA AND GREECE. MUSSOLINI RELUCTANTLY ACCEPTED HITLER'S WISHES AS HE WAS DEPENDENT ON GERMANY FOR RAW MATERIALS NEEDED FOR ARMAMENTS.

Q Which World War II leader said: "One death is a tragedy, one million is a statistic"?

A Joseph Stalin.

Q Who was Chief of the Army General Staff in the German Army in 1940?

A General Franz Halder.

Q Which three countries did the Soviet Union occupy in June 1940?

A Lithuania, Latvia, and Estonia.

Q What was a T-34?

A A Russian medium tank.

Q What were the design features that made the T-34 such a good tank?

A One of the most innovative designs was its sloped armor, which not only saved weight compared with rolled plate, but was also more difficult for antitank rounds to penetrate. In addition, its Christie-type suspension, combined with a diesel powerplant, gave it an excellent power-to-weight ratio and good cross-country mobility.

Q Why did the Winter War encourage Hitler to attack the Soviet Union?

A The performance of the Red Army did little to lessen the disdain with which Hitler and the Nazis viewed the Soviet regime. Indeed, the fact that a small "Nordic" country had withstood the onslaught of a nation of 180 million Slavs further convinced Hitler of the overall superiority of the Aryan race. How much worse would the Red Army fare against the mighty Wehrmacht?

DID YOU KNOW

THE DICTATOR OF THE SOVIET UNION WAS NOT RADICALLY DIFFERENT FROM ADOLF HITLER. BOTH MEN SHARED A DISLIKE OF LIBERALISM AND WEAKNESS, AND BOTH SAW TREASON AND INCOMPETENCE EVERYWHERE. UNLIKE HITLER, STALIN HAD NOT SEEN WAR SERVICE (HE WAS FOUND TO BE UNFIT FOR MILITARY SERVICE BY THE RUSSIAN AUTHORITIES). THIS PUT HIM AT A DISADVANTAGE WHEN IT CAME TO CONFERENCES WITH SENIOR RED ARMY COMMANDERS DURING THE WAR, DUE TO HIS LACK OF PRACTICAL MILITARY KNOWLEDGE. HOWEVER, HE WAS QUITE HAPPY TO GIVE A CERTAIN LATITUDE TO HIS GENERALS, SECURE IN THE KNOWLEDGE THAT HIS SECRET POLICE MAINTAINED AN IRON GRIP OVER THE SOVIET PEOPLE AND THAT HE COULD ALWAYS HAVE INCOMPETENT OFFICERS EXECUTED OR SENT TO THE GULAG IF THEY FAILED IN THEIR DUTY TO MOTHER RUSSIA.

Q Which two Romanian provinces did the Soviet Union seize in June 1940?

A Bessarabia and Northern Bukovino.

Q What was the name of Hitler's retreat in the Bavarian Alps?

A The Berghof.

" THE ICY WATER WAS ALREADY TAKING A
GRIP ON ME AND I LOOKED AROUND
FOR SOMETHING TO
FLOAT ON "
RONALD HEALISS, ON THE TORPEDOED
HMS *GLORIOUS*, JUNE 1940

57

Q What was the Iron Guard?

A A Romanian fascist movement

Q Which Romanian leader was nicknamed "Red Dog"?

A Romanian dictator Ion Antonescu. He was nicknamed "Red Dog" because of his hair color.

Q Who said "If Russia is laid low, then Britain's last hope is wiped out, and Germany will be master of Europe and the Balkans."?

A Adolf Hitler in July 1940.

Q Who commanded Italian forces in Libya in 1940?

A Marshal Rodolfo Graziani.

Q How many Italian troops invaded Egypt in September 1940?

A 250,000.

Q Who was the British commander who opposed them?

A General Sir Richard O'Connor.

"FIRE A BOW TORPEDO AT A LARGE FREIGHTER OF ABOUT 6000 TONS AT A RANGE OF 750 METERS"
Captain Otto Kretschmer, *U-99*, October 1940

Q What was the British Selective Service Bill of September 1940?

A It authorized the conscription of men aged 21–35.

Q Why did the Germans suspend Operation Sealion?

A In September 1940 Adolf Hitler decided to suspend Operation Sealion after Germany's failure to achieve aerial supremacy over southern England.

DID YOU KNOW

THE PANZER IV BECAME THE BACKBONE OF THE GERMAN PANZER ARM ON THE EASTERN FRONT. CONTINUALLY UPGRADED IN TERMS OF ARMAMENT AND ARMOR THROUGHOUT THE WAR, THE PANZER IV SOLDIERED ON UNTIL THE SURRENDER OF GERMANY IN 1945, BY WHICH TIME 8,600 OF ALL VARIANTS HAD BEEN BUILT. ORIGINALLY ARMED WITH THE SHORT-BARRELLED 75MM GUN, EXPERIENCE IN RUSSIA REVEALED THIS WEAPON TO BE TOTALLY INADEQUATE AGAINST SOVIET T-34 AND KV-1 TANKS. THE PANZER IV HAD ORIGINALLY BEEN DESIGNED TO DESTROY "SOFT" TARGETS SUCH AS INFANTRY, SOFT-SKINNED VEHICLES, AND ANTITANK EMPLACE-MENTS, WHILE THE PANZER IIIS WERE FOR TANK-VERSUS-TANK COMBAT. THEREFORE, THE LONG-BARRELLED 75MM L/43 OR L/48 GUNS WERE INSTALLED IN PANZER IVS TO ENABLE THEM TO KNOCK OUT SOVIET TANKS. THE PANZER IV WAS NOT AN IDEAL DESIGN, HAVING RELATIVELY THIN, NON-SLOPING ARMOR THAT PRODUCED MANY SHOT TRAPS AND A HIGH, BOX SHAPE. HOWEVER, IT WAS A PLATFORM WHERE THE GUNS AND ARMOR COULD BE CONTINUALLY UPGRADED.

Q In naval warfare, what was a "Wolf Pack"?

A In this tactic, some 15–20 U-boats were deployed across the approaches to Britain. When a U-boat found a convoy, it tracked the vessels and awaited the gathering of the entire "Wolf Pack" for a combined attack. Germany launched its first successful "Wolf Pack" operation in the Atlantic in September 1940, sinking 12 ships.

Q What was Operation Felix?

A The codename of a German plan to capture Gibraltar.

Q Which senior Nazi served in the same regiment as Hitler in World War I?

A Rudolf Hess.

Q Which position did this individual hold in the Third Reich?

A Deputy Leader.

Q What does *panzerkampfwagen* mean in English?

A Armored fighting vehicle.

❝ HELL OF A BANG, THEY HAVE BLOWN THE BRIDGE UP. HE MUST BE ADVANCING AGAIN ❞
SERGEANT PEXTON, BRITISH SOLDIER IN FRANCE, MAY 1940

Q What was the Waffen-SS?

A The military wing of the SS.

Q Does Wehrmacht mean German Army?

A No. Wehrmacht means armed forces, which included the army.

DID YOU KNOW

THE 9MM MP38 WAS THE STANDARD GERMAN SUBMACHINE GUN OF
WORLD WAR II. AS ITS DESIGNATION SUGGESTS, IT WAS FIRST ISSUED IN
1938. TWO YEARS LATER, IT WAS REPLACED BY THE MP40, WHICH WAS
IDENTICAL EXCEPT IT UTILIZED LESS EXPENSIVE STAMPED METAL FOR
CERTAIN PARTS, WHICH WAS MORE COST EFFECTIVE FOR A MASS-PRODUCED
WEAPON. IT WAS A VERY SUCCESSFUL FIREARM, AND EVEN ALLIED FORCES
PREFERRED IT OVER THEIR OWN SUBMACHINE GUNS AND SCAVENGED
MP40S WHENEVER POSSIBLE. IT HAD A 32-ROUND MAGAZINE AND A
CYCLIC RATE OF FIRE OF 500 ROUNDS PER MINUTE. BETWEEN 1939 AND
1945 THE GERMAN ARMY RECEIVED 689,403 MP38/40 SUBMACHINE
GUNS, MOST OF WHICH WENT TO FRONTLINE UNITS, ESPECIALLY
PANZERGRENADIER FORMATIONS.

Q Which German ships sank the aircraft carrier HMS *Glorious* in June 1940?

A *Scharnhorst* and *Gneisenau*.

Q What type of warship was the *Prinz Eugen*?

A A heavy cruiser.

Q Who was the leader who replaced Neville Chamberlain as leader of the British Conservative Party in October 1940?

A Winston Churchill.

Q List the main roles of the Luftwaffe during a German ground offensive.

A First, to destroy the enemy's air force (preferably on the ground). Second, to provide close air support for ground units, which included interdicting enemy supplies and communications to bring about his paralysis.

Q Which leader said in 1940: "I make decisions; I need men who obey."?

A Adolf Hitler.

" ROUSED OUT OF IT AT 6AM AND
PUT ON THE ROAD. I'M JUST
**BEGINNING TO REALIZE
THAT I'M A PRISONER**
SERGEANT PEXTON, FRANCE, MAY 1940 **"**

Q After the defeat of France Hitler created 12 field marshals. Name at least five of them.

A Brauchitsch, Keitel, Rundstedt, Bock, Leeb, List, Kluge, Witzleben, Reichenau, Milch, Kesselring, and Sperrle.

Q How many were from the air force?

A Three: Milch, Kesselring, and Sperrle.

DID YOU KNOW

THE GREATEST RED ARMY GENERAL OF WORLD WAR II AND ONE OF THE
MOST FAMOUS COMMANDERS OF THE CONFLICT, GEORGI ZHUKOV, WAS
BORN IN 1896 INTO AN IMPOVERISHED PEASANT FAMILY NEAR MOSCOW.
HE WAS GOING TO BE A CRAFTSMAN, BUT THE OUTBREAK OF WORLD WAR
I CHANGED HIS LIFE FOREVER. DRAFTED IN 1915, BY 1918 HE WAS
SERVING IN THE RED ARMY CAVALRY AND A YEAR LATER JOINED THE
COMMUNIST PARTY. WHAT MARKED OUT THE YOUNG MAN WAS HIS THIRST
FOR KNOWLEDGE. DURING THE NEXT 20 YEARS HE DEVOURED MASSES OF
WRITTEN WORKS ON THE MILITARY ART. BY 1938 HE WAS IN COMMAND OF
THE ÉLITE 4TH CAVALRY DIVISION. HOWEVER, IT WAS WHEN IN COMMAND
OF TANKS THAT HE GAINED HIS FIRST VICTORY, OVER THE JAPANESE IN
MONGOLIA AT KHALKHIN GOL IN AUGUST 1939. BY MAY 1940 HE WAS A
GENERAL AND IN CHARGE OF THE KIEV MILITARY DISTRICT. WHEN THE
GERMANS INVADED THE SOVIET UNION IN JUNE 1941 ZHUKOV ADVOCAT-
ED ABANDONING KIEV, AN IDEA THAT PROMPTED AN OUTBURST FROM
STALIN. ZHUKOV OFFERED TO RESIGN BUT STALIN, PROBABLY RECOGNIZING
HIS GENERAL WAS RIGHT, REFUSED THE OFFER. KIEV FELL ANYWAY AND
ZHUKOV WAS GIVEN COMMAND OF THE RESERVE FORCES SITUATED TO THE
EAST OF MOSCOW. WHEN THE GERMAN MOSCOW OFFENSIVE STALLED AT
THE END OF NOVEMBER 1941, ZHUKOV LAUNCHED A COUNTEROFFENSIVE
ALONG THE WHOLE FRONT, WHICH NOT ONLY SAVED MOSCOW BUT ALSO
GAVE THE GERMANS THEIR FIRST STRATEGIC DEFEAT. IN AUGUST 1942
ZHUKOV BECAME DEPUTY SUPREME COMMANDER-IN-CHIEF OF THE RED
ARMY, SECOND ONLY TO STALIN. BY NOW HIS STAR WAS IN THE ASCEN-
DANT. HE MASTERMINDED THE OPERATION THAT DESTROYED THE GERMAN
SIXTH ARMY AT STALINGRAD AND THEN PLANNED AND EXECUTED THE RED
ARMY DEFENSE AT KURSK. AFTER THE BATTLE HE WENT ON TO LIBERATE
THE UKRAINE AND RETAKE KIEV. HIS GREATEST OPERATION WAS PROBABLY
BAGRATION IN JUNE 1944, WHICH DESTROYED THE GERMAN ARMY GROUP
CENTER. THOUGH STALIN WAS JEALOUS OF ZHUKOV'S POPULARITY AND
MILITARY VICTORIES, HE AGREED TO HIM HAVING THE HONOR OF TAKING
BERLIN IN 1945, WHICH HE DID—ALBEIT WITH TERRIBLE LOSSES AND
WITH THE HELP OF KONEV. ZHUKOV DIED IN 1974.

Q Where were the Ploesti oilfields?

A Romania.

Q Japan signed the Tripartite Pact in September 1940. Why?

A The pact pledged that each country would wage war on any state that declared war on an Axis state. Japan was keen to deter intervention by the United States in the Far East and thus signed the pact.

Q Who commanded Italian troops during the invasion of Greece in October 1940?

A General Sadasiano Visconti-Prasca.

DID YOU KNOW

THE FAMOUS GERMAN 88MM FLAK 18 PROVED ITSELF TO BE NOT ONLY AN EXCELLENT ANTIAIRCRAFT WEAPON BUT ALSO AN IDEAL TANK-KILLER DUE TO ITS HIGH MUZZLE VELOCITY AND EFFICIENT HEAVY PROJECTILE. BY MID-1943 IT HAD BUILT UP AN IMPRESSIVE REPUTATION. IN FRANCE IN 1940 IT HAD TRIUMPHED AGAINST THE HEAVILY ARMORED FRENCH CHAR B1-BIS HEAVY TANKS AND BRITISH MK II MATILDA INFANTRY TANKS. IN NORTH AFRICA IT WAS A FEARED TANK-KILLER THAT COULD KNOCK OUT ANY ALLIED TANK AT RANGES WELL OVER 3,280 FT (1,000 M). AND IN RUSSIA IT WAS THE ONLY GUN CAPABLE OF DEALING WITH SOVIET T-34/76 MEDIUM TANKS AND KV-1 HEAVY TANKS. IT HAD A MUZZLE VELOCITY OF 820 METRES PER SECOND AND A RANGE OF 9.25 MILES (14.8 KM). THE 88MM ANTIAIRCRAFT GUNS WERE USUALLY DEPLOYED IN THE HEAVY FLAK BATTERIES. THEY COULD PRISE OPEN ANY ALLIED TANK LIKE A TIN OPENER, AND WERE FEARED BY ENEMY TANK CREWS.

SUDDENLY THERE WAS A BLOODY FLASH
ON MY PORT WING
AND I FELT A BLOW ON
MY LEFT ARM
D.H. WISSLER, RAF PILOT, OCTOBER 1940

Q **Who commanded Greek forces?**

A General Alexander Papagos.

Q **Why did the Italians attack Greece?**

A Italy hoped to rival Germany's conquests of 1940.

65

Q **What factors impeded the Italian advance in Greece in October 1940?**

A The mountainous terrain and absence of maps for commanders hampered the invasion. In addition, the winter weather limited Italian air support and led to thousands of deaths from hypothermia. Finally, Greek resistance was stiffer than expected.

Q **Who was elected president of the United States in November 1940?**

A Franklin D. Roosevelt, for an unprecedented third time.

Q **When did British forces occupy the Greek island of Crete?**

A The end of October 1940.

Q What happened at the Battle of Taranto in November 1940?

A British torpedo aircraft from the carrier HMS *Illustrious* attacked Italian ships at Taranto.

Q What was the result of the battle?

A Three Italian ships were sunk and two others damaged.

Q The assault against Taranto was the blueprint for which Axis aerial assault in 1941?

A The Japanese attack against Pearl Harbor.

" IN THE MORNING, I WOULD WALK
ALONG CLARKEHOUSE ROAD
LOOKING FOR SHRAPNEL "
GEORGE MACBETH, A BOY IN SHEFFIELD,
ENGLAND, AUTUMN 1940

Q Which British general, outnumbered three to one, won a famous victory over the Italians in North Africa in December 1940?

A Major General Richard O'Connor.

Q What was the name of the force he commanded?

A The Western Desert Force.

1941

This year the Germans launched Operation
Barbarossa, the invasion of the Soviet Union.
In North Africa Rommel turned the tide
against the British, while in the Pacific Japan
mounted a surprise attack on the U.S. fleet at
Pearl Harbor. And, in the Atlantic, German
U-boats preyed on Allied merchant ships.

Q Who commanded British forces in the Sudan in early 1941?

A General William Platt.

Q What was the name of the German force formed to fight in North Africa in January 1940?

A The *Deutsches Afrika Korps* (or DAK)—the German Africa Corps.

Q Who commanded it?

A General Erwin Rommel.

> **"** DEAREST LU, WE'VE BEEN ATTACKING
> # SINCE THE 31ST WITH
> # DAZZLING SUCCESS **"**
> ROMMEL TO HIS WIFE, NORTH AFRICA, APRIL 1941

Q What was the DAK composed of in early 1941?

A Initially, just two German divisions: the 5th Light (which later became the 21st Panzer) and the 15th Panzer, formed the core of the Africa Corps.

Q When he arrived in North Africa, was Rommel under German or Italian command?

A He was technically under Italian command, though he did have the right to refer to Berlin if he was unhappy concerning the way his command was being handled.

DID YOU KNOW

WHEN ROMMEL ARRIVED IN LIBYA IN FEBRUARY 1941, ITALIAN FORCES
HAD BEEN PUSHED BACK TO EL AGHEILA. THE INITIAL GERMAN FORCE,
WHICH COMPRISED JUST THE 5TH LIGHT DIVISION, BENEFITED FROM A
REDIRECTION OF MANY OF THE BRITISH COMMONWEALTH FORCES
DEPLOYED IN EASTERN LIBYA AWAY FROM THAT THEATER TO DEFEND
MAINLAND GREECE. THIS REDEPLOYMENT LEFT JUST INEXPERIENCED
COMMONWEALTH TROOPS, PARTLY EQUIPPED WITH CAPTURED ITALIAN
WEAPONS, TO DEFEND THE BRITISH FRONT IN LIBYA. ROMMEL, EVER THE
AUDACIOUS ARMORED COMMANDER, IGNORED THE ADVICE OF HIS
SUPERIORS AND SEIZED THE OPPORTUNITY PRESENTED BY THIS MOMENTARY
BRITISH WEAKNESS BY INITIATING AN IMMEDIATE OFFENSIVE.

Q In February 1941 the U.S. Navy was divided into three fleets.
What were they?

A Atlantic, Asiatic, and Pacific.

Q Who became chief of the Soviet general staff and deputy
commissar for defense in February 1941?

A Georgi Zhukov.

Q Why did Hitler wish to see a stable Balkans that was either
neutral or, preferably, pro-German?

A Hitler desired these conditions to ensure that events in the Balkans
did not disrupt Germany's preparations for Barbarossa, the planned
invasion of the Soviet Union, slated to begin in late spring 1941.

" MECHILI LANDING GROUND WAS LITTERED WITH DESTROYED PLANES
Heinz Werner, Africa Corps, April 1941

Q Why did the Italian invasion of Greece threaten Germany's preparations for the invasion of the USSR?

A Hitler feared that Greece would secure a military alliance with Great Britain against the Italians, an agreement that the British could then fashion into an antiGerman front to threaten the southern flank of the German concentration areas for Barbarossa. Even worse, from Greek air bases British long-range bombers could attack the Ploesti oilfields in Romania, from where the Wehrmacht obtained most of its fuel.

Q How did Hitler intend to resolve this issue?

A Hitler decided to initiate decisive military action during the spring of 1941 to settle permanently the Balkan imbroglio before Barbarossa commenced. This action comprised nothing less than an intended German conquest of Greece, staged from Bulgarian soil.

Q Who raided the Lofoten Islands in March 1941?

A An Anglo–Norwegian commando raid and naval assault on the Lofoten Islands, off Norway, destroyed fish-oil plants used in explosives production, captured 215 Germans, rescued 300 Norwegians, and sank 10 ships.

Q What was the U.S. Lend-Lease Bill of March 1941?

A President Franklin D. Roosevelt signed the Lend-Lease Bill that allowed Britain to obtain supplies without having immediately to pay for them in cash.

Q What was the Japanese "Greater East Asia Co-Prosperity Sphere"?

A An East Asia free of colonial influence and united under Japanese hegemony. Japan hoped that the Co-Prosperity Sphere would lead many colonial Asian countries to work, violently or otherwise, toward their independence from British, Dutch, and U.S. influence.

Q What was the position of Yugoslavia in early 1941?

A In early 1941, Hitler began the necessary diplomatic moves to bring Romania and Bulgaria into the Axis pact, a situation that placed the Yugoslav government, certainly not a staunch enemy of Berlin, in a difficult position. During February and March, German forces moved first on to Romanian and then Bulgarian soil. Bowing to the political wind, the Yugoslavs reluctantly discussed with Germany plans for a joint invasion of Greece, thereby intending to avoid a German violation of Yugoslav sovereignty as a stepping-stone for its attack on Greece.

Q Why did Germany invade Yugoslavia in April 1941?

A A pro-British regime had seized power in Yugoslavia on 27 March.

71

DID YOU KNOW

FOLLOWING THE FALL OF FRANCE IN JUNE 1940, U.S. PRESIDENT FRANKLIN D. ROOSEVELT PURSUED A POLICY OF SUPPLYING BRITAIN WITH THE SUPPLIES IT REQUIRED TO CARRY ON THE FIGHT AGAINST NAZI GERMANY. AS DEPENDENCE ON THESE IMPORTS INCREASED, IN DECEMBER 1940 THE BRITISH PRIME MINISTER, WINSTON CHURCHILL, PROPOSED AN ARRANGEMENT WHEREBY THE ALLIED NATIONS COULD OBTAIN ESSENTIAL U.S. GOODS AND EQUIPMENT BUT WOULD REPAY THE UNITED STATES AFTER THE WAR.

Q Who was the British commander at the Battle of Cape Matapan in March 1941?

A Admiral Sir Andrew Cunningham.

Q What was the result of the battle?

A British torpedo-bombers damaged the Italian battleship *Vittorio Veneto* and crippled the cruiser *Pola*. Three British battleships then engaged two cruisers sent to cover the *Pola*. The Battle of Cape Matapan claimed five Italian ships and 3,000 men killed. The British lost only one aircraft in the action.

Q What was the strategic situation of Yugoslavia in early April 1941?

A In strategic terms the defensive power of the Yugoslav Army was fundamentally compromised by the fact that it faced hostile Axis powers—Italy (including Albania), the Austrian parts of the Reich, Romania, Hungary, and Bulgaria—on three sides.

Q What was the strategic situation of Greece in early April 1941?

A Though the Greek Army enjoyed a strong geostrategic position, the inconclusive war with Hitler's Italian allies had already tied down some two-thirds of the Greek Army in the northwestern part of the country, leaving a small force to resist the German invasion.

" SUDDENLY, THE U-BOAT SPOTTED US
AND IN A CLOUD OF SPRAY
HE CRASH-DIVED "
CAPTAIN DONALD MACINTYRE, ROYAL NAVY,
MARCH 1941

DID YOU KNOW

ERWIN ROMMEL (1891–1944) WAS A DECORATED WORLD WAR I OFFICER WHO COMMANDED HITLER'S BODYGUARD AND WAS RESPONSIBLE FOR THE FÜHRER'S PERSONAL SAFETY DURING THE POLISH CAMPAIGN. HE THEN TOOK COMMAND OF THE 7TH PANZER DIVISION FOR THE 1940 INVASION OF FRANCE. HIS SPEEDY ADVANCE ACROSS THE MEUSE RIVER AND DRIVE TO THE ENGLISH CHANNEL EARNED HIM A REPUTATION AS A DARING TANK COMMANDER. FOLLOWING THE FAILED ITALIAN CAMPAIGN IN NORTH AFRICA, HE WAS SENT THERE TO LEAD THE AFRIKA KORPS IN 1941. ROMMEL BECAME A MASTER OF DESERT WARFARE TACTICS WITH HIS ABILITY TO EXPLOIT OPPORTUNITIES, EMPLOY UNORTHODOX METHODS, AND DEPLOY HIS ARMORED FORCES TO MAXIMUM EFFECT. AFTER RECAPTURING TOBRUK IN 1942, HE PUSHED THE ALLIES BACK TO EL ALAMEIN IN EGYPT. THE "DESERT FOX" WAS PROMOTED TO FIELD MARSHAL, HAVING LED THE AFRIKA KORPS TO A STRING OF VICTORIES.

Q Turkey and the Soviet Union were allies of Yugoslavia in April 1941. True or false?

73

A True. But when Germany attacked Yugoslavia neither wished to get involved in a conflict against Europe's premier military machine, and so avoided criticizing the German invasion. Stalin, in particular, wished to avoid worsening his already delicate relations with Hitler, in the hope that the Führer would not invade the Soviet Union while Britain remained undefeated.

Q Which German general accepted the Greek capitulation in April 1941?

A Colonel-General Alfred Jodl, chief of staff of OKW.

Q What was Operation Demon?

A The British evacuation from Greece in April 1941.

Q How did the SS *Leibstandarte* Division cross the Corinth Canal in April 1941?

A In requisitioned fishing boats.

Q Why did the Germans decide to invade Crete in May 1941?

A The Allied possession of Crete posed a major threat to Axis operations. From there, British aircraft could interdict the naval convoys crossing the Mediterranean to resupply Rommel's forces in North Africa and could still undertake long-range missions to attack the Ploesti oilfields in Romania.

❝ THE WAR AGAINST RUSSIA WILL BE SUCH THAT IT CANNOT BE CONDUCTED
IN A CHIVALROUS FASHION
❞
ADOLF HITLER, MARCH 1941

Q What was the codename of the German invasion of Crete?

A Operation Mercury.

Q What happened at the Battle of Keren, Eritrea, in March 1941?

A Italian troops were forced to retreat toward the capital, Asmara. The Italians lost 3,000 men compared to British fatalities of 536. Asmara fell five days later.

DID YOU KNOW

DURING THE NORTH AFRICAN CAMPAIGN, BOTH THE GERMANS AND
BRITISH DENIGRATED THE FIGHTING CAPABILITIES OF ITALIAN TROOPS.
AFTER THE WAR, THE ANGLO-GERMAN ACCOUNTS OF THE CAMPAIGN
DEVELOPED THE IDEA OF THE ITALIANS AS A "NONMARTIAL" RACE, IN A
CARICATURE BASED ON THE ALLEGED "LATIN" TEMPERAMENT. THE
ITALIANS SUPPLIED THE BULK OF THE AXIS TROOPS FIGHTING IN NORTH
AFRICA, AND TOO OFTEN THE GERMAN ARMY UNFAIRLY RIDICULED
ITALIAN MILITARY EFFECTIVENESS EITHER DUE TO ITS OWN ARROGANCE OR
TO CONCEAL ITS OWN MISTAKES AND FAILURES. IN REALITY, A SIGNIFICANT
NUMBER OF ITALIAN UNITS FOUGHT SKILLFULLY IN NORTH AFRICA, AND
MANY "GERMAN" VICTORIES WERE THE RESULT OF ITALIAN SKILL-AT-ARMS
AND A COMBINED AXIS EFFORT. THE BRITISH CREATED SOMETHING OF A
MYTH AROUND ROMMEL, SINCE THEY PREFERRED TO JUSTIFY THEIR
DEFEATS WITH THE PRESENCE IN THE ENEMY CAMP OF AN EXCEPTIONAL
GENERAL, RATHER THAN RECOGNIZE THE SUPERIOR QUALITIES OF THE
COMBATANTS, WHETHER ITALIAN OR GERMAN. THAT CERTAIN ITALIAN
FORMATIONS FOUGHT AS EFFECTIVELY AS THEY DID REMAINED AN
IMPRESSIVE FEAT CONSIDERING THAT ON THE HOME FRONT ITALY'S
POPULATION HAD LITTLE STOMACH FOR THE WAR.

75

Q Why did the United States occupy Greenland in April 1941?

A To prevent the Danish colony falling into German hands.

Q Who was the commander of the Crete garrison in May 1941?

A Major General Bernard Freyberg.

" THE FIRST SALVO FROM HOOD FELL JUST
ASTERN—ONE COULD SEE THE GREAT
TOWERING COLUMNS OF
WATER SPURTING INTO
THE AIR **"**

ESMOND KNIGHT, ON BOARD
HMS *PRINCE OF WALES*,
MAY 1941

Q **What was the size of the Allied garrison on Crete?**

A 42,000 troops, including 11,000 Greek soldiers.

Q **What were the problems facing the garrison on the eve of the German assault?**

A First, many of the British, Commonwealth, and Greek forces that had withdrawn from the mainland had managed to transport only a fraction of their equipment with them. Second, the RAF had taken heavy casualties on the mainland and was able to offer only minimal air cover to the ground forces.

Q **How did the Germans plan to conquer Crete?**

A Some 16,000 élite airborne troops—both paratroopers and gliderborne soldiers—of the 7th Parachute Division would land on Crete's three main airfields at Maleme, Retimo, and Heraklion, as well as near the capital, Canea. Once these forces had captured these landing strips, German aircraft would transport some 3,000 reinforcements from the 5th Mountain Division to these locations. Simultaneously, maritime convoys would carry a further 7,000 mountain soldiers to Crete for amphibious assault operations.

Q Who was the commander of Germany's paratroopers in 1941?

A General Kurt Student.

Q What was the main gun on the Panzer III Ausf G?

A The 50mm KwK L/42 gun.

Q What was the decisive moment in the battle for Crete in May 1941?

A On May 23 Freyberg ordered his forces at Maleme to withdraw to Canea. The Germans immediately followed up the enemy withdrawal, and prepared themselves for an attack that would break through the British defenses at Canea and enable them to race east to rescue their encircled comrades at Retimo and Heraklion.

77

DID YOU KNOW

DURING GERMANY'S EARLY BLITZKRIEG CAMPAIGNS, PARTICULARLY THAT IN FRANCE DURING MAY–JUNE 1940, THE GERMAN ARMY HAD EXTENSIVELY USED AIR ASSAULTS BY PARACHUTE AND GLIDERBORNE TROOPS TO SUSTAIN THE TEMPO AND MOMENTUM OF THE ADVANCING GROUND TROOPS. THE CATASTROPHIC LOSSES THAT THE GERMAN AIRBORNE FORCES SUFFERED DURING THEIR MAY 1941 AIR ASSAULT ON CRETE, HOWEVER, CONVINCED HITLER THAT SUCH OPERATIONS WERE NOW TOO COSTLY TO REMAIN STRATEGICALLY JUSTIFIED. AT A MEDAL CEREMONY IN MID-JULY 1941, HITLER INFORMED GENERAL STUDENT, COMMANDER OF GERMAN AIRBORNE TROOPS, THAT THE EXPERIENCE OF CRETE HAD LED HIM TO CONCLUDE THAT THE DAY OF THE LARGE-SCALE AIR ASSAULT WAS OVER.

Q Why did Rudolf Hess fly to Britain in May 1941?

A Hess believed a diplomatic coup was possible if he could have an audience with George VI, whom he believed he could persuade to dismiss Churchill. Peace could then be implemented between the two countries and they could act in concert against a common enemy: the Soviet Union.

Q What name did Hess give on landing in Britain by parachute?

A On landing he gave his name as Captain Horn and asked to be escorted to the Duke of Hamilton, whom he had met at the 1936 Berlin Olympic Games.

DID YOU KNOW

AS WITH OTHER BLITZKRIEG CAMPAIGNS, THE USE OF THE LUFTWAFFE WAS CRUCIAL TO GERMAN SUCCESS IN THE BALKANS. IN YUGOSLAVIA ACTUAL OPERATIONS WERE CARRIED OUT BY VIII AIR CORPS UNDER LIEUTENANT GENERAL WOLFRAM VON RICHTHOFEN. THE WEHRMACHT INAUGURATED ITS ATTACK ON YUGOSLAVIA, AT HITLER'S PERSONAL INSISTENCE, WITH OPERATION RETRIBUTION, A TERROR BOMBING ATTACK ON BELGRADE, THE YUGOSLAV CAPITAL. DESPITE THE YUGOSLAV DECLARATION OF APRIL 4 THAT BELGRADE WAS AN "OPEN CITY" FREE OF MILITARY UNITS, SOME 500 GERMAN AIRCRAFT POUNDED THE CITY DURING APRIL 6–7. THESE AERIAL ATTACKS DEVASTATED LARGE PARTS OF THE CITY AND KILLED PERHAPS AS MANY AS 6,000 CIVILIANS. IN ADDITION TO THE PROPAGANDA BENEFITS OBTAINED FROM THIS DEMONSTRATION OF GERMAN AERIAL POWER, THE OPERATION ALSO ACHIEVED THE USEFUL TACTICAL MISSION OF SMASHING THE YUGOSLAV COMMAND AND CONTROL FACILITIES LOCATED IN THE CITY.

Q Did Hess meet George VI?

A No. He was immediately arrested.

Q Which ship sank the British battlecruiser HMS *Hood* in May 1941?

A The German battleship *Bismarck*.

"
IF WE SEE THAT GERMANY IS
WINNING THE WAR WE
OUGHT TO HELP
RUSSIA
HARRY S. TRUMAN, JULY 24, 1941
"

79

Q What was the Soviet-Japanese Neutrality Pact of April 1941?

A The pact stated that each party would "respect the territorial integrity and inviolability of the other party; and should one of the Contracting Parties become the object of hostilities on the part of one or several third powers, the other Contracting Party will observe neutrality throughout the duration of the conflict." The pact would initially last for five years.

Q How did the signatories to the pact benefit?

A The pact freed up Red Army divisions facing the Japanese in the East for deployment elsewhere and allowed Japan to concentrate on its ambitions in China and Southeast Asia.

Q What was Operation Brevity?

A A British offensive in North Africa in May 1941. The British attacked the Axis positions at Sollum, the Halfaya Pass, and Capuzzo.

Q Was it a success?

A No. After a successful initial British advance some 15 miles (24 km) west, Rommel counterattacked and recaptured all the ground his forces had just relinquished.

Q Who led the pro-Axis coup in Iraq in April 1941?

A Rashid Ali.

Q What was the codename of the German attack on the Soviet Union in June 1941?

A Operation Barbarossa.

Q Who was Barbarossa?

A A medieval German emperor who had fought the Slavs.

"" GIVE US THE TOOLS, AND WE WILL
FINISH THE JOB
WINSTON CHURCHILL TO PRESIDENT ROOSEVELT,
FEBRUARY 9, 1941

DID YOU KNOW

THE OBJECTIVES OF OPERATION BARBAROSSA REMAINED A CONFUSED MIXTURE OF CONTRADICTORY AIMS. THE PLAN INCLUDED ECONOMIC OBJECTS SUCH AS THE AGRICULTURE OF THE UKRAINE, THE INDUSTRY OF THE DON BASIN, AND THE OIL OF THE CAUCASUS; IT TARGETED THE POPULATION CENTERS THAT DOUBLED AS KEY COMMUNICATIONS NODES, SUCH AS MOSCOW, KIEV, AND KHARKOV; AND IT ALSO AIMED FOR MARITIME CENTERS SUCH AS LENINGRAD, ROSTOV, AND SEVASTOPOL, WHOSE CAPTURE WOULD PROTECT THE FLANKS OF THE AXIS ADVANCE. THE PURSUIT OF SO MANY DIFFERENT TARGETS LEFT THE AXIS INVASION FORCES WITHOUT A CLEAR, OVERRIDING OBJECTIVE TOWARD WHICH THEIR MAIN EFFORT COULD BE DIRECTED.

Q In Barbarossa, who commanded Army Group North?

A Field Marshal Ritter Wilhelm von Leeb.

Q In Barbarossa, who commanded Army Group Center?

A Field Marshal Fedor von Bock.

Q In Barbarossa, who commanded Army Group South?

A Field Marshal Gerd von Rundstedt.

Q What was Army Group North's Barbarossa mission?

A To capture Leningrad, link up with Finnish forces pushing south from Karelia, and then push on to capture Archangel on the White Sea.

Q What was Army Group Center's Barbarossa mission?

A To advance through Belorussia along the direct route via Smolensk to Moscow, and thence through Gorky and Kazan to the Ural Mountains.

Q What was Army Group South's Barbarossa mission?

A To advance through the Ukraine—via Kiev and Kharkov—to Rostov on the Sea of Azov, and thence thrust southeast into the oil-rich Caucasus and east through Kazakhstan to the southern Urals around Orsk.

Q Führer Directive 21 (Case Barbarossa) set out the strategic objective of Barbarossa. What was this?

A The destruction of the bulk of the Red Army located in the western areas of the Soviet Union. The Germans sought to destroy the Red Army in the 250 mile (400 km) border region up to the Dnieper and Dvina rivers. Once the German Army had achieved this task, it was to push on toward the Ural mountains.

Q Who was the commander of the German Second Panzer Group during Operation Barbarossa?

A Colonel General Heinz Guderian.

Q What was Hitler's Commissar Order of June 1941?

A Hitler's Directive for the Treatment of Political Commissars stated that Red Army commissars would be immediately shot when captured.

Q What was the Soviet equivalent of a German army group?

A A front.

Q What was the Lucy Spy Ring?

A A Soviet espionage group, part of the so-called Red Orchestra spy group. It contained senior German figures.

DID YOU KNOW

IN DECEMBER 1940, A SERIES OF OKH WAR GAMES AND INDEPENDENT STUDIES REGARDING A GERMAN WAR IN THE EAST, CONDUCTED UNDER THE DIRECTION OF HEAD QUARTERMASTER OF THE GENERAL STAFF, MAJOR GENERAL FRIEDRICH PAULUS, CONCLUDED THAT GERMAN FORCES WERE "BARELY SUFFICIENT FOR THE PURPOSE" ASSIGNED TO THEM. IN ADDITION, THE WEHRMACHT WOULD HAVE NO RESERVES LEFT BY THE TIME IT REACHED MOSCOW, FORCING THE ARMY TO UNDERTAKE AN ATTACK AGAINST THE CITY WITH NO REINFORCEMENTS. AND THE VOLGA–ARCHANGEL LINE WAS A TARGET THAT WAS BEYOND THE REACH OF THE WEHRMACHT. MORE WORRYINGLY, THE STUDIES REVEALED THAT IN A CAMPAIGN AREA THE SIZE OF THE WESTERN USSR, THE PANZER COLUMNS AND SLOWER-MOVING INFANTRY WOULD QUICKLY BECOME SEPARATED, LEAVING THE FLANKS OF THE PANZER FORCES DANGEROUSLY EXPOSED.

Q What important piece of intelligence did the Lucy Spy Ring send to Moscow in mid-June 1941?

A That the German attack on the USSR would begin on June 22.

Q Who was the president of Turkey in 1941?

A President Inönü.

Q What was Turkey's position in 1941?

A Despite German pressure on Turkey to side with the Axis powers, President Inönü was of the opinion that the Axis powers could not win the war. And despite pressure, Turkey did not allow Axis troops, ships, or aircraft to pass through or over Turkey and its territorial waters.

Q What was the strength of a Soviet mechanized corps in June 1941?

A 36,000 men and 1,031 tanks.

DID YOU KNOW

THERE IS LITTLE DOUBT THAT THE GERMAN CAMPAIGN IN THE BALKANS IN THE SPRING OF 1941 HAD A DETRIMENTAL EFFECT ON THE OUTCOME OF BARBAROSSA. THE DECISION TO INVADE YUGOSLAVIA AND GREECE WAS MADE ON MARCH 27, POSTPONING THE START OF BARBAROSSA FROM MID-MAY. ON APRIL 7, OKH DELAYED BARBAROSSA AGAIN, BY FOUR WEEKS, THUS PUTTING THE START DATE IN MID-JUNE. ONLY ON JUNE 17 DID HITLER SET THE START DATE FOR THE INVASION OF THE SOVIET UNION FOR JUNE 22.

Q **What was the Soviet Stavka?**

A *Shtab vierhovnogo komandovani*—Headquarters of the Main Command.

Q **What prompted Finland to declare war on the Soviet Union in June 1941?**

A On June 25, a force of 500 Soviet bombers attacked cities and airfields in Finland. Finnish Prime Minister Rangell announced that, as a result, Finland was at war with the USSR.

Q **Who became commander of the Soviet Northwest Front at the end of June 1941?**

A General Petr Sobennikov.

Q **At the end of June how were the German Second and Third Panzer Groups reorganized?**

A They were brought under the overall command of Field Marshal Günther von Kluge's Fourth Army, which was renamed the Fourth Panzer Army.

Q **What was a Pak 38?**

A A German 50mm antitank gun.

Q **What was a Soviet *glavkom*?**

A A theater command. Several were established in July 1941 to coordinate front defenses more effectively. *Glavkom* Northwest was headed by Marshal Voroshilov (Northern and Northwest Fronts and Baltic and Northern Fleets), Marshal Timoshenko commanded *Glavkom* West (Western Front and Pinsk Flotilla), and *Glavkom* Southwest was under Marshal Budenny (Southwestern and Southern Fronts and the Black Sea Fleet).

"" **BELIEVE! OBEY! FIGHT!**
ITALIAN WAR SLOGAN
""

Q **Who replaced General Sir Archibald Wavell as the Middle East commander of British forces in July 1941?**

A General Sir Claude Auchinleck.

Q **Why was he replaced?**

A Wavell's Middle East Command had achieved considerable success against numerically superior Italian forces despite supply shortages. Further commitments in Greece, Iraq, and Syria then overstretched his forces. Nevertheless, Churchill wanted a decisive offensive in the desert, and his failure to achieve this led to his transfer.

DID YOU KNOW

A MUTUAL ASSISTANCE AGREEMENT WAS SIGNED IN MOSCOW BETWEEN THE SOVIETS AND THE BRITISH IN JULY 1941. IT STATED: "THE TWO GOVERNMENTS MUTUALLY UNDERTAKE TO RENDER EACH OTHER ASSISTANCE AND SUPPORT OF ALL KINDS IN THE PRESENT WAR AGAINST HITLERITE GERMANY. THEY FURTHER UNDERTAKE THAT DURING THIS WAR THEY WILL NEITHER NEGOTIATE NOR CONCLUDE AN ARMISTICE OR TREATY OF PEACE EXCEPT BY MUTUAL AGREEMENT."

Q What does *Einsatzgruppen* mean?

A Special Action Groups.

Q What was their task?

A To follow immediately behind the German armies as they advanced into the USSR, and round up Jews, gypsies, political commissars, and anyone else who was perceived by the Nazis as being a real or potential threat to the "New Order" being established in the East. All persons thus taken were to be executed immediately

Q What was their composition?

A Each one contained a mixture of Waffen-SS, Gestapo, Kripo (Criminal Police), SD (Security Police), and regular uniformed police personnel.

Q Who commanded Einsatzgruppe A?

A SS-Brigadeführer Franz Stahlecker.

Q Who commanded *Einsatzgruppe* B?

A SS-Gruppenführer Arthur Nebe.

Q Who commanded *Einsatzgruppe* C?

A SS-Oberführer Dr Otto Rasch.

Q Who commanded *Einsatzgruppe* D?

A SS-Gruppenführer Otto Ohlendorf.

> " I RECEIVED MY FIRST WAR DECORATION,
> NAMELY, THE TANK ASSAULT
> ## MEDAL. I WEAR
> ## IT PROUDLY "
> SERGEANT KARL FUCHS, GERMAN SOLDIER,
> EASTERN FRONT, JUNE 1941

Q Why did U.S. troops move into Iceland in July 1941?

A To protect shipping from German U-boat attacks.

Q To which position did Stalin appoint himself on July 21, 1941?

A Defense Commissar.

Q Why was the Fourth Panzer Army disbanded at the end of July 1941?

A The Fourth Panzer Army was disbanded, with the Fourth Army becoming an infantry force once again. Guderian's Second Panzer Group was thus removed from under Kluge's command and placed directly under the control of Army Group Center. This was due to disagreements between Guderian and Kluge regarding strategy and objectives, which were having an adverse effect on operations.

Q Which was the most successful U-boat of the war?

A *U-48*. During her career she sank 51 merchant vessels and one warship. She was scuttled on May 3, 1945.

Q Which Vichy French commander surrendered Syria to the Allies in July 1941?

A General Henri Dentz.

DID YOU KNOW

IN MARCH 1941, THE U.S. CONGRESS PASSED THE LEND-LEASE ACT AND GAVE ROOSEVELT WIDE-RANGING POWERS TO SUPPLY GOODS AND SERVICES TO "ANY COUNTRY WHOSE DEFENSE THE PRESIDENT DEEMS VITAL TO THE DEFENSE OF THE UNITED STATES." ALMOST $13 BILLION HAD BEEN ALLOCATED TO THE LEND-LEASE ARRANGEMENT BY NOVEMBER 1941. ALTHOUGH BRITAIN NOW HAD THE OPPORTUNITY TO INCREASE THE AMOUNT OF U.S. IMPORTS, HER OWN WAR PRODUCTION HAD BEEN INCREASING DURING THIS PERIOD. FOOD AND OIL FROM THE UNITED STATES, HOWEVER, WAS STILL CRUCIAL TO HER SURVIVAL.

Q Who headed the Czech government-in-exile?

A Edouard Benes.

Q With which state did this government sign a mutual assistance agreement in July 1941?

A The Soviet Union.

Q What was the British Operation Substance of July 1941?

A The British transportation of supplies from Gibraltar to Malta.

Q Name the two Soviet pockets destroyed on the Eastern Front in early August 1941.

A The Smolensk and Uman Pockets.

DID YOU KNOW

IN AUGUST 1939, HITLER AND STALIN HAD SIGNED A NONAGGRESSION TREATY, THE MOLOTOV-RIBBENTROP PACT. THE PACT DID NOT, HOWEVER, ALTER THE UNDERLYING TENSION THAT EXISTED BETWEEN THE TWO COUNTRIES. RATHER, THE TREATY WAS SIMPLY A TEMPORARY PIECE OF CYNICAL EXPEDIENCY BY BOTH LEADERS. IN THE PACT THE TWO AGREED JOINTLY TO INVADE AND THEN DIVIDE POLAND, WHILE STALIN ALSO GUARANTEED TO SEND LARGE GRAIN EXPORTS TO GERMANY UNTIL MID-JUNE 1941—NOTE THAT DATE! THUS, HITLER OBTAINED A FREE HAND FROM A QUIESCENT STALIN TO DEAL WITH THE WEST IN 1940 WITHOUT FEAR OF THE TRADITIONAL GERMAN STRATEGIC SPECTER OF A TWO-FRONT WAR. THE PERIOD ALSO GAVE STALIN TIME TO PREPARE FOR A WAR HE WAS CERTAIN WOULD COME.

" THE HEAT WAS TREMENDOUS, THOUGH INTERSPERSED WITH SUDDEN SHOWERS "

GENERAL BLUMENTRITT, GERMAN ARMY,
RUSSIA, JULY 1941

Q **What was the Russian Katyusha multiple rocket launcher better known as?**

A Stalin's Organ.

Q **Why did Britain and the Soviet Union invade Iran in August 1941?**

A Because of the British and American need to transport war materials across Iran to the Soviet Union, which would have violated Iranian neutrality.

Q **Was the invasion justified?**

A Yes. The occupation of Iran was vital to the Allied cause. Britain, the USSR, and the United States together would ship more than 5 million tons (5.08 million tonnes) of munitions and other war materiel across Iran to the USSR between 1941 and 1945.

Q **At which port did the first convoy of aid from Britain to the Soviet Union land?**

A Archangel.

Q What was the German Operation Beowulf of September 1941?

A An amphibious assault against the Estonian islands on the Eastern Front, which were defended by 23,600 troops and 140 artillery pieces of the Soviet Eighth Army.

Q Who took command of Vichy French forces in North Africa in August 1941?

A Admiral Jean Darlan.

Q What was the base of the Soviet Baltic Fleet?

A Leningrad.

❝ CARELESS TALK COSTS LIVES ❞
BRITISH POSTER, 1941

Q What was the codename for the German assault on Moscow?

A Operation Typhoon.

Q How did the Germans intend to capture Moscow?

A The Ninth Army and Third Panzer Group would drive to the north of the city, and the Second Panzer Group and Second Army would attack from the south. In this way Moscow would be enveloped by a double pincer movement, with the panzer formations forming the outer pincers.

DID YOU KNOW

TIMING HAD A CRITICAL INFLUENCE ON THE OUTCOME OF THE MOSCOW
ATTACK, CODENAMED TYPHOON, BUT THERE WERE OTHER FACTORS THAT
INFLUENCED ITS COURSE. FIRST, ALTHOUGH ARMY GROUP NORTH HAD
SUCCEEDED IN ENCIRCLING LENINGRAD IN EARLY SEPTEMBER, THE FACT
THAT THE CITY WAS STILL IN SOVIET HANDS MEANT THAT ARMY GROUP
NORTH COULD NOT CONTRIBUTE TO OPERATION TYPHOON BY MOUNTING
A FLANKING ATTACK AGAINST THE SOVIET CAPITAL FROM THE NORTHWEST.
IN ADDITION, HITLER'S INSISTENCE THAT ARMY GROUP SOUTH SHOULD
DIRECT ITS COMBAT STRENGTH TOWARD THE CONQUEST OF THE DONETS
BASIN, ROSTOV, AND THE CRIMEA MEANT IT COULD NOT PARTICIPATE
DIRECTLY IN TYPHOON. NEVERTHELESS, BOTH HITLER AND OKH
BELIEVED THAT ARMY GROUP CENTER, SUITABLY REINFORCED, COULD
DEFEAT RED ARMY FORCES IN FRONT OF MOSCOW AND CAPTURE THE CITY
BEFORE THE END OF THE YEAR.

Q How many Soviet troops were captured in the Kiev Pocket in September 1941?

A 665,000.

Q What happened at Babi Yar in September 1941?

A A German SS unit, *Sonderkommando* 4a, working in conjunction with Ukrainian auxiliary police, began the mass murder of Kiev's Jews at Babi Yar ravine. In two days of shooting, 33,771 Jews were murdered. Tens of thousands of others would be slaughtered at Babi Yar over the next months.

Q Which Luftwaffe ace sank the Soviet battleship *Marat* in September 1941?

A Hans-Ulrich Rudel.

> ## MY JU 87 KEEPS PERFECTLY STEADY AS
> ## I DIVE; SHE DOES NOT
> ## SWERVE AN INCH
> HANS ULRICH RUDEL, STUKA PILOT,
> EASTERN FRONT, SEPTEMBER 1941

Q What was the Atlantic Charter?

A Formulated in August 1941 by Winston Churchill and Franklin D. Roosevelt, it was an ideology that asserted liberal policies that articulated their intentions not to acquire any territories or change national borders without the support of the populations concerned. People were also to be granted self-determination regarding how they were governed, and equal access was to be given to economic resources.

Q Jews in Germany were forced to wear what symbol from September 1, 1941?

A A yellow Star of David.

Q Which post was Reinhard Heydrich appointed to in September 1941?

A Protector of Bohemia and Moravia.

Q What ancient curse did Heydrich violate when he assumed his new position?

A Heydrich was shown the crown jewels of Czechoslovakia by President Hacha, who told him of an intriguing legend that surrounded them. It was said that any person not the true heir who put the crown on his head was sure to die. It is said that Heydrich laughed and placed the crown on his head.

Q Which German auxiliary cruiser fought the Australian cruiser HMAS *Sydney* in November 1941?

A The *Kormoran*.

Q What happened in this encounter?

A The cruiser was deceived by the disguised German raider's pretence of being an innocent Dutch freighter and came too close. The concealed guns quickly inflicted serious damage and a torpedo hit damaged the *Sydney* seriously. The cruiser replied effectively with her guns, but both ships caught fire and were heavily damaged. The *Sydney* drifted away and was never seen again, and the *Kormoran* sank.

DID YOU KNOW

HITLER'S DIRECTIVE 33 OF JULY 19, 1941, SHIFTED THE GERMAN MAIN EFFORT SOUTH AWAY FROM MOSCOW TOWARD THE UKRAINE. HERE, AFTER MID-AUGUST, THE GERMANS PLANNED TO ENACT ANOTHER GREAT DOUBLE ENVELOPMENT THROUGH THE COOPERATION OF KLEIST'S FIRST PANZER GROUP FROM ARMY GROUP SOUTH WITH GUDERIAN'S SECOND PANZER GROUP FROM ARMY GROUP CENTER. BACK IN MID-JULY, KLEIST'S ARMOR HAD COMMENCED ITS PREPARATORY OPERATIONS WITH A THRUST SOUTHEAST TOWARD THE RIVER DNIEPER TO TURN THE SOUTHERN FLANK OF A MASS OF IMMOBILE ENEMY INFANTRY WEST OF KIEV. ELEMENTS OF KLEIST'S FORMA-TION ALSO THRUST SOUTH TO LINK UP ON AUGUST 3 WITH THE SEVENTEENTH ARMY TO CREATE AN ANCILLARY ENCIRCLEMENT OF 200,000 SOVIET INFANTRYMEN AT UMAN. MEANWHILE, KLEIST'S FORCES CONTINUED TO THRUST RAPIDLY EAST UNTIL, ON AUGUST 12, THEY CAPTURED KREMENCHUG ON THE DNIEPER RIVER, 110 MILES (177 KM) BEHIND THE MAIN NORTH-SOUTH SOVIET DEFENSIVE LINE BETWEEN GOMEL AND KIEV. IF KLEIST'S PANZERS COULD PUSH NORTH TO MEET THE INTENDED THRUST SOUTH BY GUDERIAN'S ARMOR, THE ENSUING ENCIRCLEMENT WOULD ENGULF FIVE SOVIET ARMIES. THEY COULD AND DID, AND THE TRAP CLOSED ON 665,000 RED ARMY SOLDIERS IN THE KIEV POCKET.

Q Was the German Army that invaded the Soviet Union in 1941 fully motorized?

A No. Contrary to popular belief, the 1941 German Army was not a motorized force. Outside its small number of elite mechanized divisions, the bulk of the army comprised infantry divisions equipped with horse-drawn vehicles; some 625,000 German Army horses invaded the Soviet Union in 1941.

Q Why did the Germans have problems using the Russian rail network in 1941?

A The Germans planned to use Soviet railroads to resupply their troops, but as these were on a wider gauge than the European lines, engineers had to regauge every mile of track before German locomotives could operate along them.

Q What was a *Vernichtungskrieg*?

A A war of racial annihilation, as waged by Nazi Germany against Bolshevik Russia.

DID YOU KNOW

ON JUNE 23–24, 1941, THE SECOND AND THIRD DAYS OF OPERATION BARBAROSSA, ELEMENTS OF BOTH HOEPNER'S FOURTH PANZER GROUP IN LITHUANIA AND KLEIST'S FIRST PANZER GROUP NEAR THE BUG RIVER EXPERIENCED THEIR FIRST ENCOUNTER WITH THE NEW SOVIET KV-1 HEAVY TANK. TO THE GERMAN TROOPS' DISMAY, AT RANGES AS LOW AS 2700 FT (820 M), EVEN THE ROUNDS FIRED BY THE 50MM KWK L/42 GUN MOUNTED IN THEIR MOST MODERN PANZER III TANKS SIMPLY BOUNCED OFF THE FRONT OF THESE SOVIET HEAVY TANKS.

❝ A NEW ORDER FOR EUROPE ❞
THE SLOGAN TAKEN FROM
THE REPORT OF A MEETING BETWEEN
HITLER AND MUSSOLINI, AUGUST 1941

Q What were panzergrenadiers?

A German motorized infantry.

Q During the first 48 hours of Operation Barbarossa the Luftwaffe destroyed enemy aircraft at a rate of one every 80 seconds. True or false?

A True. During the first 48 hours of Barbarossa the Luftwaffe committed its 2,150 available first-line aircraft to a concentrated counter-air campaign to secure aerial superiority over the theater. Aided by total surprise, massed German aerial formations attacked the rows of enemy planes sitting on the runways of the western Soviet Union. In these first 48 hours alone, the Luftwaffe succeeded in destroying 2,200 Soviet aircraft.

Q Why did Stalin lift the ban on religion throughout the USSR in October 1941?

A To boost civilian morale.

Q Why did the Finns refuse to attack Leningrad in 1941?

A Following the Winter War of 1939–1940, Finland was eager to get back the territory she had lost to the USSR. When Operation Barbarossa was launched, the Finns were quick to point out that they were participating only to retake Finnish territory lost in 1940.

Q Which leader stated in November 1941: "The German invaders are straining their last forces. There is no doubt that Germany cannot keep up such an effort for any long time"?

A Joseph Stalin in Red Square, Moscow, on the anniversary of the October Revolution.

Q Which general was placed in command of U.S. forces in the Far East in July 1941?

A Douglas MacArthur.

Q Which firm manufactured the German Bf 109 fighter?

A Messerschmitt.

Q What was the Royal Air Force's first monoplane fighter?

A The Hawker Hurricane.

> **"** IT WAS A STRANGE FEELING TO
> BE DROPPED SUDDENLY INTO AN
> ALIEN LAND WITH ORDERS
> TO CONQUER IT **"**
> BARON VON DER HEYDTE, GERMAN PARATROOPER,
> CRETE, MAY 1941

DID YOU KNOW

THE INVASION OF THE USSR BY NAZI GERMANY WAS A DISASTER FOR THE SOVIET ECONOMY. BY THE END OF 1941, FOR EXAMPLE, THE USSR HAD LOST THE GRAIN LANDS OF BELORUSSIA AND THE UKRAINE; ONE-THIRD OF ITS RAIL NETWORK; THREE-QUARTERS OF ITS IRON ORE, COAL, AND STEEL SUPPLY; AND 40 PERCENT OF ITS ELECTRICITY GENERATING CAPACITY. THIS CATASTROPHE WOULD HAVE BEEN MUCH WORSE HAD IT NOT BEEN FOR THE EVACUATION OF HUNDREDS OF FACTORIES AND TENS OF THOUSANDS OF WORKERS EAST TO THE URALS, TO THE VOLGA REGION, TO KAZAKHSTAN, AND TO EASTERN SIBERIA. THE SCALE OF THE MOVEMENT WAS ASTOUNDING: BETWEEN JULY AND DECEMBER 1941, 1,523 ENTERPRISES, THE MAJORITY STEEL, IRON, AND ENGINEERING PLANTS, WERE TRANSPORTED EAST.

Q What type of aircraft was the British Handley Page Hampden?

99

A A medium bomber.

Q How many crew did it have?

A Four.

Q What was its nickname?

A The "Flying Suitcase."

Q Which German battlecruiser was torpedoed by British aircraft at Brest in April 1941?

A *Gneisenau.*

Q What type of warship was the German *Emden*?

A Light cruiser.

DID YOU KNOW

TIMING HAD A CRITICAL INFLUENCE ON THE OUTCOME OF THE MOSCOW ATTACK, CODENAMED TYPHOON, BUT THERE WERE OTHER FACTORS THAT INFLUENCED ITS COURSE. FIRST, ALTHOUGH ARMY GROUP NORTH HAD SUCCEEDED IN ENCIRCLING LENINGRAD IN EARLY SEPTEMBER, THE FACT THAT THE CITY WAS STILL IN SOVIET HANDS MEANT THAT ARMY GROUP NORTH COULD NOT CONTRIBUTE TO OPERATION TYPHOON BY MOUNTING A FLANK- ING ATTACK AGAINST THE SOVIET CAPITAL FROM THE NORTHWEST. IN ADDI- TION, HITLER'S INSISTENCE THAT ARMY GROUP SOUTH SHOULD DIRECT ITS COMBAT STRENGTH TOWARD THE CONQUEST OF THE DONETS BASIN, ROSTOV, AND THE CRIMEA MEANT IT COULD NOT PARTICIPATE DIRECTLY IN TYPHOON. NEVERTHELESS, BOTH HITLER AND OKH BELIEVED THAT ARMY GROUP CENTER, SUITABLY REINFORCED, COULD DEFEAT RED ARMY FORCES IN FRONT OF MOSCOW AND CAPTURE THE CITY BEFORE THE END OF THE YEAR. THUS, ON SEPTEMBER 15, OKH ORDERED THE FOURTH PANZER GROUP TO WITH- DRAW HALF ITS ARMOR AND TRANSFER IT TO ARMY GROUP CENTER. THIS TRANSFER BEGAN TWO DAYS LATER. UNFORTUNATELY FOR ARMY GROUP CENTER, THE LATE CONCLUSION OF THE BATTLE OF KIEV AND THE TIME- CONSUMING REGROUPING OF REINFORCEMENTS FROM THE NORTH AND SOUTH MEANT THAT PREPARATIONS FOR TYPHOON WERE CONCLUDED ONLY BY THE END OF SEPTEMBER. IN ADDITION, THE PANZER DIVISIONS INVOLVED WERE ONLY 40–50 PERCENT OF THEIR ORIGINAL COMBAT STRENGTH.

> THE MESSERSCHMITTS COME IN CLOSE FOR THE KILL. AT THIS **RANGE THEIR CAMOUFLAGE LOOKS DIRTY**
>
> "JOHNNIE" JOHNSON, RAF FIGHTER PILOT, AUGUST 1941

Q Which German pocket battleship was damaged by British aircraft off Norway in June 1941?

A The *Lützow*.

Q Which British aircraft carrier supported the British offensive against the Italians in Somaliland in 1941?

A HMS *Hermes*.

Q Which British warship was made famous in the film *In Which We Serve*?

A HMS *Kelly*.

Q What calibre was the German Light Field Howitzer 18 (le FH 18)?

A 105mm.

Q What was a *Nebelwerfer*?

A A German multiple rocket launcher.

Q On the Eastern Front, the Sinyavino Offensive took place near which city?

A Leningrad.

Q What was the title of the 1st SS Panzer Division?

A The *Leibstandarte* Division.

Q Who commanded this division in 1941?

A Josef "Sepp" Dietrich.

> ❝ THE EXPLOSION HAD TORN KING'S
> HEAD AND SHOULDERS FROM
> THE REST OF HIS BODY ❞
> CYRIL JOLY, 7TH ARMOURED DIVISION, LIBYA,
> JUNE 15,1941

Q What was the name of the area of the Ukraine controlled by the Romanians between the Rivers Bug and Dniester?

A Transnistria.

Q Which city, the capital of the Crimea, was captured by the Germans in early November 1941?

A Simferopol.

DID YOU KNOW

THE QUESTION OF HOW MUCH THE UNITED STATES KNEW ABOUT THE
JAPANESE ATTACK ON PEARL HARBOR HAS EXCITED CONSPIRACY THEORISTS
AND HISTORIANS ALIKE EVER SINCE THAT FATEFUL DAY. THE MORE
FANCIFUL THEORIES SUGGEST THAT THE U.S. KNEW AN ATTACK WAS
IMMINENT, BUT ALLOWED IT TO HAPPEN SO THAT THE U.S. COULD ENTER
THE WAR ON THE ALLIES' SIDE. THEY POINT TO THE FACT THAT U.S.
CARRIERS WERE NOT IN THE HARBOR WHEN THE ATTACK TOOK PLACE, AND
THAT THE WEALTH OF INTELLIGENCE POINTING TO A JAPANESE ATTACK
LEADING UP TO DECEMBER 1941 WAS IMPOSSIBLE TO MISS. WHILST IT WAS
CERTAINLY UNFORTUNATE THAT THE INTELLIGENCE COLLECTED DID NOT
RAISE THE ALARM EARLIER, AND THE COINCIDENCE THAT THE CARRIERS
WERE ABSENT IS ALMOST UNBELIEVABLE, SIMPLE INTELLIGENCE FAILURE
SEEMS TO BE THE MOST LIKELY CAUSE OF THE SURPRISE.

Q When the Japanese sent their forces into the south of
Indochina in July 1941, how did the Western powers retaliate?

A Japanese assets in the U.S. were seized, and the U.S. placed a
ferocious trade embargo on Japan, which reduced her oil supplies by
90 percent. The British and the Dutch also imposed their own economic
sanctions, and in total Japan's foreign trade was cut by 75 percent.

Q Did the Allied response push the Japanese toward war?

A Yes. The oil embargo meant that the Japanese fleet would be
confined to port by the spring of 1942.

Q Who commanded the Imperial Japanese Navy in 1941?

A Admiral Isoroku Yamamoto.

Q What was the size of the Japanese Army in 1941?

A 1.8 million men.

Q How many aircraft did the Japanese Air Force have on the eve of Pearl Harbor?

A 2,000.

> " NOTHING IN THE LANDSCAPE TO REST
> OR DISTRACT THE EYE; NOTHING
> ## TO HEAR BUT ROARING
> ## TRUCK ENGINES
> PRIVATE CRIMP, 7TH ARMOURED DIVISION, LIBYA,
> OCTOBER 1941 "

Q What was the U.S. Two Ocean Naval Expansion Act?

A A massive naval building program which would set a ratio of Japanese to U.S. ships of 3:10 by 1944.

Q Which panzer group was nearing the Soviet city of Rostov in early November 1941?

A The First Panzer Group.

Q Which panzer corps captured the Soviet city of Tikhvin on November 9, 1941?

A XXXIX Panzer Corps.

Q Who was the leader of fascist Italy?

A Benito Mussolini.

Q Which country first introduced a series of radar stations on her home soil?

A Britain, in 1938, in response to the threat of German bomber raids.

Q Which Soviet front defended Moscow against the German Operation Typhoon?

A The Western Front.

DID YOU KNOW

AIRCRAFT RADAR, INTRODUCED IN 1941, INITIALLY ENABLED NIGHTFIGHTERS TO LOCATE TARGETS AND EVENTUALLY AIDED BOMBER NAVIGATION. U-BOATS THAT SURFACED IN DARKNESS FOR SAFETY COULD ALSO BE DETECTED BY AIRCRAFT, WHICH THEN ILLUMINATED THE SUBMARINES WITH LIGHTS BEFORE ATTACKING THEM. GROUND-BASED RADAR ALSO HELPED BOMBER CREWS HIT TARGETS BY PRECISELY TRACKING AND RELAYING INFORMATION TO THE AIRCRAFT. IN THE WAR AT SEA, RADAR WAS USED TO DETECT ENEMY AIRCRAFT AND ALSO DIRECTED GUNFIRE, WHICH COULD BE EFFECTIVELY EMPLOYED EVEN IN COMPLETE DARKNESS WITH THE NEW TECHNOLOGY. RADAR THEREFORE BECAME A KEY TECHNOLOGY IN LAND, SEA, AND AIR OPERATIONS DURING THE WAR.

Q Name one of the three Soviet fronts that took part in the Soviet counteroffensive that began on December 5, 1941?

A The Kalinin Front, Western Front, and Southwestern Front.

Q Name the two German panzer groups that took the full fury of Zhukov's offensive.

A The Second and Third Panzer Groups. The Third Panzer Group was forced to conduct a fighting retreat to Klin. The Tenth Army ploughed into the southern flank of the Second Panzer Group, forcing Guderian to order a withdrawal to the Don, Shat, and Upa Rivers.

DID YOU KNOW

BENITO MUSSOLINI, JOURNALIST, SOLDIER, AND POLITICIAN, EXPLOITED THE INSTABILITY OF INTERWAR ITALY TO BECOME THE DICTATOR OF A FASCIST STATE. AFTER RISING TO POWER IN 1922, HE SUPPRESSED OPPOSITION AND PROMISED THE NATION THAT A NEW ROMAN EMPIRE WOULD ARISE. MUSSOLINI PRESENTED HIMSELF AS A TOUGH ALTERNATIVE TO PREVIOUS LIBERAL STATESMEN AND A PATRIOTIC ENEMY OF COMMUNISM. FASCIST PROPAGANDA HID HIS REGIME'S ECONOMIC INSTABILITY, AND THE CONQUEST OF ETHIOPIA (1935–36) AND ALBANIA (1939) ATTEMPTED TO DIVERT PUBLIC ATTENTION AWAY FROM DOMESTIC PROBLEMS. MUSSOLINI ESTABLISHED CLOSE RELATIONS WITH ADOLF HITLER, BUT INSISTED THAT ITALY WOULD NOT BE READY TO ENTER INTO WAR UNTIL 1942. AFTER THE FALL OF FRANCE IN JUNE 1940, HOWEVER, HE WAS KEEN TO CAPITALIZE ON GERMANY'S CONQUESTS AND DECLARED WAR ON THE ALLIES. MILITARY BLUNDERS IN FRANCE, NORTH AFRICA, AND GREECE LEFT ITALY DEPENDENT ON GERMANY MILITARY ASSISTANCE. MUSSOLINI, PHYSICALLY AND MENTALLY WEAKENED, FACED GROWING PUBLIC APATHY AND POLITICAL THREATS AS HIS COUNTRY FALTERED.

Q Who was Chief of the German Army General Staff in December 1941?

A Field Marshal Walter von Brauchitsch.

Q What happened to him at the end of 1941?

A He suffered a heart attack and tendered his resignation, an offer not immediately accepted by Hitler.

> **FOUR OF MY TANKS WERE BLAZING INFERNOS; THREE OTHERS JUST**
> # SAT THERE, SAD AND ABANDONED
> CAPTAIN ROBERT CRISP, 3RD ROYAL TANK REGIMENT, SIDI REZEGH, NOVEMBER 28, 1941

107

Q The Soviet December 1941 counteroffensive prompted Hitler to issue which directive?

A Führer Directive Number 39.

Q What were its main points?

A (a) To hold areas which are of great operational or economic importance to the enemy.
(b) To enable forces in the East to rest and recuperate as much as possible.
(c) Thus to establish conditions suitable for the resumption of large-scale offensive operations in 1942.

DID YOU KNOW

ON DECEMBER 17, 1941, HITLER ISSUED AN ORDER TO ALL GERMAN SOLDIERS ON THE EASTERN FRONT: "MAJOR WITHDRAWAL MOVEMENTS CANNOT BE MADE. THEY WILL RESULT IN THE COMPLETE LOSS OF HEAVY WEAPONS AND EQUIPMENT. UNDER THE PERSONAL LEADERSHIP OF COMMANDERS AND OFFICERS ALIKE, THE TROOPS ARE TO BE FORCED TO PUT UP A FANATICAL RESISTANCE IN THEIR LINES, REGARDLESS OF ANY ENEMY BREAKTHROUGH IN THEIR FLANKS AND REAR. ONLY THIS KIND OF FIGHTING WILL WIN THE TIME WE NEED TO MOVE UP THE REINFORCEMENTS I HAVE ORDERED FROM THE HOME COUNTRY AND THE WEST."

Q Which city, recaptured by the Red Army on December 9, 1941, allowed supplies to be sent into Leningrad?

A Tikhvin.

Q Which dam did the Germans blow up on December 11, 1941, in an effort to slow the Red Army's advance?

A The Istra Dam.

Q What cargo was the old cattle boat the *Struma* carrying when it sailed from Romania in December 1941?

A A total of 769 Jews who had spent their savings to avoid Nazi persecution.

Q What was the ship's destination?

A Istanbul.

Q Did it get there?

A Yes, but the Jews were not allowed off the boat (the British refused to allow them passage to Palestine). The boat was towed out to sea by the Turks, where it was sunk by a Soviet submarine.

Q How many citizens of Leningrad starved to death on Christmas Day 1941?

A 3,700.

Q What was the daily death rate in the city at this time?

A 1,500. Very few due to German bombs or shells; most to starvation and hypothermia.

Q Why did Hitler dismiss Heinz Guderian at the end of December 1941?

A For his retreats and insubordination.

Q Who replaced him as commander of the Second Panzer Group?

A General Rudolf Schmidt.

" IN THE LONG RUN
NATIONAL SOCIALISM AND RELIGION WILL
NO LONGER BE ABLE
TO EXIST TOGETHER **"**
ADOLF HITLER, JULY 1941

Q Estimate the total number of Luftwaffe aircraft lost on the Eastern Front in 1941?

A 2,100.

Q How many tanks did the Soviets lose on the Eastern Front in 1941?

A 20,000.

Q What were Soviet losses in combat aircraft in 1941?

A 10,000.

"" I WAS WORKING ON THE USS SHAW. IT WAS ON A FLOATING DRY DOCK, IT WAS IN FLAMES ""
JOHN GARCIA, PEARL HARBOR, DECEMBER 7, 1941

Q What was the Soviet scorched earth policy?

A First used in 1941 on the Eastern Front, in the words of Stalin: "In case of a forced retreat ... all rolling stock must be evacuated, the enemy must not be left a single engine, a single railway car, not a single pound of grain or gallon of fuel. The collective farmers must drive off all their cattle and turn over their grain to the safe keeping of the state authorities for transportation to the rear. All valuable property, including non-ferrous metals, grain, and fuel that cannot be withdrawn, must be destroyed without fail. In areas occupied by the enemy, guerrilla units must set fire to forests, stores, and transports."

DID YOU KNOW

THE SOVIET KV-1 HEAVY TANK SHARED MANY COMPONENTS WITH THE T-34 TANK, SUCH AS THE ENGINE AND 76.2MM MAIN GUN. ALTHOUGH UNRELIABLE (IN 1941 MANY OF THE 639 KV-1S BROKE DOWN ON THE WAY TO THE BATTLEFIELD), IT WAS CONTINUALLY UPGRADED THROUGHOUT THE WAR. DESIGN "FEATURES" INCLUDED TRANSMISSION GEARS THAT WERE SO DIFFICULT TO SHIFT THAT DRIVERS WERE ISSUED WITH A HAMMER TO KNOCK THEM INTO PLACE!

Q What were *Feldgendarmerie*?

A German field police.

Q What does *Festung* mean?

A It is German for fortress.

111

Q What is Flak short for?

A *Fliegerabwehrkanone*—a German term meaning antiaircraft gun.

Q In the German armed forces, what were *Freiwilligen* units?

A Used mainly by the Waffen-SS to denote units composed of foreign volunteers.

Q What is an artillery airburst?

A The bursting of a high-explosive shell in the air above the target.

Q What happens in a gun's chamber?

A The cartridge explodes and is thus fired from the barrel.

Q What is an artillery piece's cradle?

A The part of the gun that supports the barrel and recoil system.

" I REPEAT THAT THE UNITED STATES
CAN ACCEPT NO RESULT SAVE
VICTORY, FINAL AND
COMPLETE
PRESIDENT ROOSEVELT, RADIO BROADCAST,
DECEMBER 9, 1941 "

Q In artillery parlance, what is direct fire?

A Artillery fire in which there is a direct line of sight between gun and target.

Q Define the term howitzer.

A A gun that uses variable charges and fires at an angle up to and above 45 degrees to enable it to drop shells behind obstacles.

Q What is a muzzle brake?

A An attachment to the muzzle of a gun which deflects propellant gases sideways or slightly to the rear.

Q What is its function?

A It reduces the rearward thrust of recoil and thus permits the firing of heavy charges without the need for a heavy carriage.

Q Define field artillery.

A Artillery that is part of an infantry or armored division, and which provides the division's fire support.

DID YOU KNOW

THERE WERE CRUCIAL PIECES OF EVIDENCE IN THE MONTHS PRIOR TO THE JAPANESE ATTACK ON PEARL HARBOR. U.S. INTELLIGENCE OFFICIALS NOTED THAT THE JAPANESE CARRIERS HAD DISAPPEARED FROM THEIR USUAL MOORINGS. SIMILARLY, IN NOVEMBER 1940, LOW-FREQUENCY SIGNALS, THE KIND USED BY JAPAN'S CARRIERS, WERE DETECTED NORTHWEST OF HAWAII BUT NOT INVESTIGATED. DUTCH INTELLIGENCE INTERCEPTED AN ENCRYPTED MESSAGE SENT TO THE JAPANESE AMBASSADOR IN BANGKOK SUGGESTING AN ATTACK ON THE PHILIPPINES AND HAWAII, AND THE DUTCH INFORMED THE U.S., BUT THE WARNING WAS DISMISSED (THE U.S. WAS ALSO AWARE THAT THE JAPANESE WERE TELLING THEIR DIPLOMATIC OFFICIALS TO DESTROY CODE BOOKS AND TO PREPARE FOR WAR). SADLY FOR SERVICEMEN WHO LOST THEIR LIVES AT PEARL HARBOR, THESE WARNINGS WERE MISSED OR MISREAD.

Q What is the difference between armor-piercing shell and armor-piercing shot?

A The shell is hollow and carries a charge of explosive, while shot is solid steel.

Q What is homogeneous armor?

A Armor that is of a similar density and hardness all the way through.

Q What is face-hardened armor?

A Armor that has had carbon absorbed into the face of the plate, making it extremely hard.

114

DID YOU KNOW

AS THE RELATIVELY FEW AXIS MECHANIZED FORMATIONS PUSHED FORWARD DURING OPERATION BARBAROSSA, THE BULK OF THE INVADING FORCE, SOME 126 INFANTRY DIVISIONS—WITH 625,000 HORSES—WOULD MARCH FORWARD TRYING DESPERATELY NOT TO FALL TOO FAR BEHIND THE PANZER SPEARHEADS. IN ADDITION TO OCCUPYING GROUND AND MOPPING UP, THESE INFANTRY FORMATIONS WOULD HELP THE FOUR PANZER GROUPS TO REDUCE THE SOVIET POCKETS. TOGETHER THESE ACTIONS WERE CONCEIVED AS PARTS OF A SINGLE, CONTINUOUS, OFFENSIVE EFFORT THAT WOULD WIN THE WAR IN A MATTER OF MONTHS. THE KEY QUESTION REMAINED, HOWEVER, AS TO WHETHER THE GERMAN ARMY COULD MAINTAIN ITS ADVANCE IN A COUNTRY OF THIS SIZE AGAINST AN ENEMY AS POWERFUL AS THE SOVIETS IF THE LATTER'S COHESION DID NOT SWIFTLY COLLAPSE. THE FIRST FEW WEEKS INDICATED THAT IT COULD.

Q In British artillery nomenclature, what does QF mean?

A Quick firing.

Q What does the abbreviation APDS mean?

A Armor-Piercing Discarding Sabot.

" WE FLEW THROUGH AND OVER THICK
CLOUDS WHICH WERE
AT 2000 METERS
TAISA MITSUO, JAPANESE PILOT AT PEARL HARBOR **"**

115

Q What was a *Kettenkrad*?

A A German tracked motorcycle.

Q What is an artillery limber?

A A wheeled carriage that can be attached to the trail end of a gun to support it for transport.

Q What is a mortar?

A In specific terms, any gun that fires only at elevation angles greater than 45 degrees. However, in reality, the term is confined to infantry mortars.

DID YOU KNOW

A KEY REASON FOR THE GERMAN INABILITY TO REPLACE THE LOSSES SUFFERED DURING BARBAROSSA WAS HITLER'S SPRING 1941 DECISION TO SCALE BACK SIGNIFICANTLY ARMAMENTS PRODUCTION FOR THE GROUND FORCES, ESPECIALLY LIGHT HOWITZERS AND MORTARS. DURING THE WINTER OF 1941–42, THE BADLY WEAKENED GERMAN ARMY IN THE EAST FOUND ITSELF—DESPITE ALL THE VAST TACTICAL SUCCESSES IT HAD ACHIEVED—FACING A MORE POWERFUL ENEMY THAN EVER BEFORE THAT WAS RUTHLESSLY DETERMINED TO DRIVE THE BRUTAL AXIS FORCES OFF SOVIET SOIL. IN ADDITION, HITLER WAS MAKING EXORBITANT DEMANDS ON THE ALREADY SHAKEN TROOPS, AS GUDERIAN NOTED: "WE HAD SUFFERED A GRIEVOUS DEFEAT IN THE FAILURE TO REACH THE CAPITAL, WHICH WAS TO BE SERIOUSLY AGGRAVATED DURING THE NEXT FEW WEEKS THANKS TO THE RIGIDITY OF OUR SUPREME COMMANDER [HITLER]: DESPITE ALL OUR REPORTS, THESE MEN FAR AWAY IN EAST PRUSSIA COULD FORM NO TRUE CONCEPT OF THE REAL CONDITIONS OF THE WINTER WAR IN WHICH THEIR SOLDIERS WERE ENGAGED."

Q Name two of the the six Japanese aircraft carriers that were involved in the attack on Pearl Harbor.

A *Akagi, Kagi, Hiryu, Soryu, Zuizaku,* and *Shokaku.*

Q Who commanded the Japanese carrier strike force at Pearl Harbor?

A Vice Admiral Chuichi Nagumo.

Q How many Japanese air strikes were launched against Pearl Harbor?

A Two.

Q Why was the Japanese attack against Pearl Harbor a strategic failure?

A The strike at Pearl Harbor failed to destroy any U.S. aircraft carriers, which were out at sea. Many of the damaged ships were repaired quickly. Furthermore, Nagumo called off a third strike aimed at destroying Pearl Harbor's oil and shore facilities. Such a raid could have rendered Pearl Harbor inoperable. Instead, it continued to function.

Q Why was Singapore so vital to the Allies in late 1941?

A It was the Allies' main port for control of the Malacca Strait between Malaya and the Dutch East Indies.

Q Which Japanese army launched the Burma offensive in December 1941?

A The Fifteenth Army.

117

Q Who commanded the army?

A Lieutenant General Shojiro Iida.

" FAMINE HAD PECULIAR EFFECTS ON
PEOPLE. WOMEN WERE SO RUN DOWN
THEY STOPPED MENSTRUATING
ALEXANDER WERTH, LENINGRAD,
WINTER OF 1941–42 **"**

Q Which two British battleships were sunk by the Japanese in the South China Sea in December 1941?

A HMS *Prince of Wales* and HMS *Repulse*.

Q What was at Victory Point in Burma?

A An important Allied air base. It fell to the Japanese on December 16, 1941.

Q Who was the Thai prime minister in 1941?

A Field Marshal Pibul Songgram.

“ PRINCE OF WALES LOOKED MAGNIFICENT.
WHITE-TIPPED WAVES RIPPLED OVER
HER PLUNGING BOWS ”
O.D. GALLAGHER, WAR CORRESPONDENT

Q Why was the conquest of the Dutch East Indies in December 1941 of such importance to the Japanese?

A Conquest of the Dutch East Indies gave the Japanese vital natural resources, including oil and rubber. It consolidated their control of southwest Pacific seas, and enabled them to dominate or even invade Australia.

Q Who replaced Admiral Husband Kimmel as commander of the U.S .Pacific Fleet in December 1941?

A Rear Admiral Chester Nimitz.

DID YOU KNOW

THE JAPANESE ASSAULT ON PEARL HARBOR WAS PLANNED BY ADMIRAL ISOROKU YAMAMOTO (COMMANDER-IN-CHIEF, IMPERIAL JAPANESE NAVY) AND COMMANDED BY VICE ADMIRAL CHUICHI NAGUMO. IT WAS DELIVERED BY A STRIKE FORCE OF SIX AIRCRAFT CARRIERS, TOGETHER CONTAINING AROUND 450 AIRCRAFT, WITH A DEFENSIVE/LOGISTICAL ACCOMPANIMENT OF TWO BATTLESHIPS, TWO CRUISERS, SEVERAL DESTROYERS, AND EIGHT SUPPORT VESSELS. THIS LARGE BODY OF SHIPPING MANAGED TO SAIL COMPLETELY UNDETECTED FROM THE KURILE ISLANDS NORTH OF JAPAN TO ATTACK POSITIONS ONLY 275 MILES (443 KM) NORTH OF HAWAII.

Q Who was the governor of Hong Kong in 1941?

A Sir Mark Young.

Q What was the Mitsubishi A6M fighter better known as?

A The Zero.

Q What was its armament?

A Two 20mm cannon and two 7.7mm machine guns.

Q Whose words are these: "Yesterday, December 7, 1941—a date that will live in infamy—the United States of America was suddenly and deliberately attacked by naval and air forces of the Empire of Japan."

A U.S. President Franklin Delano Roosevelt.

Q In the Pacific theater, where was the port of Davao?

A On Mindanao in the southern Philippines.

Q Why was its fall to the Japanese in December 1941 a major blow to the Allies?

A It was used as a staging post for subsequent Japanese invasions of the Dutch East Indies, and it opened another front in the Japanese offensive against the Philippines, which until this point has been concentrated in the north against Luzon.

> **AS THE P-40S DIVED TO ATTACK, EVERYBODY WENT A LITTLE CRAZY WITH EXCITEMENT**
> CLAIRE CHENNAULT, "FLYING TIGERS", CHINA, DECEMBER 1941

Q Who was the prime minister of Australia in 1941?

A John Curtin.

Q Why did U.S. troops on Luzon withdraw to the Bataan Peninsula in December 1941?

A To avoid the Japanese encirclement of Manila.

1942

In North Africa and on the Eastern Front Axis offensives were initially successful, but were halted and then defeated by a series of Allied and Soviet counterattacks. In the Pacific, meanwhile, the Japanese juggernaut was at first successful. But then the U.S. Navy won a decisive victory at Midway in June.

Q What was the name of General Rommel's halftrack in North Africa?

A "Griffin."

Q What was signed at the Arcadia Conference in January 1942?

A Allied countries signed the United Nations Declaration pledging to follow the Atlantic Charter principles.

Q What does *Sturmgeschütz* mean?

A It is the German word for assault gun.

> ❝ NEVER BEFORE HAVE WE HAD SO LITTLE
> # TIME IN WHICH TO DO
> ## SO MUCH
> PRESIDENT ROOSEVELT, FEBRUARY 1942 ❞

Q The SS was a Nazi organization. But what do the letters SS mean?

A *Schutzstaffel*: literally Protection Force or Defense Squad.

Q What was the ABDACOM?

A The American, British, Dutch, and Australian (ABDA) Command.

DID YOU KNOW

The Japanese surprise attack on the American fleet at Pearl Harbor was designed to cripple the American Pacific Fleet to such an extent that the Greater East Asia Co-Prosperity Sphere, Japan's innocent-sounding name for her territorial acquisitions, would be beyond the range of U.S. forces after the American carriers had been destroyed. Though the carriers were never found and destroyed, Japanese strategy for 1942 was built upon this same precept: protection. The Japanese high command in Tokyo decided that the Greater East Asia Co-Prosperity Sphere had to be protected by a defensive line extending south and north of the Marshall Islands. This meant that certain islands that lay within this perimeter had to be taken and fortified. This included the Philippines, where the U.S. had 130,000 men stationed, the key strategic island of Corregidor, New Guinea, the Solomon Islands, and the Gilbert Islands.

123

Q **Who was the commander of ABDACOM?**

A The British General Sir Archibald Wavell.

Q **Who was made commander-in-chief of Allied forces in China in January 1942?**

A The Chinese Nationalist leader Chiang Kai-shek.

Q **Was the Japanese Type 95 tank a light, medium, or heavy tank?**

A Light tank.

> # " THERE ARE NO ATHEISTS IN FOXHOLES
> W.T. Cummings, sermon on Bataan, March 1942 "

Q Who was the prime minister of Burma in early 1942?

A U Saw.

Q Why was he arrested by the British in January 1942?

A He was planning Burmese independence.

Q Why did the government of Thailand declare war on Britain and the USA in January 1942?

A It believed Japan would win the war.

Q What threat did the Japanese prime minister, General Hideki Tojo, issue to Australia in January 1942?

A "If you continue your resistance, we Japanese will show you no mercy."

Q Which U.S. aircraft carrier was damaged by a Japanese suicide aircraft attack in February 1942?

A USS *Enterprise*.

Q Why did Colonel General Ernst Udet, head of Luftwaffe aircraft production and development, commit suicide in January 1942?

A Over his failure to provide adequate replacements and new improved aircraft models.

Q What was Operation Drum Beat in January 1942?

A The first coordinated attack carried out by five U-boats initially against U.S. shipping along the East Coast of the United States.

Q How many ships were sunk by German U-boats during the first month of Drum Beat?

A 20.

DID YOU KNOW

THE INFANTRY UNITS OF THE RED ARMY WERE IN A CONSTANT STATE OF FLUX DURING THE FIRST TWO YEARS OF THE WAR ON THE EASTERN FRONT. HUGE LOSSES REQUIRED CONSTANT REORGANIZATION TO KEEP THE UNITS IN SOME SORT OF FIGHTING ORDER. THE REASONS FOR THESE MASSIVE LOSSES ARE NOT HARD TO FIND: DURING 1941–42, UNITS WERE QUICKLY FORMED AND OFTEN THROWN INTO BATTLE WITH LITTLE OR NO TRAINING. STALIN'S PURGES IN THE 1930s MEANT THAT THOUSANDS OF INEXPERIENCED OFFICERS WERE PROMOTED BEYOND THEIR LEVEL OF COMPETENCE. THIS RESULTED IN POOR LEADERSHIP ON THE BATTLEFIELD. TO COMPOUND PROBLEMS, EACH RIFLE DIVISION HAD AN INADEQUATE NUMBER OF RADIOS, WHICH MADE COORDINATING ARTILLERY SUPPORT ALL BUT IMPOSSIBLE (GERMAN COMMENTATORS DURING BARBAROSSA NOTED THE ALMOST TOTAL ABSENCE OF ARTILLERY SUPPORT FOR ATTACKING RED ARMY INFANTRY UNITS).

Q What was the "Channel Dash" in February 1942?

A Protected by Luftwaffe fighters and smaller naval units, the German battleships *Scharnhorst* and *Gneisenau* and the cruiser *Prinz Eugen* made a dash from Brest up the English Channel to reach ports in Germany. Taken by complete surprise, the British Royal Navy and Royal Air Force were unable to stop the operation, losing a considerable number of planes and naval vessels in the attempt.

Q Which German city was devastated by an RAF bomber raid on March 28, 1942?

A Lübeck on the Baltic.

Q What did Hitler and Mussolini discuss at Berchtesgaden in April 1942?

A Future Axis strategy in North Africa and the Mediterranean, the main objectives being the reduction of Malta and the seizure of the Suez Canal.

Q Why did the commander of the German Army Group North, Field Marshal von Leeb, resign in January 1942?

A Red Army units were threatening to cut off 100,000 troops around Demyansk. Leeb requested permission to retreat. Hitler refused, whereupon Leeb resigned.

" WE'RE THE BATTLING
BASTARDS OF BATAAN,
NO MAMA, NO PAPA,
NO UNCLE SAM **"**
ANONYMOUS

DID YOU KNOW

HITLER'S AIM IN THE EAST WAS VERY CLEAR: ACQUIRING *LEBENSRAUM* IN THE EAST UP TO THE URAL MOUNTAINS. THESE LANDS WERE OCCUPIED BY GROUPS THAT HITLER AND NAZISM DESPISED: BOLSHEVIKS, SLAVS, AND JEWS. UNDER THE NEW ORDER, THESE PEOPLES WOULD EITHER BECOME SLAVES UNDER GERMAN OVERLORDS OR WOULD BE EXTERMINATED. HITLER WAS TO STATE IN 1942: "IF WE DO NOT COMPLETE THE CONQUEST OF THE EAST UTTERLY AND IRREVOCABLY, EACH SUCCESSIVE GENERATION WILL HAVE WAR ON ITS HANDS." FOR HIM THE WAR IN RUSSIA WAS A RACIAL CONFLICT, IN WHICH THE RACIALLY SUPERIOR GERMAN ARYAN RACE WAS LOCKED IN A STRUGGLE WITH THE "SUB-HUMAN" SLAVS. THIS MADE RETREAT IN THE FACE OF "INFERIOR" PEOPLES UNIMAGINABLE, FOR THE FÜHRER COULD NOT CONCEIVE OF THE RACIALLY INFERIOR SLAVS BEING ABLE TO DEFEAT A SUPERIOR RACE. AS HE STATED ON THE EVE OF KURSK: "GERMANY NEEDS THE CONQUERED TERRITORIES OR SHE WILL NOT EXIST FOR LONG. SHE WILL WIN HEGEMONY OVER THE REST OF EUROPE. WHERE WE ARE—WE STAY."

127

Q Who replaced Leeb as Army Group North's commander?

A Georg von Küchler.

Q On the Eastern Front, what was the Demyansk Pocket?

A In February 1942, the jaws snapped shut on 90,000 German troops around Demyansk as the Soviet First Shock and Eleventh Armies linked up on the Lovat River, northern Russia. Inside the German pocket were the 12th, 30th, 123rd, and 290th Infantry Divisions, plus the 3rd SS *Totenkopf* Division.

Q How did the Germans intend to supply those troops trapped in the Demyansk Pocket?

A The units had to rely on the Luftwaffe for supplies of food and ammunition.

Q What was the PTRD?

A A Red Army 14.5mm antitank rifle.

Q What was the main armament of the Panzer III Ausf G?

A A 50mm gun.

DID YOU KNOW

THE FAILURE OF OPERATION TYPHOON HERALDED A CRISIS FOR THE GERMAN ARMY ON THE EASTERN FRONT AT THE END OF 1941. UNDERSTRENGTH AND EXHAUSTED DIVISIONS LACKED THE MANPOWER WITH WHICH TO DEFEND EVERY MILE OF THE FRONT, ESPECIALLY IN THE FACE OF THE RED ARMY COUNTEROFFENSIVE THAT BEGAN IN EARLY DECEMBER. TO COMPOUND THE PROBLEM, PREWAR TRAINING HAD LARGELY SHUNNED ANYTHING TO DO WITH DEFENSIVE OPERATIONS IN WINTER CONDITIONS. INDIVIDUAL COMMANDERS AND UNITS THEREFORE HAD TO LEARN FAST IF THEY WERE TO AVOID BEING ANNIHILATED BY THE MORE NUMERICAL AND OFTEN BETTER EQUIPPED ENEMY. IN RESPONSE, THE GERMANS ADOPTED SO-CALLED HEDGEHOG TACTICS TO BEAT OFF RED ARMY ATTACKS AND PRESERVE THEIR LINES.

REMEMBER
PEARL HARBOR!
U.S. SLOGAN

Q **What was the standard main armament of all British cruiser and infantry tanks up to 1942?**

A The two-pounder gun.

Q **What caliber was the BESA machine gun?**

A 7.92mm.

Q **Was the Panzer 38(t) a German tank?**

A No. It was originally built by the Czechs. It was taken into German service when the Third Reich absorbed Czechoslovakia before the war.

Q **Which German medium bomber was nicknamed "The Flying Pencil"?**

A The Dornier Do 17.

Q **Why did it have this name?**

A It had a slender rear fuselage.

Q What was a *Bergepanzer?*

A A German armored recovery vehicle.

Q Who chaired the Wannsee Conference in Berlin in January 1942?

A The deputy chief of the SS, Reinhard Heydrich.

Q What was the purpose of the conference?

A To decide the fate of the Jews in German-occupied territory.

“ WHEN I THINK ABOUT IT I REALIZE
THAT I'M EXTRAORDINARILY
HUMANE
HITLER DISCUSSING THE JEWS, APRIL 1942 **”**

Q What was the decision of the conference?

A Heydrich received permission to begin deporting all Jews in German-controlled areas to Eastern Europe to face forced labor or extermination (the killing of Jews in Eastern Europe was already commonplace).

Q Why did the Nazis use poison gas to exterminate people?

A Execution by shooting was inefficient and a strain for the troops engaged. Using poison gas was more efficient.

DID YOU KNOW

THE SECRET WANNSEE CONFERENCE IN BERLIN OFFICIALLY LAUNCHED
THE NAZI PROGRAM TO EXTERMINATE THE JEWISH PEOPLE, WHO WERE
REGARDED AS THE RACIAL ENEMY OF THE "ARYAN" GERMANS. THE
PREVIOUS PERSECUTION AND KILLING OF JEWS IN NAZI-OCCUPIED EUROPE
WAS TRANSFORMED INTO A HIGHLY EFFICIENT OPERATION. EUROPEAN JEWS
WERE SYSTEMATICALLY HERDED INTO CONCENTRATION CAMPS IN EASTERN
EUROPE WHERE THEY WERE WORKED LIKE SLAVES. MILLIONS DIED FROM
MALTREATMENT, EXHAUSTION, DISEASE, AND STARVATION. IN EXTER-
MINATION CAMPS, POISON GAS CHAMBERS WERE USED TO KILL THOUSANDS
OF PEOPLE. MANY OTHER PEOPLE DEEMED "UNDESIRABLE" BY THE NAZIS,
INCLUDING GYPSIES, POLITICAL OPPONENTS, AND THE MENTALLY AND
PHYSICALLY HANDICAPPED, ALSO SHARED THE SAME FATE AS THE JEWS.

Q Which Axis garrison in Libya fell to British troops on January 17, 1942?

A Halfaya.

Q Who became Norwegian prime minister in February 1942?

A Vidkun Quisling.

Q What position did Lieutenant General Joseph Stilwell assume in February 1942?

A Commander-in-chief of the U.S. forces in the China-Burma-India theater, and chief of staff to Chiang Kai-shek. The fact that he spoke Chinese and had an understanding of Chinese culture made him especially suitable for this position.

A TSAR ONCE REMARKED THAT TWO OF HIS BEST GENERALS IN HIS ARMY WERE JANUARY AND FEBRUARY

BRYAN PERRETT, *A HISTORY OF BLITZKRIEG*

Q The Italian torpedo boat *Circe* sank which British submarine off Taranto on February 13, 1942?

A HMS *Tempest*.

Q How many Axis air raids were launched against the island of Malta in March 1942?

A 275.

Q What type of weapon was the Beretta Model 1938A?

A A submachine gun.

Q What was the Carro M13/40?

A An Italian medium tank.

Q What was the Semovente da 75/18?

A An Italian assault gun.

Q How many engines did the Italian Savoia Marchetti SM.81 bomber have?

A Three.

Q What caliber was the Cannone Da 75/18 Modello 37 field gun?

A 75mm.

DID YOU KNOW

THE GERMANS NEVER RECOVERED FROM THE HORRENDOUS LOSSES OF THE 1941 CAMPAIGN IN RUSSIA. BY APRIL 1942 THE ARMY HAD LOST ONE-THIRD OF THE TROOPS, 40 PERCENT OF THE ANTITANK GUNS, HALF THE HORSES, AND 79 PERCENT OF THE ARMOR THAT HAD BEGUN THE CAMPAIGN. MASSIVE VEHICLE LOSSES HAD SIGNIFICANTLY REDUCED MOBILITY, WHILE MUNITIONS STOCKS HAD FALLEN TO ONE-THIRD OF JUNE 1941 LEVELS. NEW PRODUCTION AND REPLACEMENTS COULD NOT OFFSET LOSSES; AND, AS A RESULT, INFANTRY, OFFICER, AND EQUIPMENT STRENGTHS PLUMMETED. MOREOVER, LIMITATIONS IMPOSED BY TERRAIN AND WEATHER, BY SHORTAGES IN TROOPS, EQUIPMENT, AND SUPPLIES, AS WELL AS BY HITLER'S HOLD-FAST ORDERS, PREVENTED THE GERMANS DURING THE WINTER OF 1941–42 FROM CONDUCTING THE ELASTIC DEFENSE IN DEPTH PROSCRIBED BY ESTABLISHED DOCTRINE. INSTEAD, THE ADAPTABLE GERMANS SWIFTLY ADOPTED EXPEDIENT, IMPROVISED DEFENSIVE TECHNIQUES DICTATED BY THE CIRCUMSTANCES THAT FACED THEM. THE RED ARMY LAUNCHED HEAVY, IF UNSOPHISTICATED, ILL-COORDINATED, AND DISPERSED, FRONTAL ASSAULTS ALL ALONG THE CENTRAL SECTOR OF THE FRONT TO DRIVE THE GERMANS BACK FROM MOSCOW AND GAIN SOME OPERATIONAL ROOM FOR MANEUVER. THIS COUNTEROFFENSIVE EMBROILED THE DEPLETED AND EXHAUSTED PANZER DIVISIONS THAT HAD SPEARHEADED THE GERMAN ADVANCE ON THE SOVIET CAPITAL IN HEAVY DEFENSIVE FIGHTING, FOR WHICH THEY WERE ILL-SUITED.

Q What was the Persian Corridor?

A When the Germans invaded Russia, the United States set up a mission to provide Lend-Lease aid to the Soviets. One of the supply routes was through the Middle East, called the Persian Corridor.

Q Which American organization coordinated operations along the Persian Corridor?

A The U.S. Military Iranian Mission.

Q Where was its headquarters?

A Baghdad, Iraq.

DID YOU KNOW

GERMAN MILITARY OPERATIONS IN THE EAST REMAINED DOMINATED BY THE NOTION, BASED ON A DISTORTED INTERPRETATION OF CLAUSEWITZ'S MILITARY THOUGHT, THAT WAR OVERWHELMINGLY CONSTITUTED A CLASH OF MORAL FORCES. WHILE THIS CONCEPT DID—AND STILL DOES—SHED CONSIDERABLE LIGHT ON MILITARY OPERATIONS, DURING WORLD WAR II THE IMPACT OF NAZI IDEOLOGY FURTHER DISTORTED GERMAN UNDER-STANDING OF THE CONCEPT. GIVEN THE NAZIS' SUPREME BELIEF IN THE SUPERIOR RACIAL WILL OF THE ARYAN GERMANS, MOST GERMAN COMMANDERS BELIEVED THAT THE WILL OF THE "SEMILITERATE" SLAVIC SOVIETS WOULD NOT BE ABLE TO RESIST THE ONSLAUGHT OF THE TECHNO-LOGICALLY ADVANCED WEHRMACHT. CONSEQUENTLY, BARBAROSSA WOULD PROVE A SHORT AND DECISIVE CAMPAIGN. THE APPALLINGLY BRUTAL, 900-DAY GERMAN SIEGE OF LENINGRAD, HOWEVER, PROVED HOW WRONG WAS THE GERMAN APPRECIATION OF THE ENEMY FACING THEM. THE SIEGE DEMONSTRATED HOW MUCH SUFFERING THE SOVIETS COULD ENDURE IN THEIR DESPERATE STRUGGLE TO RESIST THE AXIS ONSLAUGHT.

I SHALL RETURN
DOUGLAS MACARTHUR, LEAVING THE PHILIPPINES,
MARCH 11, 1942

Q What was the U.S. Air Force's Halverson Detachment?

A A special group of B-24 bombers that found itself in the Middle East in early June 1942. It was named after its commander, Colonel Harry A. Halverson. It consisted of 23 B-24D Liberator heavy bombers with hand-picked crews.

Q Who was Chief of Staff of the U.S. Army in 1942?

A General George C. Marshall.

Q On the Eastern Front, what was a "flak nest"?

A A German strongpoint containing multiple antiaircraft guns.

Q Which Red Army units took part in the Soviet Barvenkovo-Lozavaia Offensive of January 1942?

A The Southwestern and Southern Fronts.

Q What was the aim of the offensive?

A To recapture Kharkov, Krasnograd, and Pavlograd in the Ukraine.

135

Q In January 1942, Hitler ordered the setting up of the *Luftflotte* 2 command on Sicily. What units did it contain?

A *Fliegerkorps* II and X.

Q What was *Luftflotte* 2's mission?

A To command the waters around Malta and in the eastern Mediterranean.

Q Which Allied aircraft carriers were used to fly in Spitfire fighters to the island of Malta in spring 1942?

A The British carriers HMS *Argus* and *Eagle* and the American carrier HMS *Wasp*.

> " WE GOT RUN OUT OF BURMA,
> ## AND IT IS HUMILIATING
> ### AS HELL
> JOSEPH STILWELL, PRESS STATEMENT, MAY 25, 1942 "

Q What type of aircraft was the Vickers Wellesley?

A A British general-purpose bomber.

Q What was the size of its crew?

A Two.

DID YOU KNOW

THROUGHOUT THE COMBAT ON THE EASTERN FRONT IN 1942, THE
FIGHTING QUALITIES OF THE INDIVIDUAL GERMAN SOLDIER REMAINED
HIGH. THIS WAS UNDOUBTEDLY BOLSTERED BY IDEOLOGICAL TRAINING. IN
LATE SPRING 1942, FOR EXAMPLE, THE GERMANS STEPPED UP THEIR
EFFORTS TO MOTIVATE PSYCHOLOGICALLY THEIR FRONTLINE SOLDIERS IN
THE EAST. DURING MAY, UNIVERSITY LECTURERS VISITED THE ELITE
GROSSDEUTSCHLAND DIVISION—ONLY RECENTLY EXPANDED FROM
REGIMENTAL SIZE—AND DELIVERED DISCUSSIONS ON THE EVILS OF
COMMUNISM. IN ADDITION, THE DIVISION CREATED A NEW APPOINTMENT,
THAT OF EDUCATION OFFICER, WHO COORDINATED ALL THE ACTIVITIES
UNDERTAKEN TO BOLSTER THE MORALE AND DETERMINATION OF THE
TROOPS. THE OFFICER PROCURED SEVERAL HUNDRED NEW
PROPAGANDISTIC BOOKS FOR THE DIVISION'S LIBRARY VAN, AND GAVE
SEMINARS THAT STRESSED BOTH THE INHERENT SUPERIORITY OF THE
GERMAN ARMY AND THE INEVITABILITY OF ITS ULTIMATE VICTORY TO
"STRENGTHEN SOLDIERLY QUALITIES" AND INSTILL "STEADFASTNESS DURING
CRISES" WITHIN THE TROOPS.

137

Q Which British aircraft was nicknamed the "Shagbat"?

A The Supermarine Walrus.

Q What type of aircraft was this?

A A seaplane designed to operate from Royal Navy aircraft carriers.

Q What was the most successful variant of the British Spitfire fighter?

A The Mk XI version. Some 5,665 were built.

Q What was the Supermarine Seafire?

A A Spitfire configured for service on aircraft carriers.

Q What hampered its performance as a carrier-borne aircraft?

A It had a long nose and narrow-track main landing gear units.

Q Which British aircraft was nicknamed the "Flying Suitcase"?

A The Handley Page Hampden.

Q Which British bomber built by Avro was retired in June 1942?

A The Avro Manchester.

Q How many engines did it have?

A Two.

Q What was the RAF's most successful heavy bomber in World War II?

A The Avro Lancaster.

Q The German Bf 110 aircraft was a heavy fighter. What did this term mean?

A During the 1930s air strategists believed twin-engine "heavy fighters" to be essential to offensive air operations.

Q The Bf 110 was dubbed *Zerstörer*. What does this mean?

A Destroyer.

Q What was the Organization Todt?

A A paramilitary construction organization of the Nazi Party, auxiliary to the Wehrmacht. Named after its founder, Dr Todt.

> DEFEAT IS BITTER.
> BITTER TO THE COMMON
> SOLDIER, BUT TREBLY
> BITTER TO HIS GENERAL
> WILLIAM SLIM

Q What was the aircraft that provided the Germans with the bulk of their battlefield reconnaissance capability in World War II?

A The Henschel Hs 126.

Q What type of aircraft was the German Henschel Hs 129?

A A close-support, antitank aircraft.

Q What was its main armaments?

A Two 20mm cannon.

“ SEAS ARE RUNNING MUCH ROUGHER AND
HUGE SWELLS ARE ROLLING US
40 AND 50 DEGREES
AT A ROLL
FRANK CURRY, ROYAL CANADIAN NAVY,
JANUARY 1942 **”**

Q What was Operation Munich on the Eastern Front in March 1942?

A Joined by a Luftwaffe detachment, German troops attacked partisan bases around Yelnya and Dorogobuzh.

Q What was Operation Bamberg launched in the same month?

A Another German anti-partisan mission on the Eastern Front, near Bobruisk.

DID YOU KNOW

THE KATYUSHA MULTIPLE ROCKET LAUNCHER WAS BETTER KNOWN AS "STALIN'S ORGAN," NAMED THUS BY GERMAN TROOPS DUE TO ITS RESEMBLANCE TO A PIPE ORGAN. STALIN'S ORGAN WAS SEEN IN MANY FORMS DURING WORLD WAR II, THE ROCKETS BEING MOUNTED ON VARIOUS TRUCKS (OFTEN AMERICAN LEND-LEASE STUDEBAKER US6 VEHICLES), TANKS, AND EVEN ON FARM TRACTORS. BEFORE THE GERMAN INVASION, THE RED ARMY'S ARTILLERY BRANCH WAS UNIMPRESSED BY THE KATYUSHA BECAUSE IT TOOK UP TO 50 MINUTES TO LOAD AND FIRE THE ROCKETS IN ONE SALVO (A HOWITZER COULD FIRE UP TO 150 ROUNDS IN THE SAME TIME). HOWEVER, THE GREAT ATTRIBUTE OF THE KATYUSHA WAS ITS SIMPLICITY. IT COMPRISED A RACK OF PARALLEL RAILS ON WHICH 16 OR MORE ROCKETS WERE MOUNTED, WITH A FOLDING FRAME TO RAISE THE RAILS TO LAUNCH POSITION.

Q Which general, who later defected to the Nazis, commanded the Soviet Second Shock Army in early 1942?

141

A General Andrei Vlassov.

Q What happened to Vlassov's army?

A Surrounded in northern Russia by German forces, it was annihilated in June 1942.

Q Who was the commander of the SS *Totenkopf* Division in 1942?

A Theodor Eicke.

Q What was the subject of Führer Directive No. 41 of April 1942?

A The forthcoming summer offensive on the Eastern Front.

Q Was the offensive to be along the whole Eastern Front?

A No. As Hitler stated: "In pursuit of the original plan for the Eastern campaign, the armies of the central sector will stand fast, those in the north will capture Leningrad and link up with the Finns, while those on the southern flank will break through into the Caucasus."

Q What was the codename of the German offensive into the Caucasus in 1942?

A Operation Blue.

DID YOU KNOW

DESIGNED BY GEORGE SHPAGIN, THE RUSSIAN PPSH-41 SUBMACHINE GUN ENTERED SERVICE SHORTLY BEFORE THE GERMAN INVASION OF THE SOVIET UNION IN JUNE 1941. THE PPSH-41 WAS DESIGNED TO BE AS SIMPLE AS POSSIBLE. IT USED A MINIMUM NUMBER OF PARTS, A SIMPLE BLOW-BACK ACTION, AND FIRED FROM THE OPEN BOLT POSITION. IT SOON PROVED ITSELF TO BE EFFECTIVE AS A WEAPON AS WELL AS EASY TO MANUFACTURE, AND BECAME ONE OF THE MOST FAMOUS SMALL ARMS OF WORLD WAR II. FACTORIES AND WORKSHOPS THROUGHOUT THE SOVIET UNION BEGAN TURNING OUT THIS RELIABLE WEAPON, AND MORE THAN FIVE MILLION WERE PRODUCED BY 1945.

❝ AS DARKNESS APPROACHED, THE FIGHTING
INTENSIFIED, THE SHELLING
INCREASED
BRITISH GUNNER, BATTLE OF GAZALA,
JUNE 1942 **❞**

Q On the Eastern Front, what was Operation Bustard in May
1942?

A The German Eleventh Army launched Operation Bustard to destroy
enemy forces in the Kerch Peninsula. For this task it deployed
XXXII, VII Romanian, and XXX Corps (LIV Corps covered Sevastopol).

Q What was the function of the Central Staff of the USSR Partisan
Movement?

A To direct partisan operations behind German lines.

Q Where was its headquarters?

A In Moscow.

Q Did the Red Army consider Soviet troops who surrendered to
the enemy to be traitors?

A Yes. The Red Army field manual stated that a loyal soldier was
either fighting or was dead; surrender was considered to be
treason. The wartime edition of the official Soviet encyclopedia stated
that "the penalty for premeditated surrender into captivity not
necessitated by combat conditions is death by shooting."

Q Who was the Allied commander at the Battle of the Java Sea in February 1942?

A Dutch Rear Admiral Karel Doorman.

Q Who was the Japanese commander?

A Vice Admiral Takagi Takeo.

Q What happened at the battle?

" THE DOMINANT FEELING OF THE
BATTLEFIELD IS
LONELINESS
WILLIAM SLIM, ADDRESSING THE 10TH INDIAN DIVISION,
JUNE 1942
"

A Two Allied cruisers and three destroyers were sunk, the British cruiser HMS *Exeter* withdrew owing to battle damage, and Doorman was killed. The Japanese force under the command of Takeo suffered only one damaged destroyer.

Q What was the composition of the Allied force at the Battle of the Java Sea?

A It was a mixed unit of U.S., Dutch, British, and Australian warships.

DID YOU KNOW

THOUGH THE U.S. HAD BELIEVED THAT A WAR AGAINST JAPAN WAS INEVITABLE LONG BEFORE PEARL HARBOR—INDEED, AIR BASES AND OTHER FACILITIES WERE BEING CONSTRUCTED ON WAKE ISLAND AND THE MARSHALL ISLANDS IN THE MONTHS LEADING UP TO WAR—THE JAPANESE SURPRISE ATTACK CAUGHT THE U.S. OFF GUARD. THEREFORE, THE INITIAL U.S. STRATEGY FOR 1942 WAS AT FIRST DISORGANIZED AND LACKING COHERENCE. THE U.S. LACKED THE MANPOWER OR THE EQUIPMENT TO HOLD ON TO WHAT PACIFIC TERRITORY IT HAD, AND HAD LITTLE WAY OF REINFORCING THE PHILIPPINES OR ANY OTHER ISLANDS IN THE FACE OF JAPANESE INVASION. THUS, U.S. STRATEGY WAS TO HOLD ON FOR AS LONG AS POSSIBLE WHILST U.S. STRATEGISTS CAME UP WITH A PLAN. HOWEVER, STRATEGIC THINKING IN 1942 WAS LIMITED BY SEVERAL FACTORS. FIRSTLY, THE SHOCK OF PEARL HARBOR AND THE DESTRUCTION OF VITAL SHIPPING THERE TOOK ITS TOLL. SECONDLY, SUPERIOR JAPANESE PLANNING IN THE LEAD-UP TO 1942 GAVE THEM AN ADVANTAGE OVER THE AMERICANS. LASTLY, THE CONDITION OF U.S. UNPREPAREDNESS COULD BE IMPROVED ONLY OVER A PERIOD OF TIME, NOT OVERNIGHT.

145

Q Name the Japanese commander who led the attack on Singapore in February 1942.

A Lieutenant General Yamashita.

Q Which army did he command?

A The Twenty-Fifth Army.

Q Who was the British commander at Singapore?

A Lieutenant General Percival.

Q What was a decisive factor in the fall of Singapore?

A The defense of Singapore became futile when Japanese forces took control of the island's reservoirs and severed Singapore City's water supply.

" THE JAPS MADE NO MOVE TO
FEED US. MANY HAD TASTED
NO FOOD IN FOUR DAYS "
WILLIAM DYESS, THE "BATAAN DEATH MARCH,"
APRIL 1942

Q What was the U.S. Government's Executive Order 9066?

A Executive Order 9066 enabled the war secretary to displace people from military areas; and Japanese-Americans, already alienated following Pearl Harbor, were the primary victims of this policy. Some 11,000 Japanese-Americans were initially moved from the Pacific coast to camps in Arkansas and Texas.

Q How many Japanese-Americans were interned during the war?

A 112,000.

Q Was California attacked by the Japanese in 1942?

A Yes. In February the Japanese submarine *I-17* shelled an oil refinery at Ellwood, California. In total, 17 rounds were fired, inflicting only minor damage to a pier and an oil well derrick.

Q Which Japanese army captured Rangoon in March 1942?

A The Fifteenth Army.

Q Who replaced Douglas MacArthur as commander of Allied forces on Bataan in March 1942?

A Lieutenant General Jonathan Wainwright.

Q What was the Allied codename for the Japanese Nakajima B5 bomber?

A Kate.

DID YOU KNOW

AS C-IN-C OF THE COMBINED FLEET FROM JULY 1939, ISOROKU YAMAMOTO (1884–1943) WAS JAPAN'S GREATEST WARTIME NAVAL STRATEGIST. BORN IN 1884 IN NAGAOKA, HE JOINED THE NAVAL ACADEMY SHORTLY AFTER THE TURN OF THE CENTURY, GAINING COMBAT EXPERIENCE IN THE RUSSO-JAPANESE WAR OF 1904. HE WENT TO THE U.S. IN 1919 TO STUDY ENGLISH, AND ALSO TO LEARN ABOUT U.S. NAVAL AND INDUSTRIAL STRENGTHS. YAMAMOTO RETURNED TO JAPAN IN 1921 AND ROSE QUICKLY THROUGH A SERIES OF INFLUENTIAL POSITIONS. MOST SIGNIFICANTLY, HE BECAME AN EXPERT IN THE NEW ART OF NAVAL AVIATION WARFARE, SOME-THING HE LATER PUT TO DEVASTATING EFFECT AS ARCHITECT OF THE PEARL HARBOR ATTACK. HOWEVER, YAMAMOTO WAS NOT A SUPPORTER OF JAPANESE AGGRESSION, CORRECTLY BELIEVING THAT U.S. INDUSTRIAL POWER WOULD TRIUMPH IN A SUSTAINED CAMPAIGN. BUT ONCE WAR WAS INEVITABLE HE COMMITTED HIMSELF TO JAPANESE VICTORY. PEARL HARBOR ABLY DEMONSTRATED THE FORWARD-THINKING AND TACTICAL CAPABILITIES OF YAMAMOTO, AND IT FULFILED ALL HIS CLAIMS FOR NAVAL AVIATION BEING THE FUTURE OF WAR AT SEA.

Q Which British aircraft carrier was sunk by Japanese aircraft in early April 1942?

A Near Ceylon a Japanese scout plane spotted the carrier HMS *Hermes* and the destroyer HMAS *Vampire*. The subsequent air strike sank HMS *Hermes* in only 10 minutes after 40 bomb hits, and the *Vampire* went down after suffering 13 explosions. This effectively finished the British Pacific Fleet as a significant force in the region.

Q What was the "Bataan Death March"?

A In April 1942, 78,000 U.S. and Filipino troops fell into Japanese hands on Bataan and were made to walk 65 miles (104 km) in the most dreadful conditions to prison camps. Around one in three men died in what became known as the "Bataan Death March."

"" WE KNEW NOW THE JAPS WOULD RESPECT NEITHER AGE NOR **RANK. THEIR FEROCITY GREW AS WE MARCHED "**
WILLIAM DYESS, THE "BATAAN DEATH MARCH,"
APRIL 1942

Q Who was the leader of the Indian Congress Party?

A Pandit Nehru.

Q What was the Doolittle Raid in April 1942?

A Sixteen U.S. B-25 Mitchell bombers flying from the aircraft carrier USS *Hornet* and led by Colonel James Doolittle achieved a major propaganda victory by bombing the Japanese capital, Tokyo.

DID YOU KNOW

THE USS *ENTERPRISE* WAS ONE OF THE MOST INFLUENTIAL WARSHIPS OF WORLD WAR II. A "YORKTOWN" CLASS AIRCRAFT CARRIER THAT JOINED THE PACIFIC FLEET IN 1938, THE USS *ENTERPRISE* WAS IMMEDIATELY SENT INTO ACTION FOLLOWING THE JAPANESE ATTACK ON PEARL HARBOR. THE SHIP MADE ITS FIRST SUCCESSFUL ENGAGEMENT OF THE WAR ON DECEMBER 11, 1941, WHEN ITS AIRCRAFT SANK THE JAPANESE SUBMARINE *I-170*. THE USS *ENTERPRISE*'S DEFINING ENGAGEMENT CAME IN JUNE 1942 DURING THE BATTLE OF MIDWAY. AIRCRAFT FLYING FROM THE USS *ENTERPRISE*, PARTICULARLY THE DOUGLAS SBD DAUNTLESS DIVE-BOMBER, SANK THE JAPANESE CARRIERS *KAGA* AND *AKAGI*, ASSISTED IN THE SINKING OF THE CARRIER *HIRYU*, AND LATER SANK THE HEAVY CRUISER *MIKUMA*.

Q What was the first major carrier battle of World War II?

A The Battle of the Coral Sea in May 1942.

Q Which American carrier was lost during the battle?

A USS *Lexington*.

Q Which Japanese aircraft carrier was sunk in the battle?

A The *Shoho*.

Q Why was the Battle of the Coral Sea a decisive engagement?

A The battle halted Japanese expansion plans in Papua and the Solomon Islands, and signaled the first major Japanese reverse in the war.

Q What was Australia's first home-produced wartime aircraft?

A The Commonwealth CA-12 Boomerang.

Q When did it make its first flight?

A May 1942.

Q Around which Pacific island did the Japanese plan to destroy the US Pacific Fleet in mid-1942?

A Midway.

" LOWERED AWAY TO HOUSETOPS
AND SLID OVER WESTERN OUTSKIRTS
INTO LOW HAZE
AND SMOKE "
COLONEL JAMES DOOLITTLE, RAID ON TOKYO,
APRIL 1942

Q Three new panzer divisions were formed in 1942. Name two of them.

A The 25th, 26th, and 27th Panzer Divisions.

Q What was the main armament of an M4 Sherman tank?

A A 75mm gun.

Q On the Eastern Front, what German armies took part in Operation Blue into the Caucasus in June 1942?

A Sixth Army (330,000 troops and 300 tanks and assault guns); Second Army (95,000 troops); Seventeenth Army (150,000 troops and 180 tanks and assault guns); First Panzer Army (220,000 troops and 480 tanks and assault guns); and Fourth Panzer Army (200,000 troops and 480 tanks).

Q Which non-German formations took part in Operation Blue?

A The Hungarian Second and Italian Eighth Armies.

Q From which country did the Allied convoy PQ-17 sail in July 1942?

A Iceland.

Q How many ships were lost to German attack?

A 24 out of 35.

DID YOU KNOW

IN JUNE 1942 HITLER VISITED MARSHAL MANNERHEIM IN FINLAND TO OFFER CONGRATULATIONS ON THE FINN'S 75TH BIRTHDAY, AND TO STRENGTHEN THE MUTUAL RELATIONSHIPS BETWEEN GERMANY AND FINLAND. THE TWO MEN MET NEAR THE QUIET FINNISH BORDER TOWN OF IMATRA. THE MEETING WAS NOT A SUCCESS: AT ONE POINT HITLER DEMANDED THAT FINNISH JEWS BE DEPORTED; MANNERHEIM ANSWERED, "OVER MY DEAD BODY."

Q Summarize the reorganization of the German Army Group South in July 1942 as it advanced into the Caucasus.

A Army Group South was divided into Army Groups A and B.

Q What was the purpose of this reorganization?

A Army Group B (Second, Fourth Panzer, and Sixth Armies and the Hungarian Second Army) was ordered to destroy Soviet forces between the upper Donets and middle Don and secure a crossing of the Don near Voronezh. The Fourth Panzer and Sixth Armies would then race east to Stalingrad, from whence they would sweep south to support Army Group A in the Caucasus.

152

DID YOU KNOW

IN JULY 1942, IN THE FACE OF GERMAN ADVANCES IN THE CAUCASUS, STALIN ISSUED ORDER NO. 227. IN THIS HE ALLUDED TO HIS CONCERN ABOUT GERMAN GAINS: "THE TERRITORY OF THE SOVIET UNION IS NOT A WILDER-NESS, BUT PEOPLE—WORKERS, PEASANTS, INTELLIGENTSIA, OUR FATHERS AND MOTHERS, WIVES, BROTHERS, CHILDREN. TERRITORY OF USSR THAT HAS BEEN CAPTURED BY THE ENEMY AND WHICH THE ENEMY IS LONGING TO CAPTURE IS BREAD AND OTHER RESOURCES FOR THE ARMY AND THE CIVILIANS, IRON AND FUEL FOR THE INDUSTRIES, FACTORIES AND PLANTS THAT SUPPLY THE MILITARY WITH HARDWARE AND AMMUNITION; THIS IS ALSO RAILROADS. WITH THE LOSS OF UKRAINE, BELORUSSIA, THE BALTICS, DONETS BASIN, AND OTHER AREAS WE HAVE LOST VAST TERRITORIES; THAT MEANS THAT WE HAVE LOST MANY PEOPLE, BREAD, METALS, FACTORIES, AND PLANTS. WE NO LONGER HAVE SUPERIORITY OVER THE ENEMY IN HUMAN RESOURCES AND IN BREAD SUPPLY. CONTINUATION OF RETREAT MEANS THE DESTRUCTION OF OUR MOTHERLAND. THE CONCLUSION IS THAT IT IS TIME TO STOP THE RETREAT. NOT A SINGLE STEP BACK! THIS SHOULD BE OUR SLOGAN FROM NOW ON."

WORLD WAR II TRIVIA BOOK

"
THE SUN BEATS DOWN—AS USUAL—
AND WHEN IT GETS HOT ENOUGH—
A COOL SHOWER
COMES ALONG
Sergeant Kazazkow, U.S. Army, south Pacific,
March 1942

Q In July 1942 SS chief Heinrich Himmler ordered the start of Operation Reinhard. What was this?

A Its objectives were: to kill Polish Jews; to exploit the skilled or manual labor of some Polish Jews before killing them; to secure the personal property of the Jews (clothing, currency, jewellery); and to identify and secure immovable assets such as factories, apartments, and land. The camps used for the extermination were Belzec (opened March 1942), Sobibor (opened May 1942), and Treblinka (opened July 1942).

153

Q How many people did Operation Reinhard kill?

A In total 1.7 million Jews were killed during Reinhard, plus an unknown number of Poles, gypsies, and Soviet prisoners of war.

Q Who attended the First Moscow Conference in August 1942?

A British Prime Minister Winston Churchill and US Ambassador W. Averell Harriman, representing President Roosevelt.

Q What was the purpose of the conference?

A To discuss a common war strategy. Churchill, with the support of Ambassador Harriman, informed Stalin that it would be impossible for the British and Americans to open a second front in Europe in 1942.

Q Why was the city of Stalingrad an important symbol to both Hitler and Stalin?

A Stalingrad, "the city of Stalin," acted as a magnet for German forces because, for Hitler, it assumed a massive psychological significance—he became obsessed by it. Similarly, for Stalin the city was also an obsession. It had been named after him as a result of his defense of the city during the Russian Civil War. He insisted that it should be held at all costs. On a more practical level, he knew that if the Germans took the city Moscow would be vulnerable to an attack from the south.

Q How many citizens of Stalingrad were killed in the Luftwaffe air raids over two days in August 1942?

A 40,000.

" FROM EARLY MORNING OUR
BATTERIES KEPT POURING A
MASSED SHELL-FIRE
INTO THE ENEMY TANKS "
PRIVATE WOLFGANG KNOBLICH, GERMAN ARMY,
RUSSIA, APRIL 1942

Q Who commanded the Japanese First Carrier Striking Force at the Battle of Midway?

A Vice Admiral Chuichi Nagumo.

Q Name at least two carriers that made up the First Carrier Striking Force.

A There were four carriers in total: *Akagi*, *Kaga*, *Hiryu*, and *Soryu*.

DID YOU KNOW

THE JAPANESE PLANS FOR THE BATTLE OF MIDWAY CENTERED AROUND THEIR EFFORTS TO LURE THE U.S. PACIFIC FLEET INTO THE OPEN AND DESTROY IT. HOWEVER, AS WAS COMMON IN JAPANESE STRATEGIC PLANNING, THE OPERATION WAS OVER COMPLEX, MADE UNJUSTIFIED ASSUMPTIONS ABOUT HOW U.S. NAVAL FORCES WOULD REACT, AND FAILED TO CONCENTRATE FORCE. INDEED, EVEN THE CHOICE OF MIDWAY ISLAND WAS FLAWED, AND DEEPLY UNPOPULAR WITH IMPERIAL JAPANESE NAVY CAPTAINS. A DIVERSIONARY FORCE WOULD BE SENT TO THE ALEUTIANS TO DRAW OFF PART OF THE U.S. FLEET, WHILST THE JAPANESE FORCES UNDER ADMIRAL YAMAMOTO WOULD CAPTURE MIDWAY. THIS WOULD FORCE THE AMERICANS TO TRY TO RETAKE THE ISLAND, WHICH WOULD GIVE YAMAMOTO THE OPPORTUNITY TO DESTROY NIMITZ'S CARRIERS WITH HIS CARRIER-BASED AIRCRAFT, AIDED BY LAND-BASED BOMBERS STATIONED ON THE NEWLY CAPTURED ISLAND. THIS WOULD LEAVE THE WEST COAST OF AMERICA AT THE MERCY OF THE JAPANESE AND FORCE THE U.S. TO NEGOTIATE A PEACE, OR SO THE THEORY WENT.

155

Q What forces did the American deploy at the Battle of Midway?

A Task Force 17 commanded by Rear Admiral Fletcher and containing the carrier USS *Yorktown* (patched up from the Coral Sea action), and Rear Admiral Spruance's Task Force 16 with the carriers USS *Hornet* and USS *Enterprise*.

Q How many aircraft carriers did the Japanese lose at Midway?

A Four.

Q How many aircraft carriers did the Americans lose at Midway?

A One, USS *Yorktown*.

Q The fortress of Bir Hacheim featured in which North African battle?

A The Battle of Gazala in mid-1942.

Q At this battle, what was the "Cauldron"?

A German forces were temporarily encircled by Commonwealth forces during part of the battle. The area in which they were encircled was called the "Cauldron," mainly because it was under artillery fire and German forces had their backs to British minefields.

Q Which major North African port fell to Erwin Rommel in June 1942?

A Tobruk.

Q What was the name of the British Army that fought the Battle of Alam Halfa in autumn 1942?

A The Eighth Army.

Q Who was its commander?

A General Bernard Montgomery.

> **OUR ARTILLERY OPENED UP IN ITS FULL FURY BY WAY OF A PRELUDE TO THE INFANTRY ASSAULT**
> GENERAL VON MANSTEIN DIRECTING THE
> GERMAN ASSAULT ON SEVASTOPOL, JUNE 1942

DID YOU KNOW

THE BURMA-THAILAND RAILWAY WAS ONE OF THE GREATEST, AND MOST APPALLING, ENGINEERING FEATS OF WORLD WAR II. IN MID-1942, THE JAPANESE WERE FACED WITH CHRONIC PROBLEMS IN SUPPLYING THEIR FORCES FIGHTING IN BURMA, PARTICULARLY AS SHIPPING ROUTES TO RANGOON WERE INCREASINGLY INTERDICTED BY ALLIED AIRCRAFT, SHIPS, AND SUBMARINES. THE SOLUTION WAS TO BUILD A RAILROAD EXTENSION BETWEEN THANBYUZAYAT IN BURMA AND NONG PLADUK IN THAILAND, WHICH, WHEN LINKED TO EXISTING RAIL ROUTES, WOULD PROVIDE A LOGISTICAL LIFELINE THROUGHOUT BURMA AND GIVE BETTER ACCESS TO SHIPPING SUPPLIES RUNNING UP THROUGH THE GULF OF SIAM.

Q How many Allied prisoners and forced laborers worked on the Burma-Thailand railway?

A 61,000 Allied prisoners and more than 270,000 laborers from Japanese-occupied territories.

Q How many died due to the inhuman working conditions?

A Some 12,000 Allied prisoners and 90,000 other laborers—an average of 425 deaths for every mile of track laid.

Q Why did the island of Guadalcanal become so important to the Japanese after the Battle of Midway?

A After the setback at the Battle of Midway in June 1942, the Japanese concentrated their efforts on defense of their territorial gains—what they euphemistically called the Greater East Asia Co-Prosperity Sphere—basically the areas of Asia that gave Japan the raw materials and resources she needed to fight the war. This strategy of defense included building an airfield on Guadalcanal as a way of using land-based aircraft in support of carrier-borne units against any U.S. attack.

Q Which American four-engined bomber mounted a slender wing above a tall fuselage bay?

A The Consolidated B-24 Liberator.

Q What was the U.S. Navy's first cantilever monoplane flying boat?

A The Consolidated PBY Catalina.

Q Which American warplane sank more Japanese shipping than any other Allied aircraft during the war?

A The Douglas SBD Dauntless dive-bomber.

" A PINT OF SWEAT WILL SAVE A
GALLON OF BLOOD
GEORGE S. PATTON, TO U.S. FORCES
AT CASABLANCA, NOVEMBER 8, 1942 "

Q The Douglas DC-3 transport aircraft is better known in its military form. What was this?

A The C-47 Skytrain, known as the Dakota in British service.

Q General Eisenhower said that the Dakota was one of the four decisive weapons of World War II. What were the other three?

A The Jeep, the Bazooka, and the M4 Sherman tank.

Q Which company developed the SBD Dauntless dive-bomber?

A Northrop.

Q Who was chief designer on the project?

A Ed Heinemann.

DID YOU KNOW

THE .30IN-CALIBER M1 GARAND RIFLE WAS THE FIRST SELF-LOADING RIFLE ISSUED AS A STANDARD FIREARM TO AN ARMY. IT WAS ACTUALLY ACCEPTED INTO MILITARY SERVICE IN 1932, BUT HAD A LONG TECHNICAL GESTATION PERIOD IN WHICH ITS DESIGNER, JOHN C. GARAND, REFINED IT INTO A FIRST-CLASS COMBAT WEAPON. THE M1 WAS A GAS-OPERATED RIFLE FED BY AN INTERNAL MAGAZINE HOLDING EIGHT ROUNDS, REFILLED BY PUSHING AN EIGHT-ROUND CLIP DOWN THROUGH THE OPENED BOLT. IF ANYTHING, THE MAGAZINE SYSTEM PROVED TO BE THE ONLY PRACTICAL FLAW OF THE M1; THE RIFLE COULD BE LOADED ONLY WHEN EMPTY, AND THE MAGAZINE COULD NOT BE TOPPED UP WITH INDIVIDUAL ROUNDS. ALSO, THE EMPTY CLIP WAS EJECTED WITH AN EMPHATIC "PING," SIGNALING TO ENEMY SOLDIERS THAT THE INFANTRYMAN HAD TO RELOAD. HOWEVER, IN OTHER RESPECTS THE M1 WAS A SUPERB WEAPON. IT WAS EXTREMELY RUGGED, AND PROVIDED UTTERLY DEPENDABLE SERVICE TO U.S. SOLDIERS IN ALL THEATERS OF WAR. ITS SEMIAUTOMATIC ACTION ALLOWED UNITS TO GENERATE THE HEAVY FIREPOWER SO ESSENTIAL IN THE JUNGLE COMBAT OF THE PACIFIC WAR, AND ITS .30IN ROUND HAD DECISIVE STOPPING POWER. THE M1 WAS ALSO ACCURATE, THOUGH ONLY IN TRAINED HANDS, EXPLAINING WHY TWO LATER SNIPER VERSIONS—THE M1C AND M1D—NEVER SAW LARGE-SCALE PRODUCTION.

> **" ANIMALS FLEE THIS HELL; THE HARDEST STORMS CANNOT BEAR IT FOR LONG; ONLY MEN ENDURE "**
>
> ANONYMOUS GERMAN OFFICER AT STALINGRAD,
> OCTOBER 1942

Q What cargo ships were nicknamed "American ugly ducklings"?

A Liberty ships.

Q Who replaced Rommel as the commander of Panzer Army Africa in September 1942?

A General George Stumme.

Q What happened to this commander during the Battle of El Alamein in October 1942?

A He died of a heart attack.

Q The British attack plan at the Battle of El Alamein was divided into two distinct phases. What was the first phase?

A Codenamed Operation Lightfoot, it involved a diversionary assault in the south by XIII Corps, while farther to the north XXX Corps launched the main British break-in thrust to open up two corridors in the enemy minefields.

Q What was the second phase of the British plan?

A Codenamed Operation Supercharge, the armor of XXX Corps would advance through the corridors in the enemy minefields.

Q What was the size of a Tiger I's crew?

A Five.

Q What task did each crew member perform?

A Commander, gunner, loader, radio operator, and driver.

Q What was distinctive about the Tiger's suspension?

A It was composed of driving sprocket, rear idler, and interleaved road wheels (36 in total).

Q What problems did this present in cold weather?

A Mud, ice, and rocks could jam the track mechanism and immobilize the tank.

DID YOU KNOW

FOLLOWING ENCOUNTERS WITH SOVIET T-34 AND KV-1 TANKS IN 1941, GERMAN TANK DESIGNERS WERE INSTRUCTED TO PRODUCE A HEAVY TANK THAT WOULD RESTORE MASTERY OF THE BATTLEFIELD TO THE GERMANS. THE RESULT WAS THE PANZER VI AUSF E—THE TIGER I—WHICH ENTERED SERVICE IN AUGUST 1942. IT WAS ARMED WITH THE POWERFUL 88MM GUN (ORIGINALLY DEVELOPED FROM THE 88MM FLAK 36 L/56 GUN), WHICH MEANT IT COULD KNOCK OUT ANY ALLIED TANK THEN IN SERVICE. ITS THICK (BUT NOT SHOT-DEFLECTING) ARMOR MADE IT VIRTUALLY INDESTRUCTIBLE (THE U.S. SHERMAN, ARMED WITH A 76MM GUN, AND RUSSIAN T-34/85, ARMED WITH AN 85MM GUN, STOOD A CHANCE ONLY AGAINST A TIGER AT CLOSE RANGE, AND ONLY WITH A SHOT AGAINST ITS SIDE OR REAR).

Q Which Soviet army defended the city of Stalingrad in 1942?

A The Sixty-Second Army.

Q Who was its commander?

A General Vasily Chuikov.

Q What was the German army that tried to capture Stalingrad in 1942?

A The Sixth Army.

DID YOU KNOW

CONVOYS PROVIDED PROTECTIVE ESCORTS FOR MERCHANT VESSELS AGAINST ENEMY SURFACE, SUBMERGED, OR AIR ATTACK. ALLIED CONVOYS, OFTEN CONTAINING MORE THAN 50 VESSELS, SAILED IN COLUMNS AND WEAVED THEIR WAY ACROSS THE SEA-LANES. IN THE ATLANTIC AND ARCTIC, THE BAD WEATHER REDUCED VISIBILITY, FROZE THE CREWS, AND CREATED GREAT WAVES THAT LEFT VESSELS VULNERABLE TO COLLISION. THE MAIN THREAT TO ALLIED CONVOYS WERE THE U-BOATS, WHICH INFLICTED CRITICAL LOSSES UPON SHIPPING. ANTISUBMARINE MEASURES GRADUALLY IMPROVED, HOWEVER, WITH ENHANCED AIR–SEA COORDINATION, NEW TACTICS, AND SCIENTIFIC INNOVATIONS. SHIPBUILDING WAS ALSO INCREASED TO REPLACE LOST VESSELS. THE INTERCEPTION OF GERMAN RADIO TRANSMISSIONS, CENTIMETRIC RADAR, ESCORT CARRIERS, U-BOAT-DETECTION TECHNOLOGY (ASDIC AND SONAR), IMPROVED DEPTH CHARGES, AND LAUNCHERS ALL HELPED PROTECT CONVOYS. GERMANY'S CAMPAIGN TO DESTROY ALLIED CONTROL OF THE ATLANTIC SEA-LANES WAS ESPECIALLY CRITICAL AS BRITAIN CAME TO RELY UPON NORTH AMERICAN AID. IN THE NORTH ATLANTIC ALONE, SOME 2,232 VESSELS WERE SUNK, BUT THE DESTRUCTION OF 785 U-BOATS SECURED ALLIED COMMAND OF THE SEA-LANES.

Q The Soviets planned to encircle Axis units fighting in and around Stalingrad by launching a massive offensive. What was its codename?

A Operation Uranus.

Q When did this operation commence?

A November 19, 1942.

> **"** I'VE ONLY GOT DISMAL AND DEPRESSING NEWS FOR YOU TODAY. OUR MANY **JEWISH FRIENDS ARE BEING TAKEN AWAY**
> ANNE FRANK, DIARY ENTRY, OCTOBER 9, 1942 **"**

163

Q Which South American country declared war on Germany and Italy in August 1942?

A Brazil.

Q The Nazis cleared a Jewish ghetto in which city in September 1942?

A Warsaw. More than 50,000 Jews were killed by poison gas or sent to concentration camps.

Q Which German field marshal was dismissed in September 1942?

A Field Marshal Wilhelm List, commander of Army Group A.

Q Who replaced Franz Halder as chief of the German General Staff in September 1942?

A Kurt Zeitzler.

Q What was the codename for the British and American landings in Morocco and Algeria (French North Africa) in November 1942?

A Operation Torch.

164

❝ THIS IS NOT THE END. IT IS NOT EVEN THE
BEGINNING OF THE END. BUT
**IT IS, PERHAPS, THE END
OF THE BEGINNING** **❞**
WINSTON CHURCHILL, NOVEMBER 10, 1942,
AFTER EL ALAMEIN

Q Why did the Allies invade French North Africa in 1942?

A To seize French North Africa as a springboard for future operations to clear the whole of North Africa of Axis forces.

Q Who was Vichy commissioner in Africa at the time?

A Admiral Jean François Darlan.

DID YOU KNOW

DURING 1942 EFFORTS WERE MADE TO STRENGTHEN THE GERMAN PANZER DIVISIONS AT THE FRONT. ON AVERAGE, THE PANZER DIVISIONS THAT COMMENCED BLUE FIELDED JUST 126 TANKS EACH—40 PERCENT FEWER THAN IN BARBAROSSA. TO OFFSET THIS, HOWEVER, A TINY PROPORTION OF THESE AFVs—JUST 133 IN FACT—WERE THE LATEST PANZER IV MODEL F2 VEHICLES THAT MOUNTED THE POTENT LONG-BARRELLED 75MM KwK 40 L/48 CANNON AND FEATURED FRONTAL ARMOR INCREASED TO 1.96 IN (50 MM) THICKNESS. THE GUN OF THE F2 DELIVERED A MUZZLE VELOCITY OF 2,430FPS (740MPS) AND COULD PENETRATE 3.5 IN (89 MM) OF WELL-SLOPED ARMOR AT THE TYPICAL COMBAT RANGE OF 3,282 FT (1,000 M), SUFFICIENT TO PUNCH THROUGH EVEN THE FRONTAL ARMOR OF THE T-34. WHAT THE GERMANS DESPERATELY NEEDED, THOUGH, WAS LARGER NUMBERS OF THE PANZER IV MODEL F2 TO NEUTRALIZE THE IMPACT THE T-34 THEN EXERTED ON THE TACTICAL BATTLEFIELD.

Q Which three Japanese aircraft carriers protected a Japanese supply convoy as it attempted a resupply mission to Guadalcanal in August 1942?

A The *Ryujo, Zuizaku,* and *Shokaku.*

Q What was the name of the U.S. force that intercepted the Japanese convoy?

A Task Force 61.

Q What was the result of the subsequent battle on August 24?

A U.S. and Japanese carrier aircraft dealt mutual blows, the U.S. sinking the *Ryujo* and the Japanese damaging, although not critically, the USS *Enterprise.* The carrier forces separated, but the next day U.S. Marine dive-bombers flying from Henderson Field sunk two Japanese transporters (*Jintsu* and *Kinryu Maru*) and the destroyer *Mutsuki.*

Q What was the name of the American airfield on Guadalcanal?

A Henderson Field.

Q Who led the Japanese attack by 20,000 troops against this airfield in late October 1942?

A General Masao Maruyama.

Q Which Japanese naval force moved toward Guadalcanal in support of Maruyama's offensive in late October 1942?

A The Combined Fleet.

DID YOU KNOW

ADMIRAL CHESTER W. NIMITZ WAS ONE OF THE MOST GIFTED NAVAL COMMANDERS OF WORLD WAR II. BORN IN 1885 IN TEXAS, NIMITZ FIRST SET HIS SIGHTS ON A CAREER IN THE U.S. ARMY, BUT OWING TO A LACK OF PLACES AT WEST POINT HE BEGAN ATTENDANCE AT THE NAVAL ACADEMY CLASS IN 1905. NIMITZ'S CROWNING ACHIEVEMENT CAME WHEN HE REPLACED REAR-ADMIRAL KIMMEL AS C-IN-C OF THE U.S. PACIFIC FLEET AFTER THE ATTACK ON PEARL HARBOR, NIMITZ BEING PROMOTED TO FULL ADMIRAL. THROUGHOUT THE PACIFIC CAMPAIGN, NIMITZ DEMONSTRATED AN AGGRESSIVE DEFENSIVE ATTITUDE COMBINED WITH A DEEP PRACTICAL UNDERSTANDING OF NAVAL WARFARE, AND AN AFFABLE PERSONALITY THAT MADE HIM POPULAR AND RESPECTED. NIMITZ PRESIDED OVER THE GREAT NAVAL BATTLES OF THE PACIFIC WAR, AND HAD AN EXCELLENT GRASP OF HOW TO SUPPORT AMPHIBIOUS LAND CAMPAIGNS. IT IS A SIGN OF HIS CAPABILITIES THAT, IN NOVEMBER 1945, HE WAS MADE CHIEF OF NAVAL OPERATIONS ON THE RETIREMENT OF ADMIRAL KING.

> ## RECKLESS COUNTERATTACKS, WITH HUGE LOSSES, GOT NOWHERE. IN SHORT, WE WERE SURROUNDED
> Benno Zieser, German soldier at Stalingrad, December 1942

Q Name the U.S. Navy units sent to intercept this force.

A U.S. Task Forces 16 and 17, containing the carriers USS *Hornet* and USS *Enterprise*.

Q What was the name of the resulting battle when the two naval fleets clashed?

A The Battle of Santa Cruz.

Q What happened at the Battle of Santa Cruz in October 1942?

A At first light on October 26 both the Americans and Japanese put flights of attack aircraft into the sky. Over the course of a four-hour battle, the Japanese carriers *Zuiho* and *Shokaku* were badly damaged, while the USS *Enterprise* suffered a smashed flight deck and the USS *Hornet* was destroyed by two torpedo and six bomb strikes and had to be abandoned. The Japanese claimed victory in the battle, but lost more than 100 pilots and aircraft, unacceptably high losses that rendered many of the carriers almost inoperable.

Q In the Pacific theater, where was "Ironbottom Sound"?

A Between the coast of Guadalcanal and Savo Island. So called because of the many sunken ships lying on the seabed.

> ❝ PRACTICALLY EVERY BUILDING OF THE
> DISMAL PLACE WAS EITHER FLAT
> # OR LITTLE MORE THAN
> # A HEAP OF RUBBLE
> GENERAL ERWIN ROMMEL, ON ENTERING TOBRUK,
> JUNE 21, 1942 ❞

Q On the Eastern Front, what was the aim of the Soviet Operation Little Saturn in December 1942?

A The destruction of the Italian Eighth Army and isolation of Group Hollidt west of Stalingrad.

Q The Germans mounted a relief operation in December 1942 to rescue Axis forces trapped in the Stalingrad Pocket. What was its codename?

A Operation Winter Storm.

Q Who commanded this relief operation?

A Field Marshal Erich von Manstein.

Q Who was the commander of the trapped German Sixth Army at Stalingrad?

A General Friedrich Paulus.

Q What was the codeword that was to signal the Sixth Army to break out of the Stalingrad Pocket and link up with the German relief force?

A Thunderclap.

1943

Allied victories in Papua New Guinea, the Solomon Islands, and Burma forced the Japanese on to the defensive in the Pacific. Axis forces were cleared from North Africa, allowing the Allies to invade Italy. And on the Eastern Front the Germans suffered two decisive defeats: at Stalingrad and Kursk.

Q The U.S. Fifth Army was formed in North Africa in January 1943. Who was its commander?

A General Mark Clark.

Q Who replaced Admiral Erich Raeder as commander-in-chief of German naval forces in January 1942?

A Admiral Karl Dönitz.

Q Why did Admiral Raeder resign his post?

A Because of German naval blunders made at the Battle of the Barents Sea in December 1942.

" THE DUTY OF THE MEN AT STALINGRAD
IS TO BE DEAD
ADOLF HITLER, JANUARY 1943 **"**

Q Which brother and sister were executed in Munich in February 1943 for the crime of distributing traitorous literature?

A Hans and Sophie Scholl.

Q Which anti-Nazi group did they belong to?

A The White Rose group.

DID YOU KNOW

THE RED ORCHESTRA WAS ESTABLISHED IN 1939 BY LEOPOLD TREPPER, AN AGENT IN THE SOVIET MILITARY INTELLIGENCE SERVICE. IT COLLECTED INTELLIGENCE FROM AGENTS IN NAZI-OCCUPIED EUROPE AND NEUTRAL SWITZERLAND. IT COMPRISED THREE MAIN SECTIONS: THE NETWORK IN FRANCE, BELGIUM, AND HOLLAND; A NETWORK IN BERLIN (WHICH INCLUDED HARRO SCHULZE-BOYSEN, AN INTELLIGENCE OFFICER ASSIGNED TO THE GERMAN AIR MINISTRY, AND ARVID VON HARNACK, WHO WORKED IN THE MINISTRY OF ECONOMICS); AND THE "LUCY SPY RING" THAT OPERATED FROM SWITZERLAND. THE LATTER INCLUDED SOME HIGH-RANKING GERMAN INDIVIDUALS: LIEUTENANT GENERAL FRITZ THEILE, WEHRMACHT COMMUNICATIONS BRANCH; AND RUDOLF VON GERSDORFF, WHO BECAME ARMY GROUP CENTER'S INTELLIGENCE OFFICER ON THE EASTERN FRONT.

Q On the Eastern Front, what was the Soviet Operation Ring of January 1943?

171

A The codename for the destruction of the German Sixth Army at Stalingrad.

Q On the Eastern Front, what was the Soviet Operation Iskra?

A An offensive designed to push the German Eighteenth Army out of the Schlusselburg-Mga salient and thus reopen a supply line to the besieged city of Leningrad.

Q Georgi Zhukov was promoted to marshal following his Operation Mars. Why was this somewhat surprising?

A Because Mars cost the Red Army nearly 500,000 troops killed, wounded, or captured (German casualties were around 40,000).

Q What was the last German airfield to fall in the Stalingrad Pocket?

A Gumrak, on January 23, 1943.

Q Which German airfield in the Stalingrad Pocket was captured on January 16, 1943?

A Pitomnik.

Q Why did Hitler promote the commander of the Sixth Army at Stalingrad, Friedrich Paulus, to field marshal at the end of January 1943?

A It was a cynical move to prompt the commander at Stalingrad to commit suicide rather than surrender (no German field marshal had yet surrendered to the enemy).

172

DID YOU KNOW

GERMAN PANZERGRENADIER DIVISIONS WERE INTEGRAL TO BLITZKRIEG WARFARE, WITH MOTORIZED INFANTRY ACCOMPANYING AND SUPPORTING THE FAST-MOVING PANZER DIVISIONS. THE INFANTRY TRAVELED IN HALFTRACK ARMORED PERSONNEL CARRIERS TO AND ON TO THE BATTLE-FIELD. HOWEVER, THERE WERE NEVER ENOUGH HALFTRACKS, SO EACH DIVISION ALSO USED TRUCKS TO TRANSPORT ITS MEN. IN ADDITION, EARLIER MOTORIZED DIVISIONS ALSO HAD LARGE NUMBERS OF MOTOR-CYCLE-MOUNTED TROOPS, ALTHOUGH THEY DISAPPEARED AS THE WAR WENT ON BECAUSE MOTORCYCLES WERE VULNERABLE TO SMALL-ARMS FIRE.

" TELL THEM FROM ME THEY ARE
UNLOADING HISTORY
WINSTON CHURCHILL, TELEGRAM TO THE
PORT COMMANDER AT TRIPOLI, FEBRUARY 24, 1943 "

Q Did Hitler's tactic work?

A No. Paulus surrendered at Stalingrad on January 31, 1943. Hitler was disgusted, stating: "Here is a man who can look on while fifty or sixty thousand are dying and defending themselves with courage to the end—how can he give himself up to the Bolsheviks?"

Q How many troops did the Germans lose when the Sixth Army surrendered at Stalingrad?

A 150,000 dead and another 90,000 taken prisoner, including 24 generals and 2,000 officers (only 6,000 returned home to Germany in the 1950s).

173

Q How many aircraft did the Luftwaffe lose during the abortive Stalingrad airlift?

A 488 aircraft and 1,000 air crews.

Q Why did Stalin create a communist-led Polish army in February 1943?

A As a counterweight to the Western Allied-sponsored Polish Army that was being formed in Iran. Both units were staffed by Poles who were former prisoners of the Soviets. Because of the lack of Polish cadres left in the USSR, though, many of the commanders and specialists in Stalin's Polish Army would be Russian.

Q In North Africa, where was the Mareth Line?

A On the Libyan-Tunisian border.

Q What was the name of the German army that confronted Anglo-American forces in Tunisia at the end of 1942?

A The Fifth Panzer Army.

Q Who commanded this army?

A Colonel General Hans-Jürgen von Arnim.

Q Where did Axis forces attack American troops in western Tunisia between February 14 and 22, 1943?

A At the Kasserine Pass.

Q What was the result?

A The attack successfully advanced 60 miles (96 km) in the face of collapsing American cohesion.

" GODDAMN IT, YOU'LL NEVER GET THE
PURPLE HEART HIDING IN A
FOXHOLE! FOLLOW ME! "
LIEUTENANT-COLONEL HENRY P. CROWE,
JANUARY 13, 1943

DID YOU KNOW

GERMAN PANZERGRENADIER DIVISIONS HAD A TANK ELEMENT, WHICH COULD BE QUITE SIZEABLE. AT THE BATTLE OF KURSK, FOR EXAMPLE, THE ÉLITE *GROSSDEUTSCHLAND* DIVISION HAD 45 PANZER IVs, 46 PANTHERS, 13 TIGER Is, AND 35 ASSAULT GUNS. BY THE MIDDLE OF THE WAR, THE PANZERGRENADIERS THAT TRAVELED IN HALFTRACKS PRECEDED THE PANZERS ON TO THE BATTLEFIELD, TO SEARCH OUT AND DESTROY ENEMY ANTITANK GUN POSITIONS AND ENEMY INFANTRY TANK-DESTRUCTION PARTIES LYING IN WAIT FOR THE PANZERS. ON PAPER EACH DIVISION NUMBERED ON AVERAGE 13,900 TROOPS, DIVIDED BETWEEN TWO MOTORIZED INFANTRY REGIMENTS; ONE ARMORED BATTALION; ONE ARTILLERY REGIMENT (WITH 12 105MM HOWITZERS, 16 150MM HOWITZERS AND 8 SELF-PROPELLED 105MM HOWITZERS); 1 ANTITANK BATTALION (28 75MM ASSAULT GUNS OR TANK DESTROYERS AND 12 TOWED 75MM ANTI-TANK GUNS); AN ARMORED RECONNAISSANCE BATTALION; AN ANTIAIRCRAFT BATTALION; ENGINEER BATTALION; SIGNALS BATTALION; AND VARIOUS SUPPORT SERVICES.

Q **What was Erwin Rommel's last battle in North Africa?**

A At Medinine on March 6–7, 1943.

Q **Was it a success?**

A No. He attacked Montgomery's forces that faced him on the Mareth Line. He concentrated three panzer divisions with 160 tanks that were supported by some 200 guns and 10,000 infantry. Yet. Montgomery, due to his foreknowledge of the attack (ULTRA intercepts had provided the British commander with vital intelligence), had managed to assemble a force of 400 tanks, 350 artillery pieces, and 470 antitank guns to halt Rommel. The weight of Allied numbers soon defeated Rommel's thrust and inflicted heavy casualties on Axis forces.

DID YOU KNOW

THE INTRODUCTION OF PANZER VI MODEL E TIGER I HEAVY TANKS INTO THE NORTH AFRICAN THEATER DURING DECEMBER 1942 HELPED THE AXIS RESTABILIZE THE STRATEGIC SITUATION FOLLOWING THE TWIN DISASTERS OF OPERATION TORCH AND ROMMEL'S "GREAT RETREAT" AFTER THE SECOND BATTLE OF EL ALAMEIN. THE TIGER I HEAVY TANK WAS A SQUAT AND ANGULAR 55-TON (56-TONNE) VEHICLE THAT MOUNTED THE LETHAL 88MM KwK 43 L/56 GUN. IT POSSESSED IMPRESSIVE LEVELS OF PROTECTION, WITH FRONTAL ARMOR SOME 3.9 IN (100 MM) THICK, PLUS 3.1 IN (80 MM) PLATES ON ITS SIDES AND REAR. APART FROM THE EARLIEST VEHICLES, THE TIGER WAS POWERED BY A 700HP MAYBACH HL 230 ENGINE THAT DELIVERED A SATISFACTORY TOP ROAD SPEED OF 23.5MPH (38KPH) BUT ONLY A MODEST 12.5MPH (20KPH) OFF ROAD. SINCE THE TIGER WAS TOO LARGE TO BE TRANSPORTED ON THE STANDARD GERMAN RAILROAD FLAT-CAR, THE MANUFACTURERS, HENSCHEL, DEVELOPED A NOVEL TWO-TRACK SYSTEM FOR THE VEHICLE. IN BATTLE THE TIGER UTILIZED WIDE 28.5 IN (725 MM) COMBAT TRACKS, BUT WHEN BEING MOVED BY RAIL THESE WERE REPLACED WITH NARROWER TRANSPORTATION TRACKS. THE TIGER MADE ITS OPERATIONAL DEBUT DURING AUGUST 1942 ON THE EASTERN FRONT, BUT FOUGHT MANY OF ITS EARLIEST ACTIONS IN NORTH AFRICA DURING EARLY 1943. THOUGH THE TIGER BOTH MOUNTED AN EXTREMELY POTENT GUN AND WAS HEAVILY ARMORED, ITS COMBAT EFFECTIVENESS WAS UNDERMINED SOMEWHAT BY PERSISTENT MECHANICAL UNRELIABILITY AND ITS LIMITED MOBILITY. NEVERTHELESS, WHEN EMPLOYED IN THE DEFENSIVE BATTLES THAT DOMINATED THE GERMAN ARMY'S EXPERIENCES FROM 1943 ONWARD, THE TIGER PROVED A FORMIDABLE TANK-KILLER THAT BOLSTERED GERMAN DEFENSIVE RESISTANCE AGAINST SUPERIOR ALLIED NUMBERS. UNFORTUNATELY FOR THE GERMAN ARMY, THERE ALWAYS REMAINED TOO FEW TIGERS AVAILABLE—ONLY 1,354 WERE BUILT—TO RESTORE THE STEADILY DETERIORATING STRATEGIC SITUATION DURING THE SECOND HALF OF THE WAR.

Q How many Axis troops surrendered to the Allies in North Africa in May 1943?

A 275,000.

Q What happened at the Battle of Huon Gulf in early January 1943?

A Waves of U.S. aircraft attacked Japanese supply convoys destined for Papua New Guinea, sinking three Japanese transports and downing eighty Japanese aircraft with few losses.

Q Why was the U.S. capture of Guadalcanal in February 1943 so important to Allied war aims?

> **"** GUADALCANAL IS NO LONGER MERELY THE NAME OF AN ISLAND. IT IS
> ## THE GRAVEYARD OF THE JAPANESE ARMY
> MAJOR GENERAL KIYOTAKE KAWAGUCHI, 1943 **"**

A Ejecting the Japanese from Guadalcanal was a crucial land victory for the U.S., giving it a base from which to penetrate Japan's Pacific conquests and providing security for Australia and New Zealand.

Q Who was the British general who conducted guerrilla warfare behind Japanese lines in Burma beginning in February 1943?

A Orde Wingate.

Q What was the formation he commanded?

A The 77th Indian Brigade.

Q Orde Wingate's 77th Indian Brigade, which fought the Japanese in Burma, had another name. What was it?

A The Chindits.

Q Where did this name come from?

A They were named after the stone lions seen guarding Buddhist temples.

Q What was the mission of the 77th Indian Brigade?

A To disrupt Japanese communications and tactical deployments, and pave the way for more opportunities for conventional offensives.

> **THE VULNERABLE ARTERY IS THE LINE OF COMMUNICATIONS WINDING THROUGH THE JUNGLE**
> ORDE WINGATE, BURMA, 1943

Q In the Pacific theater, what was the Allied Elkton Plan?

A Initiated in February 1943, it was the campaign to eject Japanese forces from New Guinea, New Britain, and the Solomon Islands and isolate the Japanese base at Rabaul.

Q What was the Japanese response to the plan?

A In response to Allied victories in Papua and Guadalcanal, the Japanese began pouring reinforcements into New Guinea, including the Eighteenth Army under Lieutenant General Adachi Hatazo and the Fourth Air Army.

DID YOU KNOW

Q What was the American Operation Cleanslate of February 1943?

A A force of U.S. assault battalions captured the diminutive Russell Island to the northwest of Guadalcanal.

Q Cleanslate was part of a wider Allied strategy in the Pacific in early 1943. What was this strategy?

A The occupation was the first in a series of U.S. campaigns to reclaim the Solomon Islands, and looked to cut off the Japanese naval and air base at Rabaul, New Britain, in a wider pincer operation called "Operation Cartwheel." Cleanslate was also the first element in General MacArthur and Admiral Nimitz's plan to reconquer the Pacific by working up from the south and east through Japanese-occupied territory in a systematic island-hopping strategy.

Q Who was the commander of the U.S. Fourteenth Army Air Force in China?

A Major General Claire Chennault.

Q Who attended the Casablanca Conference in January 1943?

A Winston Churchill and Franklin D. Roosevelt.

Q The conference highlighted differences between the British and Americans regarding the defeat of Hitler. What was British strategy regarding the defeat of Germany?

A The British wanted to keep fighting in the Mediterranean before the main attack on the Continent via the English Channel. They proposed invasions of Sicily and Italy as a means of drawing German reserves away from France and the Low Countries, which would cause the fall of Mussolini, and establish air bases in Italy, from where German armaments factories and Romanian oil fields could be bombed.

> **❝ THE REMAINDER OF THE TANKS WITHDREW BACK DOWN THE ROAD AND SAT ON THE HIGH GROUND ❞**
> MAJOR C. MIDDLETON, ROYAL ARTILLERY,
> NORTH AFRICA, FEBRUARY 21, 1943

Q What was American strategy for the same aim?

A The Americans believed the British plan would only dissipate resources for the cross-Channel invasion, and tie down forces in a sideshow. They believed the quickest way to defeat Hitler was an invasion of northern France. However, as a cross-Channel invasion was not possible in 1943, they grudgingly accepted that Sicily should be invaded (though Italy was not on the agenda).

Q At the conference, which took priority; the defeat of Germany or Japan?

A The defeat of Nazi Germany.

DID YOU KNOW

THERE WERE TWO FORMS OF ALLIED INTELLIGENCE IN THE PACIFIC
THEATER, KNOWN AS ULTRA AND MAGIC. ULTRA REFERRED TO THE
DECRYPTION OF MILITARY COMMUNICATIONS, WHEREAS MAGIC RELATED
TO DIPLOMATIC SOURCES. BOTH WERE PART OF THE MASSIVE ALLIED
CODE-BREAKING EFFORT WHICH HIT A HIGH SPOT WHEN THE BRITISH
DECIPHERED GERMAN ENIGMA MACHINE CODES. AS THE WAR PROGRESSED,
THE BRITISH AND U.S. INTELLIGENCE COMMUNITIES BEGAN TO COMBINE
THEIR EFFORTS TO DECIPHER JAPANESE EQUIVALENTS. ON MAY 17, 1943,
THE BRUSA (BRITAIN AND THE UNITED STATES OF AMERICA) AGREEMENT
FORMED A WORKING INTELLIGENCE PARTNERSHIP, THE U.S. ARMY
OVERSEEING DECRYPTION OF JAPANESE MILITARY CODES AND CIPHERS,
WHILE THE BRITISH CONCENTRATED MAINLY ON THE EUROPEAN THEATER.
MAGIC CODES—WHICH WERE PRODUCED ON THE FORMIDABLE "PURPLE"
CODING MACHINE—WERE ACTUALLY BEING BROKEN BEFORE DECEMBER
1941, GIVING THE U.S. AN INDICATION OF THE OUTBREAK OF WAR, BUT
NOT TELLING IT WHERE THE FIRST ATTACK WOULD COME. SUCH WAS
TYPICAL OF MAGIC INTELLIGENCE, AND IT PROVED MORE USEFUL AS A
GENERAL GUIDE TO FUTURE JAPANESE INTENTIONS THAN AS A SCRIPT TO
FUTURE JAPANESE OPERATIONS.

Q What was the Japanese Operation I of April 1943?

A A program of bombardment against Allied shipping in the Solomon Islands and New Guinea.

Q Was it a success?

A No. Three Allied transports, one destroyer, and one corvette were sunk, as well as seven Allied aircraft destroyed. The Japanese lost 19 aircraft, and the offensive was a disappointment, indicating Japanese problems in making good the loss of well-trained pilots in recent campaigns.

Q In February 1943 British and U.S. bombers launched Operation Gondola. What was this?

A A series of raids aimed at destroying German U-boats in the Bay of Biscay.

Q Who was appointed Inspector General of Armored Troops in Germany in February 1943?

A General Heinz Guderian.

Q At the beginning of March 1943 the British launched a four-month bombing offensive against which German industrial region?

A The Ruhr.

DID YOU KNOW

IN EARLY 1943, THE AMERICAN GRUMMAN F6F HELLCAT CARRIER-BORNE FIGHTER BEGAN ITS OPERATIONAL DEPLOYMENT TO THE PACIFIC THEATER, HAVING FIRST FLOWN IN PROTOTYPE FORM IN JUNE 1942. THE HELLCAT HAD THE MANEUVERABILITY, POWER, AND ARMAMENT TO TAKE ON AND SURPASS THE BEST OF JAPANESE AIRCRAFT, AND ITS KILL RATE WAS FORMIDABLE—5,156 JAPANESE AIRCRAFT DESTROYED BETWEEN 1943 AND 1945. SOME 480 F6Fs OF U.S. TASK FORCE 58 WERE AT THE FRONT-LINE OF THE SLAUGHTER OF MORE THAN 400 JAPANESE AIRCRAFT DURING THE BATTLE OF THE PHILIPPINE SEA; AND, IN TOTAL, F6Fs ACCOUNTED FOR THREE-QUARTERS OF ALL JAPANESE AIRCRAFT DOWNED DURING THE WAR. THE F6F WAS PRODUCED IN A NUMBER OF FORMS, INCLUDING THE RADAR-EQUIPPED F6F-3E AND F6F-3N AND THE F6F-5 FIGHTER-BOMBER. TOTAL PRODUCTION OF F6Fs WAS 12,275.

> **OUR MEN WILL FIGHT LIKE THE DEVIL, BUT WHEN THE BATTLE'S OVER, IT'S OVER.**
> ## THEY TREAT WAR LIKE A FOOTBALL GAME
> BRIGADIER GENERAL THOEDORE ROOSEVELT JR.,
> NORTH AFRICA, MARCH 25, 1943

Q On March 13, 1943, an attempt was made on Hitler's life. Who made it?

A German Army officers.

Q How did they attempt to kill Hitler?

A By placing a bomb in his aircraft.

183

Q Why did the assassination attempt fail?

A The bomb failed to explode.

Q Name one of the two Allied Atlantic convoys which were badly mauled by German U-boats in March 1943.

A Convoys HX-229 and SC-122. They fought a running battle with 20 U-boats, losing a total of 20 ships.

Q Which Japanese commander was killed by U.S. Lockheed P-38 Lightning fighters on April 18, 1943?

A The Commander-in-Chief of the Combined Fleet and the tactician behind the Pearl Harbor attack, Admiral Isoroku Yamamoto.

> **" THE FÜHRER HAS SOLEMNLY PROMISED TO GET US OUT OF HERE. THIS HAS BEEN READ OUT TO US "**
> ANONYMOUS GERMAN SOLDIER AT STALINGRAD, JANUARY 1943

Q How did Allied aircraft locate Admiral Yamamoto?

A Allied code breakers alerted Allied commanders in advance that Yamamoto was traveling among key bases, allowing them to prepare an ambush and demonstrate the increasingly vital role ULTRA intelligence was playing in the Allied war effort.

Q Who took over command of the Japanese Combined Fleet following the death of Admiral Yamamoto?

A Admiral Mineichi Koga.

Q On the Eastern Front, who commanded the SS Panzer Corps in early 1943?

A SS-Obergruppenführer und General der Waffen-SS Paul Hausser.

Q Why did he incur Hitler's wrath in February 1943?

A He ignored the Führer's orders and ordered a withdrawal from the city of Kharkov, which was being encircled by Soviet forces.

Q What was Hausser's nickname?

A "Papa."

Q Who commanded the German counteroffensive against Red Army forces in the Ukraine beginning on February 19, 1943?

A Field Marshal Erich von Manstein.

Q Manstein had two panzer armies in his order of battle. What were they?

A The First Panzer Army (III, XXX, and XXXX Panzer Corps) and the Fourth Panzer Army (XXXXVIII Panzer and LVII Corps).

Q What other two formations did Hausser have at his disposal?

A Army Detachment Hollidt and the SS Panzer Corps (*Leibstandarte, Das Reich,* and *Totenkopf* Divisions).

DID YOU KNOW

Nicknamed "Hitler's Buzz Saw," the MG42 machine gun was designed to replace the MG34, although in reality it never did. The MG42 would be mass produced and more rugged in the field than the high-maintenance MG34. The result of these efforts created perhaps the world's best machine gun, which had a unique delayed blow-back system of firing. Here, an additional restraint or brake is placed on the bolt or other breech closure in order to delay or slow down the opening, although not actually locking the breech. Robust, reliable, and possessing an incredible rate of fire, this weapon was the pride of the German infantry. Its rate of fire was 1,500 rounds per minute, or 25 rounds per second! This meant Red Army infantry attacks could be broken up with short bursts. Fire rates as high as this caused barrels to overheat, but the designers had thought of this and had devised a quick-change facility. This meant a trained gunner could change a barrel in less than seven seconds. A total of 414,964 MG42s were built during the war.

Q Who delivered the so-called "total war" speech in Berlin in February 1943?

A Propaganda Minister Goebbels. To thunderous applause he announced the implementation of total war: "Do you want total war? Do you want it, if necessary, more total and more radical than we could even imagine today?" Afterwards Goebbels wrote in his diary: "This hour of idiocy! If I had said to the people, jump out the fourth floor of Columbushaus, they would have done that too."

DID YOU KNOW

FOR ALLIED FORCES IN THE PACIFIC, THE STRATEGIC OUTLOOK FOR 1943 COULD NOT HAVE BEEN MORE DIFFERENT FROM THE PREVIOUS YEAR. COMPARED WITH THE POSITION OF WEAKNESS AFTER PEARL HARBOR, THE PLANNING FOR 1943 WAS AGGRESSIVE, BOLD, AND DETERMINED. OPERATION CARTWHEEL, THE TWO-PRONGED ASSAULT ON THE JAPANESE STRONGHOLD AT RABAUL ON NEW BRITAIN, BEGAN IN EARNEST. THIS CALLED FOR LARGE-SCALE ATTACKS ON NEW GUINEA AND THE SOLOMON ISLANDS. WITHIN THE HIGHEST LEVELS OF THE U.S. COMMAND THERE HAD BEEN DISAGREEMENT ABOUT WHAT KIND OF STRATEGY TO TAKE (TWO INDEPENDENT, COORDINATE COMMANDS, ONE IN THE SOUTHWEST PACIFIC UNDER GENERAL OF THE ARMY DOUGLAS MACARTHUR, AND THE OTHER IN THE CENTRAL, SOUTH, AND NORTH PACIFIC OCEAN AREAS UNDER FLEET ADMIRAL CHESTER W. NIMITZ, WERE CREATED EARLY IN THE WAR). EXCEPT IN THE SOUTH AND SOUTHWEST PACIFIC, EACH CONDUCTED ITS OWN OPERATIONS WITH ITS OWN GROUND, AIR, AND NAVAL FORCES IN WIDELY SEPARATED AREAS. THE ARGUMENT CENTERED ON WHETHER TO MOVE THROUGH THE SOUTHWEST PACIFIC TOWARD THE PHILIPPINES (THE PLAN FAVORED BY GENERAL MACARTHUR) OR TO STRIKE AT FORMOSA THROUGH THE CENTRAL PACIFIC (THE METHOD FAVORED BY ADMIRAL NIMITZ). IT WAS THE ENDORSEMENT OF MACARTHUR'S PLAN THAT SAW OPERATION CARTWHEEL LAUNCHED.

> **TOMORROW MORNING I SHALL SET FOOT ON THE LAST BRIDGE. THAT'S A LITERARY WAY OF DESCRIBING DEATH** "
>
> ANONYMOUS GERMAN SOLDIER AT STALINGRAD, JANUARY 1943

Q Which major Ukrainian city was recaptured by German forces in March 1943?

A Kharkov.

Q Which Jewish ghetto did the Germans destroy in mid-March 1943?

A The Krakow Ghetto.

Q Which SS officer supervised the operation?

A SS-Untersturmführer Amon Göth.

Q What was the nickname of the German Close Combat Bar?

A The "Eyeball-to-Eyeball" medal.

Q Following the German recapture of Kharkov in March 1943, the city's Red Square was renamed. What was its new name?

A "Platz der Leibstandarte," in honor of the SS Panzer Corps' exploits in retaking the city.

Q In the Battle of the Atlantic, May 1943 was called "Black May" by the Germans. Why?

A U-boat losses rose dramatically, and Admiral Karl Dönitz admitted defeat in the Battle of the Atlantic by withdrawing U-boats from the troubled waters. Up to May there were 40 U boats in place each day in the Atlantic, but between February and May 91 U-boats had been lost and such losses could not be sustained. A combination of long-range bombers, radar, and submarine hunter groups had made the Atlantic a hazardous place for U-boats.

Q The Jews of which ghetto mounted an uprising against the Germans in April 1943?

A Warsaw.

" SURRENDER IS FORBIDDEN. SIXTH ARMY WILL HOLD THEIR POSITIONS
TO THE LAST MAN AND THE LAST ROUND
ADOLF HITLER TO THE SIXTH ARMY AT STALINGRAD, JANUARY 24, 1943 **"**

Q In air warfare, what was saturation bombing?

A A technique of mass bombing in which concentrations of bombers mounted a giant raid on a single city, with the object of completely demolishing it.

Q Which head of British Bomber Command favored using saturation bombing against German cities?

A Arthur Harris.

DID YOU KNOW

BY 1943 THE JAPANESE IN THE PACIFIC HAD SUFFERED A SERIES OF SERIOUS SETBACKS, SUCH AS THE BATTLE OF MIDWAY IN MID-JUNE 1942. THEY THEREFORE SET ABOUT DEVISING ANOTHER WAY OF HOLDING BACK THE AMERICAN TIDE. THEY WERE DETERMINED TO HOLD WHAT THEY COULD, AND THIS MEANT VIGOROUSLY FIGHTING FOR AND REINFORCING NEW GUINEA AND THE NEIGHBORING ISLANDS. BY USING THE FORTIFIED BASE AT RABAUL, THE JAPANESE HOPED TO STRIKE AT THE AMERICANS WITH AIR- AND SEA-BASED POWER. MEANWHILE, IN BURMA AND ON THE INDIAN BORDER, THE JAPANESE WENT AHEAD WITH OPERATION U-GO, THE ASSAULT ON IMPHAL, AND OPERATION HA-GO, A DIVERSIONARY ATTACK ON THE ARAKAN PENINSULA. BY STRIKING INTO INDIA, THE JAPANESE PLANNED TO TAKE THE COMMUNICATION CENTERS OF IMPHAL AND KOHIMA AND THUS DELIVER A CRIPPLING BLOW AGAINST THE BRITISH BUILD-UP FOR OPERATIONS TO RETAKE BURMA.

Q **Estimate the number of Jews captured in the Warsaw ghetto uprising of April–May 1943.**

A 56,000, of whom 7,000 were shot.

Q **Yakov Stalin, son of the Soviet dictator, died in April 1943. Where and how?**

A Lieutenant Yakov Stalin had been a German prisoner since July 1941. He died in Sachsenhausen camp after running into the electric fence surrounding the camp, apparently so overcome by shame at the news of his father's massacre of Polish officers at Katyn.

Q **The Germans had wanted to exchange Yakov Stalin for whom?**

A The Germans had wanted to exchange him for Field Marshal Paulus, but Stalin would not hear of it.

Q What was Hitler's Operational Order No. 16 dated April 12, 1943?

A The destruction of enemy forces in the Kursk salient on the Eastern Front. Codenamed Operation Citadel; it would begin on May 3, 1943.

Q In April 1943 Radio Berlin announced the discovery of a mass grave of 4,500 Polish officers who had been murdered. Where?

A Katyn Wood.

Q Whom did the Germans blame for this atrocity?

> " THE RUSSIANS STAND AT THE DOOR OF
> OUR BUNKER. WE ARE DESTROYING
> OUR EQUIPMENT "
> SIXTH ARMY HQ AT STALINGRAD TO HIGH COMMAND,
> JANUARY 31, 1943

A The Soviet NKVD.

Q What was the Soviet response?

A The Soviet government responded by counter-charging that the Germans had killed the Poles.

Q Who was responsible for the Katyn Wood massacre?

A In November 1989 the Russians admitted responsibility for the Katyn shootings.

Q Which senior U.S. commander in the European theater was killed in early May 1943?

A General Frank Andrews.

Q Who replaced him?

A General Jacob Devers.

DID YOU KNOW

IN DECEMBER 1942, THE FIRST OF THE FINAL PRODUCTION SERIES OF THE GERMAN STUG III—THE AUSF G—ROLLED OFF THE PRODUCTION LINE IN GERMANY. WHEN PRODUCTION CEASED IN MARCH 1945, A TOTAL OF 7,720 HAD BEEN BUILT. THE HULL OF THE AUSF G WAS NOT RADICALLY DIFFERENT FROM PREVIOUS MODELS, THE MAIN CHANGES BEING TO THE SUPERSTRUCTURE. A CUPOLA WITH PERISCOPES WAS ADDED FOR THE COMMANDER, WHILE A SHIELD FOR THE MACHINE GUN WAS INSTALLED IN FRONT OF THE LOADER'S HATCH. THE SUPERSTRUCTURE INCORPORATED SLANTED SIDES, WITH THE ADDITION OF SLANTED PLATES TO PROTECT THE FRONT OF BOTH PANNIERS. DURING THE PRODUCTION RUN OTHER CHANGES WERE INCORPORATED, SUCH AS THE INTRODUCTION OF THE "SOW'S HEAD" (SAUKOPF) GUN MANTLET FOR THE STUK40 L/48 GUN, A COAXIAL MACHINE GUN IN EARLY 1944, A CLOSE-IN DEFENSE WEAPON, AND A REMOTE-CONTROLLED MACHINE GUN TO THE SUPERSTRUCTURE ROOF IN THE SPRING OF 1944. BY MID-1943, THERE WERE 28 INDEPENDENT STUG DETACHMENTS, FOUR DIVISIONAL STUG DETACHMENTS, TWO RADIO-CONTROLLED COMPANIES, AND 12 STUG PLATOONS, ALL READY FOR THE KURSK OFFENSIVE IN JULY. LATER, THE STUGS WERE DISTRIBUTED AMONG PANZER AND ANTITANK UNITS.

Q On May 11, 1943, a U.S. amphibious force landed 11,000 men of the 7th Infantry Division on Attu, beginning the campaign to take which group of islands?

A The Aleutian Islands.

Q Which national leaders attended the Trident Conference in Washington in May 1943?

A British Prime Minister Churchill and U.S. President Roosevelt.

Q What was the main British concern raised at the conference?

A Despite a unified confirmation of the Germany First strategy, including setting a date for the Allied invasion of occupied Western Europe, the British were concerned that the Pacific war was diverting too many resources away from European operations.

Q Who replaced the South West Pacific and Commander-in-Chief India, Sir Archibald Wavell, in June 1943?

A Sir Claude Auchinleck.

" LIKE RAGING WOLVES, VENGEFUL
SOLDIERS FELL ON
THE HELPLESS VICTIMS TO
STEAL PERSONAL BAGGAGE **"**
JOACHIM WIEDER, GERMAN SOLDIER CAPTURED
AT STALINGRAD

DID YOU KNOW

IN THE SPRING OF 1943 ADOLF HITLER STILL BELIEVED HE WOULD ACHIEVE TOTAL VICTORY OVER HIS ENEMIES, DESPITE THE MASSIVE DEFEATS SUFFERED BY THE WEHRMACHT IN THE SOVIET UNION AND NORTH AFRICA DURING THE PREVIOUS SIX MONTHS (SOME 500,000 GERMAN TROOPS HAD BEEN KILLED OR CAPTURED IN DEFEATS AT STALINGRAD AND EL ALAMEIN, AND IN TUNISIA). EVER THE OPTIMIST, THE FÜHRER MAINTAINED A PUBLIC VENEER OF CONFIDENCE THAT THE THIRD REICH WOULD SURVIVE FOR 1,000 YEARS. HITLER WAS CONVINCED THAT HE WOULD PREVAIL BECAUSE HIS OPPONENTS, LED BY AN ALLIANCE OF SLAVS AND JEWS, WERE RACIALLY INFERIOR TO GERMANY'S ARYANS. IT WAS JUST BEYOND HIS IMAGINATION THAT THE RUSSIAN *UNTERMENSCHEN,* OR "SUB-HUMANS," COULD BE CLEVER OR STRONG ENOUGH TO CHALLENGE GERMAN SUPREMACY (SIMILAR TO THE ATTITUDE OF EUROPEAN COLONIALISTS IN THE NINETEENTH CENTURY, WHO BELIEVED THAT AFRICAN AND ASIAN ENEMIES WERE NOT IN ANY WAY EQUAL OPPONENTS).

193

Q Which U.S. bomber began its career in May 1943 as the chief medium bomber of the Eighth Air Force in the European theater?

A The Martin B-26 Marauder.

Q What record did this aircraft set in the European theater?

A The lowest loss rate of any U.S. bomber in Europe.

Q Which U.S. fighter aircraft was nicknamed the "Jug"?

A The Republic P-47 Thunderbolt.

" AM GOING ON A RAID THIS AFTERNOON
OR EARLY IN THE MORNING.
THERE IS A POSSIBILITY
I WON'T RETURN **"**
SERGEANT CARL GOLDMAN, U.S. AIR FORCE,
FEBRUARY 1943

Q Which U.S. gull-wing fighter entered service with the U.S.
Marines in the Solomons in February 1943?

A The Vought F4U Corsair.

Q What type of aircraft was the Ilyushin Il-2 Shturmovik?

A A close-support aircraft.

Q How many Il-2s were built in World War II?

A 40,000.

Q Which British Dreadnought battleship, launched in 1913, fought
at the Battle of Jutland in 1916 but also saw active service in
World War II?

A HMS *Warspite*.

Q This ship was severely damaged during the Allied invasion of
Italy in 1943. What type of weapon inflicted the damage on her?

A German air-launched glider bombs.

Q What was the codename of the Allied invasion of Sicily in July 1943?

A Operation Husky.

Q How many Axis troops defended Sicily in July 1943?

A 130,000 Italian and 30,000 German troops.

Q Name the two élite German divisions that defended Sicily against the Allies.

A The 15th Panzergrenadier Division and the *Hermann Göring* Panzer Division.

Q Why was the *Hermann Göring* Division stationed in the Mediterranean theater in 1943?

195

A Named after the flamboyant chief of the Luftwaffe, its presence in Sicily and then Italy had much to do with Göring's political support for Kesselring as the only Luftwaffe officer who commanded a major theater of operations. The prestige of the Luftwaffe was at stake in the Mediterranean, and Göring was keen to ensure his protégé was not short of men and equipment.

DID YOU KNOW

THE ITALIAN CAMPAIGN WAS BY FAR THE GERMAN ARMY'S MOST SUCCESSFUL PROLONGED DEFENSIVE EFFORT OF THE WAR. FROM THE FIRST BRITISH AND AMERICAN LANDINGS IN SICILY IN JULY 1943 TO JUST BEFORE THE FINAL SURRENDER IN MAY 1945, THE OUTNUMBERED GERMAN UNITS, LED BY THE REDOUBTABLE FIELD MARSHAL ALBERT KESSELRING, ALWAYS HELD THE LINE AND PREVENTED THE ALLIES ACHIEVING A DECISIVE BREAKTHROUGH.

Q What was the Soviet Comintern?

A Founded in 1919 by Lenin and the Bolsheviks, it was dedicated "by all available means, including armed force, for the overthrow of the international bourgeoisie and for the creation of an international Soviet republic as a transition stage to the complete abolition of the State."

Q Why did Stalin dissolve it in May 1943?

A It was a gesture designed to reassure his Western Allies that the USSR was no longer trying to foment world revolution. The Americans in particular were keen for this organization to be disbanded.

DID YOU KNOW

THE GERMANS AT KURSK WERE FACED WITH DEEP SOVIET DEFENSES AND NO WAY TO GO AROUND THEM. THEY THEREFORE DEVISED A NEW TACTICAL FORMATION TO BREAK THROUGH. THE *PANZERKEIL*, OR ARMORED WEDGE, CAN BE LIKENED TO A TIN OPENER THAT HAD TO RIP OPEN THE SOVIET PAK-FRONTS. THEY WERE LED BY TIGER I HEAVY TANKS AND FERDINAND TANK DESTROYERS, WHICH WERE HEAVILY ARMORED AND LARGELY IMMUNE TO ENEMY ANTITANK ROUNDS THAT HIT THEM HEAD ON. THE LIGHTER PANTHERS, PANZER IVS, AND PANZER IIIS FOLLOWED ON BEHIND, WITH ABOUT 328 FT (100 M) BETWEEN EACH TANK. TO AID THE ADVANCE, THERE WAS CONSTANT RADIO CONTACT BETWEEN EACH *PANZERKEIL* AND LUFTWAFFE GROUND-ATTACK AIRCRAFT AND SUPPORTING GROUND ARTILLERY. DURING THE BATTLE, RED ARMY TANKS AND ANTITANK GUNS HAD TO BE KNOCKED OUT BY THE PANZERS AND LUFTWAFFE AIRCRAFT, WHILE ENEMY TRENCHES AND PILLBOXES HAD TO BE CLEARED BY GERMAN INFANTRY USING SMALL ARMS AND HAND GRENADES. OFTEN, THE *PANZERKEILS* WERE HELD UP BY MINE-FIELDS, THROUGH WHICH A ROUTE HAD TO BE CLEARED BY ENGINEERS. AS A RESULT, THE ADVANCE WAS OFTEN AGONIZINGLY SLOW AND BLOODY, AS EACH METER OF GROUND HAD TO BE FOUGHT OVER. SOON AFTER THE BATTLE STARTED, SOME PANZER DIVISIONS WERE SUFFERING DAILY TANK LOSSES OF 10 PERCENT. THIS RATE OF ATTRITION WAS JUST WHAT THE STAVKA HAD WANTED.

BATTLE IS THE MOST MAGNIFICENT COMPETITION IN WHICH A HUMAN BEING CAN INDULGE

GEORGE S. PATTON, JULY 1943

Q Why did Hitler decide to postpone Operation Citadel, his offensive at Kursk, on May 4, 1943?

A To allow more Tiger and the new Panther tanks to take part in the offensive.

Q What was his new start date for the offensive?

A June 13.

Q What happened on this new date?

A Nothing. Hitler was still waiting for his Panther tanks.

Q The German attack against the Kursk salient involved two giant pincers, one in the north, the other in the south. What armies made up these pincers?

A In the north was the Ninth Army, under the command of Colonel General Model. In the south was the Fourth Panzer Army, commanded by Colonel General Hermann Hoth; and Army Detachment Kempf, commanded by General Walter Kempf.

Q Name the Waffen-SS corps that fought at Kursk.

A II SS Panzer Corps.

Q Which of the German pincers at Kursk was the strongest?

A The southern pincer, with nearly 350,000 men, 1,269 tanks, and 245 assault guns, excluding reserves. In the north the Germans had 335,000 men, 590 tanks, and 424 assault guns.

Q How many Russian civilians were used to construct the Red Army's defenses in the Kursk salient?

A 300,000.

Q At the Battle of Kursk, where did the decisive clash take place on July 12, 1943?

A At the village of Prokhorovka.

Q Why did Hitler halt Operation Citadel on July 13, 1943?

A He was worried about a possible Allied invasion in the south of Europe (the Allies had landed in Sicily on July 10). Hitler informed the commanders of Army Group Center and South: "I must prevent that. And so I need divisions for Italy and the Balkans. And since they can't be taken from any other place, apart from the transfer of the 1st Panzer Division from France to the Peloponnese, they will have to be released from the Kursk Front. Therefore I am forced to stop Citadel."

❝ MORTAR AND ARTILLERY FIRE BEGAN TO FALL ON THE RIDGE, AND
THERE WAS CONSIDERABLE MACHINE-GUN FIRE
GENERAL JAMES GAVIN, U.S. 82D AIRBORNE DIVISION, SICILY, 1943 **❞**

DID YOU KNOW

AT KURSK, FOR THE FIRST TIME IN THE WAR, A BATTLE WOULD BE FOUGHT ON THE RUSSIANS' TERMS, AND THE GERMANS WOULD PAY DEARLY. THE ATTACKING HEAVY GERMAN TANKS WOULD BE STOPPED BY 85MM ANTI-AIRCRAFT GUNS (USED IN THE GROUND ROLE), WITH 122MM AND 152MM HOWITZERS PROVIDING HEAVY FIRE SUPPORT. THE LENGTH OF THE RED ARMY FRONTLINE IN THE KURSK SALIENT WAS 300 MILES (450 KM) WITH A DEPTH OF 110 MILES (190 KM). INTO THIS AREA WERE DEPLOYED 20,000 ARTILLERY PIECES AND MORTARS, 6,000 ANTITANK GUNS, AND HUNDREDS OF KATYUSHA ROCKET LAUNCHERS. IN THE GROUND WERE UP TO 2,700 ANTIPERSONNEL AND 2,400 ANTITANK MINES EVERY MILE (1.6 KM). ABOVE ALL, IT WAS THE TENACITY OF THE ORDINARY RUSSIAN SOLDIER THAT WAS THE KEY TO SUCCESS AT KURSK. HE DUG IN TO HIS POSITION AND REMAINED THERE. HE WAS ORDERED TO REMAIN AT HIS POST, AND HE DID, OFTEN UNTIL HE WAS KILLED BY THE ENEMY.

Q What was the tank-busting version of the Ju 87 Stuka?

A The Ju 87G-1.

Q What was its main armament?

A Two 37mm Flak 18 cannon in under-wing pods.

Q Why did it have reduced speed and range?

A It was fitted with armor plating to protect the pilot and gunner when flying antitank missions.

Q On the Eastern Front, what was the objective of the Soviet Operation Rumyantsev that began on August 3, 1943?

A Its objectives were the destruction of both the Fourth Panzer Army and Sixth Army by reaching the Black Sea coast behind them.

Q What type of vehicle was the Soviet SU-76?

A A self-propelled gun.

DID YOU KNOW

THE APPEARANCE OF THE SOVIET T-34 TANK ON THE EASTERN FRONT IN 1941 WAS A NASTY SURPRISE FOR THE GERMANS. IN RESPONSE, DECEMBER 1941 SAW BOTH DAIMLER-BENZ AND MAN INSTRUCTED TO BEGIN DESIGNING A NEW, POWERFUL MEDIUM TANK. MAN EVENTUALLY WON THE CONTRACT WITH ITS DESIGN. THE RESULT WAS THE PANZER V PANTHER, WHICH INCORPORATED MANY FEATURES OF THE T-34, BUT WAS LARGER AND HEAVIER. FEATURES INCLUDED WIDE TRACKS FOR BETTER TRACTION AND IMPROVED CROSSCOUNTRY PERFORMANCE, A POWERFUL ENGINE, A POWERFUL MAIN GUN, AND SLOPING ARMOR FOR EXTRA PROTECTION. IN DECEMBER 1942, THE PANTHER AUSF D ENTERED PRODUCTION, THE FIRST MODELS LEAVING THE FACTORY ON JANUARY 11, 1943. THE PANTHER WAS ARMED WITH A NEWER VERSION OF THE 75MM KWK 42 L/70 GUN, WHICH WAS MOUNTED IN A HYDRAULICALLY POWERED TURRET. ITS WEAK SPOT WAS ITS SIDE ARMOR, WHICH WAS ONLY BETWEEN 1.57 IN (40 MM) AND 1.96 IN (50 MM) THICK, DEPENDING ON THE VARIANT. THE PANTHER MADE ITS COMBAT DEBUT AT THE BATTLE OF KURSK. BECAUSE OF TECHNICAL PROBLEMS, ESPECIALLY WITH THE TRANSMISSION AND SUSPENSION, MANY PANTHERS BROKE DOWN BEFORE AND DURING THE BATTLE. NEVERTHELESS, THE PANTHER'S PROBLEMS WERE IRONED OUT AND IT WENT ON TO BECOME ONE OF THE BEST TANKS OF THE WAR.

Q It was nicknamed "the bitch." Why?

A Because it was unreliable.

> " AN INDESCRIBABLE PANIC STARTED.
> MOTHERS GRABBED
> # CHILDREN AND RUSHED MADLY AWAY
> ELSE WENDEL, IN HAMBURG WHEN
> BOMBED BY THE RAF IN JULY 1943 "

Q How many tank brigades did a Japanese tank division have?

A Two.

201

Q What was the caliber of the main gun in a Japanese Type 95 tank?

A 37mm.

Q The U.S. M3 light tank was called what by the British?

A The Stuart I.

Q What was its British classification?

A It was classed as a light cruiser tank by virtue of its armament and armor.

Q What type of vehicle was the U.S.-built M22 Locust?

A An air-portable tank.

Q Why was it never used by the U.S. Army?

A Because the army lacked an aircraft or glider to transport it.

> **" WE MUDDLED THROUGH THE FIGHTER ATTACK AND STAGGERED AWAY FROM THE TARGET "**
> CAPTAIN JOHN S. YOUNG, U.S. AIR FORCE,
> AUGUST 1, 1943

Q Who did use the M22?

A The British. They could transport it in their Hamilcar glider.

Q Why was a 75mm gun mounted in the right sponson on the U.S. Medium Tank M3?

A Because insufficient development work had been done on the problems of mounting a large-caliber gun in a revolving turret.

Q What was the vehicle called the Mine Exploder T1E4?

A A Sherman tank fitted with rollers, flails, and plunger rods to detonate mines.

DID YOU KNOW

THE PETLYAKOV PE-2 WAS ONE OF THE MOST IMPORTANT AIRCRAFT IN THE USSR'S INVENTORY, FIGHTING FROM THE BEGINNING OF BARBAROSSA UNTIL THE SURRENDER OF GERMANY IN 1945. IT ENTERED SERVICE IN AUGUST 1940 AS A MULTI-ROLE DIVE- AND ATTACK-BOMBER, HAVING A CREW OF THREE AND BEING ARMED WITH FOUR 7.62MM MACHINE GUNS: TWO FIXED FIRING AHEAD ABOVE THE NOSE; ONE AIMED FROM THE UPPER REAR POSITION; AND ONE FROM A RETRACTING VENTRAL MOUNT. BECAUSE OF ITS SPEED AND MANEUVERABILITY, GERMAN FIGHTER PILOTS FOUND THE PE-2 DIFFICULT TO CATCH AND SHOOT DOWN. FROM AUGUST 1941, THE EVEN-FASTER RECONNAISSANCE PE-2 VERSION BEGAN TO APPEAR OVER THE EASTERN FRONT (THESE AIRCRAFT LACKED DIVE BRAKES AND WERE FITTED WITH ADDITIONAL FUEL TANKAGE IN THE BOMB BAY AND HAD THREE CAMERAS IN THE REAR FUSELAGE). IN TOTAL, 11,400 PE-2S OF ALL VARIANTS WERE PRODUCED.

203

Q What type of vehicle was the U.S. M10?

A A tank destroyer.

Q What was its main armament?

A A 76mm gun.

Q A few M10s saw service with the British. What was their designation?

A 3i SP Wolverines.

Q What was the main armament of the Panzer III Ausf N?

A The 75mm KwK L/24 gun.

Q Which gun did it replace on the Panzer III?

A The 50mm KwK39 L/60.

Q The Panzer III Ausf N had a specific battlefield role. What was it?

A To provide close support for the heavier Tiger tanks.

204

" I CALLED OUT: "CRASH LANDING! AS
**NEAR TO THE HOTEL AS YOU
CAN GET IT!"**
OTTO SKORZENY, DURING THE RESCUE OF
BENITO MUSSOLINI
"

Q What was the Allied Operation Pointblank which was launched in June 1943?

A An offensive by British and U.S. bomber forces that would last until the 1944 cross-Channel invasion. U.S. strategy concentrated on daylight precision raids to destroy Germany's aircraft industry and air force. British attacks concentrated on night saturation bombing to undermine Germany's economy and morale.

Q Which British RAF squadron flew the "dambuster" raid in May 1943?

A 617 Squadron.

Q Which German dams were attacked by the British bombers?

A The Möhne, Eder, and Sorpe dams.

DID YOU KNOW

ON OCTOBER 31, 1942, THE SOVIET STAVKA ORDERED THE RAISING OF 26 RED ARMY ARTILLERY DIVISIONS. THE ORIGINAL DIVISIONAL ORGANIZATION WAS THREE HOWITZER REGIMENTS (EACH WITH 20 122MM HOWITZERS), TWO GUN REGIMENTS (EACH WITH 18 122MM OR 152MM GUN-HOWITZERS), THREE TANK-DESTROYER ARTILLERY REGIMENTS (EACH WITH 24 76MM GUNS) AND AN OBSERVATION BATTALION. AS WITH INFANTRY AND ARMORED FORMATIONS, THE ARTILLERY UNDERWENT NUMEROUS REORGANIZATIONS. IN APRIL 1943, FOR EXAMPLE, FIVE ARTILLERY CORPS HEADQUARTERS WERE CREATED TO CONTROL THE GROUPINGS OF ARTILLERY DIVISIONS AND, AT THE SAME TIME, A NEW DIVISIONAL FORMAT WAS ESTABLISHED: THE BREAKTHROUGH ARTILLERY DIVISION. THE NEW DIVISION COMPRISED: AN OBSERVATION BATTALION; A LIGHT BRIGADE (THREE REGIMENTS, EACH ONE WITH 24 76MM GUNS); A HOWITZER BRIGADE (THREE REGIMENTS, EACH ONE WITH 28 122MM HOWITZERS); A GUN BRIGADE (TWO REGIMENTS, EACH ONE WITH 18 152MM GUN-HOWITZERS); AND A MORTAR BRIGADE (THREE REGIMENTS, EACH ONE WITH 36 120MM MORTARS). IN ADDITION, TWO HEAVY HOWITZER BRIGADES (ONE OF FOUR BATTALIONS, EACH ONE WITH EIGHT 152MM HOWITZERS; AND ONE OF FOUR BATTALIONS, EACH ONE EQUIPPED WITH SIX 203MM HOWITZERS) WERE ATTACHED TO DIVISIONAL HEADQUARTERS. EACH DIVISION NUMBERED 11,000 TROOPS AND WAS EQUIPPED WITH 1,100 TRUCKS, AND 175 TRACTORS.

Q The RAF "dambuster" raid used special weapons against the German dams. What were they?

A Bouncing bombs.

Q Was the raid a success?

A Partly. Only the Möhne and Eder dams were breached. The specially trained squadron led by Wing Commander Guy Gibson lost eight aircraft. The raid caused some disruption to the German war industry, and it boosted civilian morale in Britain.

Q In the air war, what were Allied "shuttle" raids?

A Flying from a base in one country to bomb the target, then flying on to land at a base in another country.

Q What was the "window" system employed by Allied bombers over Germany?

A The dropping of foil strips to confuse German radar equipment.

Q Which German city was engulfed by a firestorm at the end of July 1943 following massive British air raids?

A Hamburg.

> " THE MINUTE I WAS ON THE BEACH I FELT BETTER. IT DIDN'T SEEM LIKE EVERYBODY
> ## WAS SHOOTING AT ME
> JOHN STEINBACK, SALERNO LANDINGS,
> SEPTEMBER 9, 1943 "

Q In the Pacific theater, what was Operation Toenails in June 1943?

A The U.S. offensive to retake New Georgia.

Q Who was the leader of the pro-Japanese Indian National Army?

A Subhas Chandra Bose.

Q Who commanded the U.S. fast patrol boat *PT-109*?

A The future U.S. president, John F. Kennedy.

DID YOU KNOW

GENERAL SIR WILLIAM SLIM (1891–1970) WAS AN IMPORTANT ALLIED LEADER IN THE FAR EASTERN WAR. SLIM HAD LONG-STANDING EXPERIENCE OF SOLDIERING IN THE FAR EAST, HAVING MOVED FROM THE BRITISH ARMY TO THE INDIAN ARMY IN 1919 AND RISEN TO THE RANK OF BRIGADIER BY 1939. THIS EXPERIENCE WAS TO STAND HIM IN GOOD STEAD WITH HIS MEN, WHO APPRECIATED BOTH HIS TOUGH YET PERSONABLE CHARACTER, AND HIS ABILITY TO TALK IN URDU AND GURKHALI AS WELL AS ENGLISH. HIS FIRST CAMPAIGNS IN WORLD WAR II WERE FOUGHT IN EAST AFRICA AND SYRIA, BUT IN MARCH 1942 HE WAS TRANSFERRED TO BURMA TO OVERSEE THE ALLIED RETREAT FROM RANGOON AS COMMANDER OF BURCORPS (SLIM WAS BY THIS TIME RANKED LIEUTENANT GENERAL). BURMA WAS TO BE HIS BATTLEGROUND FOR THE REST OF THE WAR. HE LED XV INDIAN CORPS DURING ITS DISASTROUS CAMPAIGN INTO THE ARAKAN, BUT OFFSET THIS DEFEAT BY STEERING THE FOURTEENTH ARMY TO VICTORIES IN THE ARAKAN AND ALSO THE CRUCIAL DEFEAT OF THE JAPANESE OFFENSIVE AT IMPHAL. IN JULY 1945, SLIM ROSE TO THE POSITION OF C-IN-C ALLIED LAND FORCES SOUTHEAST ASIA AFTER THE DISMISSAL OF GENERAL SIR OLIVER LEESE FROM THE POSITION.

DID YOU KNOW

ITALIAN DISSATISFACTION WITH THE AXIS CAUSE CULMINATED IN THE OVERTHROW OF MUSSOLINI ON JULY 25, 1943. A TEMPORARY, AND OSTENSIBLY PRO-AXIS, REGIME WAS ESTABLISHED UNDER MARSHAL PIERTO BADOGLIO, BUT IT CAPITULATED TO THE ALLIES ON SEPTEMBER 8. FOR THEIR PART, HITLER AND KESSELRING WERE AWARE OF THE WAVERING SUPPORT OF THE ITALIANS, AND HAD BEEN STEADILY MOVING TROOPS INTO THE COUNTRY TO PREEMPT ANY ITALIAN DESERTION. BRITISH TROOPS CROSSED THE STRAITS OF MESSINA FROM SICILY AND HEADED NORTH UP THE "TOE" OF ITALY." IN THE FIRST WEEK OF SEPTEMBER THE GERMANS STRUCK, SEIZING KEY POINTS IN ROME AND THROUGHOUT THE COUNTRY, WHILE THE ALLIES LANDED THEIR FIFTH ARMY SOUTH OF NAPLES AT SALERNO ON THE 9TH TO TRY TO CUT OFF THE RETREAT OF KESSELRING'S TROOPS NORTHWARD TO ROME.

Q **Who became the head of the new South East Asia Command (SEAC) in August 1943?**

A Vice Admiral Lord Louis Mountbatten.

Q **Who was his deputy?**

A Joseph Stilwell.

Q **What were the objectives of SEAC?**

A The geographical remit of SEAC was Burma, Malaya, Sumatra, Thailand, and French Indochina. SEAC's main objectives were to draw more Japanese away from the Pacific theater and support Chinese military efforts to the north of the zone. The decision was also made to bypass the fortified port of Rabaul, previously a key objective of Operation Cartwheel.

Q Following the successful conclusion of Operation Toenails in August 1943, what was the next part of U.S. strategy in the Solomon Islands?

A An amphibious offensive against Bougainville and Choiseul, planned for October/November 1943.

Q In Italy, what was the name of the German defensive line south of Rome, which was held until May 1944?

A The Gustav Line.

Q In September 1943 the Allies landed in Italy. At which port?

A Salerno.

Q Who was the Allied commander who issued orders for the evacuation of this port in the face of heavy German attacks?

A Lieutenant General Mark Clark.

" I PULLED THE PIN OUT OF MY GRENADE, WHICH WAS STICKY WITH SWEAT, AND LOBBED IT **"**
BERNARD FERGUSSON, CHINDIT, MARCH 1943

Q Where was the German Hagen Line?

A It was a defensive line on the Eastern Front, located just to the east of Bryansk.

Q On which river did the Germans intend to make a stand in the Ukraine in the autumn of 1943?

A The Dnieper.

> **"** THEY DROVE THE MEN ON, NOT JUST TO
> MAKE THEM WORK, BUT AS A
> ## CRUEL MASTER DRIVES A
> ## BEAST OF BURDEN
> JEFFREY ENGLISH, BRITISH PRISONER OF
> THE JAPANESE, MAY 1943 **"**

Q The Red Army established a bridgehead on this river in September 1943. Where?

A At Veliki Bukrin.

Q The inmates of which German extermination camp, located in Russia, mounted a revolt in October 1943?

A Sobibor extermination camp. Several Ukrainian guards and 11 SS men were killed and some 300 prisoners managed to escape, most of whom were killed by their pursuers. Those who had refused to join the revolt were all murdered.

DID YOU KNOW

ITALY'S MOUNTAINOUS TERRAIN WAS IDEALLY SUITED TO THE DEFENSIVE TACTICS EMPLOYED BY THE GERMANS TO HOLD BACK ALLIED FORCES TRYING TO PENETRATE THE THIRD REICH'S "SOFT UNDERBELLY." WITH NAMES SUCH AS GUSTAV, BERNARD, ROME, CAESAR, ALBERT, AND GOTHIC, THE GERMAN DEFENSIVE POSITIONS IN ITALY WERE TREATED WITH GREAT RESPECT BY THE ALLIED SOLDIERS AND COMMANDERS WHO HAD TO ATTACK THEM. UNLIKE THE FAMOUS SIEGFRIED LINE AND WEST WALL IN NORTHWEST EUROPE, GERMAN POSITIONS IN ITALY NEVER HAD THE SAME AMOUNT OF MATERIAL RESOURCES DEVOTED TO THEM. GERMAN COMMANDERS HAD TO MAKE MAXIMUM USE OF THE TERRAIN, MINEFIELDS, AND EARTHWORK DEFENSES. IMPROVISATION WAS THE NAME OF THE GAME, WITH THE TURRETS OF DISABLED PANTHER TANKS PRESSED INTO SERVICE AS FIXED PILLBOXES. THE KEY TO THE SUCCESS OF THE GERMAN DEFENSIVE LINES WAS THE SIGHTING OF POSITIONS ALONG NATURAL OBSTACLES, SUCH AS RIVERS AND HIGH MOUNTAIN RIDGES. EVERY APPROACH ROUTE WAS BLOCKED BY MINEFIELDS AND COVERED BY ARTILLERY OR MACHINE GUNS. CONTROL OF THE HIGH GROUND MEANT THAT GERMAN ARTILLERY FIRE WAS ALWAYS EXPERTLY DIRECTED ON TO ITS TARGETS.

211

Q What was the SS operation codenamed Harvest Festival?

A Following the rebellion at Sobibor, and to prevent further revolts, on November 3, 1943, SS Chief Heinrich Himmler ordered Jakob Sporrenberg, senior commander of the SS and the police in the Lublin district, to liquidate the Jewish forced labor camps. The operation was codenamed Harvest Festival. The SS murdered the prisoners at Trawniki, Poniatowa, and Majdanek camps, a total of 43,000 victims.

Q Which Soviet army liberated Kiev on November 6, 1943?

A The Thirty-Eighth Army.

" MOST OF YOU KNOW WHAT IT MEANS WHEN 100 CORPSES ARE LYING SIDE BY SIDE, OR 500 OR 1,000

HEINRICH HIMMLER TO SS LEADERS IN POLAND,
OCTOBER 1943 "

Q What work was carried out at the Peenemünde center on the Baltic Sea?

A Rocket research.

Q Which projects were developed there during the war?

A The center developed a remote-controlled, pulse-jet-powered flying bomb (V1) and a faster, liquid-fuel model (V2) as terror weapons to undermine the morale of enemy populations.

Q Why did the Danish government resign at the end of August 1943?

A After refusing a German demand for the repression of "saboteurs." The Danish authorities had tried to avoid collaboration with Nazi Germany.

Q Which SS commander rescued Mussolini in September 1943?

A Otto Skorzeny.

Q Where was the Italian dictator being held prior to his rescue?

A The Gran Sasso Hotel in the Abruzzi Mountains, northern Italy.

Q Why did British forces land on the island of Kos in the
Dodecanese in September 1943?

A The islands off southwest Turkey were a potential approach to
southeast Europe and a base for air operations against German
communications and oil resources in Romania. A victory there might also
persuade Turkey to support the Allied cause as the threat of German air
raids from Rhodes would be eliminated.

Q The British occupation of Kos was intended as a springboard
for an assault on which island?

A The German stronghold on Rhodes.

Q How did the Germans retake Kos?

A A force of 1,200 German paratroopers landed on the island. Around
900 Allied and 3,000 Italian troops were captured. The Germans
shot 90 Italian officers for fighting against their former ally.

213

DID YOU KNOW

STRATEGIC BOMBING—AIR OFFENSIVES AGAINST THE ENEMY'S INDUSTRIAL
CENTERS AND POPULATION—USING FLEETS OF BOMBERS HAD BEEN CONSIDERED
A WAR-WINNING FORMULA BY ITS PREWAR PROPONENTS. AFTER GERMANY BEGAN
ITS FIRST MAJOR RAIDS AGAINST BRITAIN IN 1940, HOWEVER, ITS LIMITATIONS
WERE EXPOSED. ALTHOUGH ATTACKS WERE HIGHLY DESTRUCTIVE, THEY FAILED
TO PARALYZE THE ECONOMY OR UNDERMINE MORALE; INDEED, THE OPPOSITE
SEEMED THE CASE AS THE POPULATION STEELED ITSELF FOR THE ONSLAUGHT.
THE EFFECT OF ALLIED RAIDS ON GERMANY MET WITH SIMILAR RESULTS,
ESPECIALLY AS BOTH BELLIGERENTS SUSTAINED HEAVY LOSSES DURING DAYLIGHT
RAIDS WHERE THEY WERE EASILY TARGETED AND WERE FORCED TO MAKE LESS
ACCURATE NIGHT ATTACKS. BRITAIN'S ANSWER WAS TO USE SATURATION BOMB-
ING TO DESTROY HOMES AND FACTORIES ACROSS WIDE AREAS.

Q Who became chairman and president of the National Government of China in September 1943?

A Chiang Kai-shek.

Q Which atoll in the Gilbert Islands was captured by U.S. Marines at great cost in November 1943?

A Tarawa Atoll.

Q Which U.S. Marine division attacked Betio Island, Tarawa Atoll, in November 1943?

A The 2d Marine Division.

> A GERMAN WITH BLOOD
> POURING DOWN HIS LEG POPPED
> ## OUT OF A DOORWAY
> ## AND SURRENDERED
> ALAN MOOREHEAD, TUNIS, MAY 7, 1943

Q Which two U.S. aircraft carriers were launched at the end of November 1943?

A The USS *Wasp* and the USS *Hornet*, both named after U.S. vessels sunk at earlier actions in the war.

Q How many aircraft carriers did the United States commission in 1943?

A Nine. The Japanese, suffering from severe industrial shortages, commissioned only two, these being conversions from existing vessels.

DID YOU KNOW

THE FIRST TROOPS OF THE U.S. 2D MARINE DIVISION WENT ASHORE AT BETIO ON NOVEMBER 20, 1943, STRAIGHT INTO A HAIL OF BULLETS AND SHELLS. BEACH RECONNAISSANCE HAD BEEN INACCURATE, AND MANY OF THE "AMTRAC" AMPHIBIOUS VEHICLES GROUNDED ON A SHALLOW REEF, LEAVING THE OCCUPANTS TO WADE ASHORE UNDER BLISTERING SMALL-ARMS AND ARTILLERY FIRE. ON THE BEACH ITSELF, THE SOFT SAND MADE IT DIFFICULT FOR THE U.S. SOLDIERS TO DIG IN. RADIO COMMUNICATIONS BETWEEN U.S. UNITS BROKE DOWN, RESULTING IN 1,500 U.S. MARINE CASUALTIES BY THE END OF THE DAY. HOWEVER, A BEACHHEAD WAS ESTABLISHED THROUGH SHEER U.S. FIREPOWER, AND OVER THE NEXT TWO DAYS THE MARINES FOUGHT THEIR WAY ACROSS TARAWA, THE ENTRENCHED DEFENDERS CONTESTING EVERY METER OF GROUND TO THE DEATH. A FINAL SUICIDAL CHARGE BY THE JAPANESE ON THE 22D SIGNIFIED THAT RESISTANCE WAS FINALLY CRUMBLING, AND ON THE 23RD THE FIGHTING FINALLY STOPPED.

215

Q Which Soviet city was recaptured by XXXXVIII Panzer Corps in November 1943?

A Zhitomir.

Q The German success was part of an offensive in the Ukraine designed to retake which major Soviet city?

A Kiev.

Q Did it succeed?

A No. The German offensive ground to a halt at the end of November 1943 short of Kiev.

Q Which German industrial plant was attacked by 290 U.S. B-17 Flying Fortresses on October 14, 1943?

A The Schweinfurt ball-bearings complex.

Q Was the raid a success?

A No. Sixty aircraft were lost and 140 damaged for little gain.

DID YOU KNOW

THE QUESTION OF WHY GERMAN TROOPS CONTINUED TO FIGHT THE RED ARMY WHEN IT WAS OBVIOUS THAT GERMANY WOULD LOSE THE WAR ON THE EASTERN FRONT IS AN INTERESTING ONE. THE REASONS WHY THEY DID SO WERE PROVIDED BY A SENIOR GERMAN OFFICER WHO FOUGHT ON THE EASTERN FRONT, GENERAL VON MELLENTHIN: "IN 1943, THE FLOWER OF THE GERMAN ARMY HAD FALLEN IN THE BATTLE OF KURSK, WHERE OUR TROOPS ATTACKED WITH A DESPERATE DETERMINATION TO CONQUER OR DIE. THEY HAD GONE INTO BATTLE WITH A SPIRIT NO LESS DETERMINED THAN THAT OF THE STORM TROOPS OF 1918, AND IT MIGHT BE THOUGHT THAT A WEAKENING OF MORALE WOULD FOLLOW OUR WITHDRAWAL FROM THE ILL-FATED SALIENT OF KURSK. ACTUALLY, NOTHING OF THE SORT OCCURRED; OUR RANKS HAD BEEN WOEFULLY THINNED, BUT THE FIERCE RESOLVE OF THE FIGHTING TROOPS REMAINED UNSHAKEN. THIS IS NOT THE PLACE FOR A DETAILED DISCUSSION OF THIS QUESTION, BUT IT IS OBVIOUS THAT THE CHARACTER OF OUR ADVERSARY HAD MUCH TO DO WITH THIS UNYIELDING SPIRIT OF THE TROOPS. THE CHURCHILL-ROOSEVELT DEMAND FOR 'UNCONDITIONAL SURRENDER' GAVE US NO HOPE FROM THE WEST, WHILE THE MEN FIGHTING ON THE RUSSIAN FRONT WERE WELL AWARE OF THE HORRIBLE FATE WHICH WOULD BEFALL EASTERN GERMANY IF THE RED HORDES BROKE INTO OUR COUNTRY." OF COURSE, A GERMAN GENERAL IS GOING TO EXTOLL THE VIRTUES OF HIS TROOPS, BUT MELLENTHIN PROBABLY SUMMARIZES ACCURATELY THE VIEW OF THE WEHRMACHT'S RANK AND FILE BETWEEN 1943 AND 1945.

THE RUSSIAN SOLDIER VALUES HIS LIFE
NO MORE THAN THOSE OF
HIS COMRADES
GENERAL VON MELLENTHIN, EASTERN FRONT, 1943

Q What change did this raid bring about in U.S. bombing tactics?

A The Americans halted unescorted, daylight raids due to high losses. Henceforth the bombers would be escorted by long-range fighter escorts.

Q What type of Royal Navy vessels attacked the German battleship *Tirpitz* in September 1943?

A Midget submarines, known as X-craft.

217

Q Which former Axis state declared war on Germany in mid-October 1943?

A Italy, on October 13.

Q Who were the "Big Three" at the Tehran Conference in November 1943?

A Stalin, Roosevelt, and Churchill.

Q At the conference, what date was set for the Allied invasion of France?

A May 1944.

Q Why was the American General Joseph Stilwell known as "Vinegar Joe"?

A Because of his aggressive and difficult personality.

Q In the Pacific theater, what was the "Tokyo Express"?

A "Tokyo Express" was the Allied nickname for the Japanese supply convoys running between Rabaul in New Britain and the Solomon Islands. The Japanese ships usually traveled via the Slot, the narrow stretch of water south of Bougainville that attracted violent naval battles.

Q What was the name of the airstrip on the island of Bougainville, which was made operational by the Americans in December 1943?

A Torokina.

> **" GERMANY NEEDS THE CONQUERED TERRITORIES OR SHE WILL NOT EXIST FOR LONG "**
> ADOLF HITLER, TALKING ABOUT THE USSR, JULY 1943

Q Which division spearheaded the U.S. invasion of New Britain at the end of December 1943?

A The 1st Marine Division under Major General W.H. Rupertus.

Q Why did the Allies wish to take New Britain?

A To isolate the vital Japanese naval and air facilities at Rabaul in the north.

DID YOU KNOW

HIDEKI TOJO (1885–1948) WAS THE POLITICAL POWER BEHIND THE PACIFIC WAR. THE SON OF A JAPANESE ARMY GENERAL, HE ENTERED THE MILITARY AND QUICKLY ROSE THROUGH THE RANKS. POLITICAL RATHER THAN OPERATIONAL APPOINTMENTS BECKONED. WITHIN THE ARMY HE SERVED AS THE CHIEF OF POLICE AFFAIRS AND CHIEF OF STAFF BEFORE BECOMING THE VICE MINISTER OF WAR THEN FINALLY MINISTER OF WAR IN 1941, THE SAME YEAR HE BECAME JAPANESE PRIME MINISTER. TOJO TOOK JAPAN TO WAR IN DECEMBER OF THAT YEAR BY GIVING THE ORDER TO ATTACK PEARL HARBOR, AND HE ADVOCATED A STRATEGY OF TOTAL MILITARY AND ECONOMIC WARFARE ON THE ALLIES, WHICH HELPED MAKE THE PACIFIC WAR THE MERCILESS FIGHT IT BECAME. AFTER THE JAPANESE DEFEAT ON SAIPAN IN JULY 1944, HE WAS FORCED TO RESIGN; HE MADE A FAILED ATTEMPT AT SUICIDE AFTER THE FINAL JAPANESE SURRENDER. IN 1948, HE WAS CONDEMNED TO DEATH FOR WAR CRIMES BY THE INTERNATIONAL MILITARY TRIBUNAL IN TOKYO, AND HANGED.

219

Q Which Allied leaders met at Cairo in November 1943?

A Winston Churchill, Franklin D. Roosevelt, and Chiang Kai-shek.

Q What was the main topic at the conference?

A They mainly considered postwar planning for China and Burma.

Q In November 1943 the British commenced a five-month bomber offensive against which German city?

A Berlin.

Q Which German medium tank made its combat debut at the Battle of Kursk in July 1943?

A The Panzer V Panther.

Q Many of these tanks broke down before they reached the combat zone. True or false?

A True. There were teething problems with the transmission and suspension systems.

Q Which German Stuka pilot single-handedly destroyed 12 T-34 tanks at the Battle of Kursk?

A Hans-Ulrich Rudel.

> ## " A CITY OF ONE MILLION PEOPLE HAS BEEN DEVASTATED IN A MANNER UNKNOWN BEFORE "
> JOSEF GOEBBELS, ON THE AIR RAID AGAINST HAMBURG, JULY 29, 1943

Q Which German battleship was sunk at the Battle of the North Cape in December 1943?

A The *Scharnhorst*.

Q What was the name of the British cruiser who finished her off with torpedoes during the battle?

A The cruiser HMS *Jamaica*.

1944

IN THE PACIFIC THE JAPANESE SUFFERED MAJOR
DEFEATS AT THE PHILIPPINE SEA AND LEYTE GULF,
WHILE IN EUROPE THE ALLIES FINALLY LAUNCHED
THEIR INVASION OF FRANCE, CODENAMED
OVERLORD. ON THE EASTERN FRONT THE RED
ARMY SHATTERED ARMY GROUP CENTER, AND
ALLIED BOMBERS REDUCED GERMANY TO RUBBLE.

Q Who became commander-in-chief of Free French forces in North Africa in January 1944?

A General Jean de Lattre de Tassigny.

Q What battle was dubbed the "Stalingrad of the Italian Campaign"?

A The four-month battle to gain control of the monastery atop Monte Cassino in central Italy.

Q Why was this position so important to both sides?

A Because the German defenses around Monte Cassino guarded the route north to Rome.

> " OLDER MEN DECLARE WAR. BUT IT IS
> ## YOUTH THAT MUST FIGHT
> HERBERT HOOVER, CHICAGO, JUNE 27, 1944 "

Q Which two rivers formed part of the German Gustav Line defenses in central Italy in early 1944?

A The Rapido and Garigliano.

Q Why did the Allies make an amphibious assault at Anzio in January 1944?

A The Allies were held up at the Gustav Line. To break the stalemate, the Allies tried to bypass the Gustav Line by staging an amphibious landing at Anzio in January 1944.

DID YOU KNOW

ITALY WAS ONE OF THE FEW THEATERS WHERE THE GERMANS DECIDED NOT TO CONCENTRATE THEIR ARMOR FOR COUNTERATTACKS. WITH THE TERRAIN ALL BUT PREVENTING THE MOVEMENT OF LARGE ARMORED FORMATIONS, GERMAN COMMANDERS BROKE UP THEIR TANKS, ASSAULT GUNS, AND ANTITANK GUNS INTO SMALL UNITS, USUALLY PAIRS, AND POSTED THEM TO FORWARD STRONGPOINTS OR WITH COUNTERATTACK TEAMS. IN THE ITALIAN TERRAIN, A HANDFUL OF HEAVY WEAPONS COULD PROVIDE FIREPOWER OUT OF ALL PROPORTION TO THEIR SMALL NUMBER. DURING THE CASSINO BATTLES, A HANDFUL OF STUG III ASSAULT GUNS AND MARDER III SELF-PROPELLED 75MM ANTITANK GUNS OPERATING WITH FORWARD GERMAN PARATROOP STRONGPOINTS MADE IT IMPOSSIBLE FOR THE ALLIES TO TRY TO SPEARHEAD THEIR INFANTRY ASSAULTS WITH TANKS. DURING REARGUARD OPERATIONS, SMALL GROUPS OF TANKS ALSO PROVED VERY EFFECTIVE AT FORCING ALLIED TROOPS TO DEPLOY TO MOUNT ASSAULT OPERATIONS. THE GERMANS WOULD THEN QUICKLY RETREAT ONCE THEY HAD ACHIEVED THEIR AIM— DELAYING THE ADVANCE—BEFORE THEIR LINE OF RETREAT BECAME THREATENED.

223

Q Why were the landings at Anzio the last major amphibious operation the Allies were to mount in Italy?

A Because of the need to move the bulk of their specialist craft and shipping to England to support the planned Normandy landings.

Q What was "Anzio Annie"?

A A German Krupp K-5 280mm-caliber railway gun.

Q Where did it operate from?

A A tunnel in the Alban Hills, south of Rome. It was wheeled out at night to fire barrages into the Anzio bridgehead before retreating underground during daylight to avoid detection by Allied aircraft.

Q What was Operation Carpetbagger that commenced in January 1944?

A Regular Allied airborne supply drops to partisans in the Netherlands, Belgium, France, and Italy.

Q Count Galeazzo Ciano, the former Italian foreign secretary, was executed by Italian fascists in January 1944. Why?

A His "crime" was to have voted with other fascists to oust Mussolini in July 1943. Ciano and his wife were lured to Bavaria in August 1943 following a report that their children were in danger. Having been promised safe passage to Spain, they were handed over to Italy's puppet fascist government.

Q What relation was Ciano to Mussolini?

> ❝ WHO HAS INFLICTED THIS UPON US? WHO
> HAS MADE US JEWS DIFFERENT
> FROM ALL OTHER PEOPLE? ❞
> ANNE FRANK, APRIL 11, 1944

A He was Mussolini's son-in-law.

Q Who was the commander of the German Army Group North on the Eastern Front at the beginning of 1944?

A Field Marshal Georg von Küchler.

Q Why was he dismissed by Hitler in January 1944?

A For ordering the withdrawal of the Eighteenth Army in the face of the Soviet Leningrad Offensive.

Q Who replaced Küchler as commander of Army Group North?

A Walther Model.

Q Why was he nicknamed "lion of the defense"?

A Because after the Battle of Kursk, he conducted a magnificent fighting withdrawal in the Ukraine as his Ninth Army retreated with Army Group Center.

DID YOU KNOW

HUNDREDS OF THOUSANDS OF SOVIET WOMEN SERVED IN UNIFORM DURING WORLD WAR II. WOMEN HAD BEEN GRANTED FULL CIVIL, LEGAL, AND ELECTORAL EQUALITY IN JANUARY 1918 BY THE NEW BOLSHEVIK REGIME, AND DURING THE CIVIL WAR 74,000 WOMEN FOUGHT ON THE SIDE OF THE REDS, SUFFERING CASUALTIES OF 1,800. WHEN THE GERMANS INVADED THE USSR IN JUNE 1941, THOUSANDS OF WOMEN VOLUNTEERED FOR SERVICE (LATER THE SOVIETS DRAFTED UNMARRIED WOMEN). MORE THAN 70 PERCENT OF THE 800,000 SOVIET WOMEN WHO SERVED IN THE RED ARMY FOUGHT AT THE FRONT, WITH 100,000 BEING DECORATED FOR THEIR BRAVERY. IN ADDITION, KOMSOMOL, THE COMMUNIST YOUTH ORGANIZATION, MOBILIZED 500,000 WOMEN AND GIRLS FOR MILITARY SERVICE. WOMEN INITIALLY TRAINED IN ALL-FEMALE GROUPS BUT, AFTER TRAINING, WERE POSTED TO REGULAR ARMY UNITS AND FOUGHT ALONG-SIDE MEN. ABOUT 30 PERCENT OF SERVICEWOMEN RECEIVED ADDITIONAL INSTRUCTION IN MORTARS, LIGHT AND HEAVY MACHINE GUNS, OR AUTOMATIC RIFLES. IN COMMON WITH MANY WOMEN IN UNIFORM, LUDMILLA PAVLICHENKO WAS TRAINED AS A SNIPER. SHE IS CREDITED WITH KILLING 309 GERMANS. LANCE CORPORAL MARIA IVANOVA MOROZOVA ALSO SERVED AS A SNIPER WITH THE 62D RIFLE BATTALION AND WON 11 COMBAT DECORATIONS.

Q Which Soviet city, under siege since 1941, was finally relived in January 1944?

A Leningrad.

Q The link up of the Red Army's 1st and 2nd Ukrainian Fronts at Zvenigorodka in late January 1944 trapped the German XI and XXXXII Corps where?

A The Cherkassy Pocket.

Q Who headed the Soviet secret police, the NKVD, in World War II?

A Lavrenti Beria.

DID YOU KNOW

THE GERMANS WERE INITIALLY SLOW TO MOBILIZE WOMEN, PARTLY DUE TO NAZI IDEOLOGY, WHICH VIEWED THE MAIN ROLE OF WOMEN AS BEING AT HOME BEARING CHILDREN. INDEED, INITIALLY NAZI LEADERS PROCLAIMED THAT THE USSR'S USE OF WOMEN SOLDIERS DEMONSTRATED THE SOVIETS WERE A WEAK ENEMY WHO WOULD EASILY BE DEFEATED. A LENGTHENING WAR AND HUGE LOSSES CHANGED THIS VIEW, AND BY 1944 THERE WERE 500,000 GERMAN WOMEN IN UNIFORM SERVING AS SUPPORT TROOPS (100,000 IN LUFTWAFFE ANTI-AIRCRAFT BATTERIES). AT THE END OF THE WAR, HITLER EVEN APPROVED THE RAISING OF ALL-FEMALE VOLKSSTURM BATTALIONS. IN ADDITION, YOUNG GIRLS OF THE *BUND DEUTSCHER MADEL* REPORTEDLY FOUGHT IN THE BATTLE OF BERLIN IN APRIL 1945.

> I HAD HOPED THAT WE WERE HURLING A WILDCAT ONTO THE SHORE, **BUT ALL WE HAD GOT WAS A STRANDED WHALE**
> WINSTON CHURCHILL, ON THE ANZIO LANDINGS

Q What was the divisional title of the 5th SS Panzer Division?

A *Wiking.*

Q In February 1944, the Soviet NKVD began the mass deportation from their homelands of which Russian national groups?

A Chechens and Ingush.

Q Where were they deported to?

A Siberia and the Kazak steppes.

Q Estimate the number of people who died during the journey.

A Some 362,000 Chechens and 134,000 Ingush old men, women, and children were rounded up and packed on to 180 train convoys in the space of just over a week. Tens of thousands died during journeys which lasted up to two months. Half of all those deported perished.

Q Why did Argentina sever relations with Germany and Japan in January 1944?

A The Argentines uncovered a vast Axis spy network in the country.

Q The British Army's rifle in World War II was the SMLE. What do these letters stand for?

A Short Magazine Lee Enfield.

Q What was the rifle's caliber?

A .303in.

Q What was its magazine capacity?

A 10 rounds.

> " I CONTINUE CLOSING UPON THE
> FORTRESS, FIRING AT THE
> ## CONTROL CABIN IN
> ## THE NOSE
> HEINZ KNOKE, GERMAN FIGHTER PILOT,
> FEBRUARY 1944 "

Q What was the fire mode of the German Gewehr 41(W)?

A Semi-automatic.

Q Hitler supposedly coined the term *SturmGewehr* for the MP44 rifle. What does this term mean?

A Assault rifle.

DID YOU KNOW

Although naval infantry, such as the British Royal Marines and the U.S. Marines, had elementary amphibious skills at the beginning of World War II, it was the Japanese who truly pioneered amphibious tactics. From experience in China in the late 1930s, and from their opening campaigns of World War II, the Japanese developed a systematic doctrine for amphibious campaigns, including the establishment of naval and air superiority in the area of landing; detailed intelligence concerning landing sites and enemy defenses; and systematic disembarkation of troops, ammunition, and supplies. They were also capable of nighttime amphibious landings, with soldiers and equipment daubed in luminous paint to aid identification. Yet, despite Japanese capabilities, the undeniable master of amphibious warfare in World War II was the U.S. American amphibious landings worked in three parts. An amphibious force was responsible for landing troops on the beaches and maintaining the flow of relevant logistics. Preparatory and support bombardments were provided by a force of warships surrounding the landing zone; farther out at sea, fleet carriers and other capital ships provided air and sea cover for the landing operations—and also interdicted Japanese reinforcement convoys.

Q **What was the British Army's main machine gun in World War II, the Korean War, and into the 1960s?**

A The .303in Vickers.

Q **What was the caliber of the U.S. M1919 medium machine gun?**

A .3in.

Q The Czech ZB26 machine gun was known in British service as what?

A The Bren Gun.

Q Why was it so named by the British?

A By combining the first two letters from the original Czech factory that made the weapon (Brno) with those of the factory where it was made in Britain (Enfield).

Q What was this weapon's magazine capacity?

> " I BEGAN TO UNDERSTAND FOR THE FIRST
> TIME THAT IN WAR IT IS MOST
> ## OFTEN THE STRONG AND THE
> ## BRAVE WHO ARE KILLED "
> Howard L. Bond, U.S. 36th Infantry Division,
> May 1944

A 30 rounds.

Q Which German machine gun was designed specifically for use by paratroopers?

A The FG42.

Q In the British Army, what rank did a single crown on a shoulder strap denote?

A Major.

DID YOU KNOW

AS THE WAR DRAGGED ON, IT BECAME INCREASINGLY MORE PERILOUS FOR HITLER TO VISIT HIS TROOPS IN THE FIELD. AIR TRAVEL BECAME TOO DANGEROUS, AND THE FATE OF JAPANESE ADMIRAL ISOROKU YAMAMOTO, WHO WAS KILLED WHEN HIS AIRCRAFT WAS AMBUSHED BY AMERICAN FIGHTERS, WAS A SALUTARY LESSON IN THE PROBLEMS CAUSED BY THE LOSS OF AIR SUPREMACY BY THE LUFTWAFFE. HITLER RETREATED INTO A SERIES OF SOME 21 UNDERGROUND BUNKER COMPLEXES CONSTRUCTED IN CONDITIONS OF GREAT SECRECY. THEY WERE BUILT AROUND GERMANY TO ALLOW HITLER TO REMAIN PROTECTED WHEN VISITING EACH OF THE MAIN BATTLE FRONTS. UNTIL THE SOVIETS BROKE THROUGH TO THE BALTIC COAST IN THE WINTER OF 1944, HITLER SPENT MOST OF HIS TIME AT THE FAMOUS WOLF'S LAIR COMPLEX IN THE FORESTS OF EAST PRUSSIA. PARANOID THAT THE BRITISH WOULD DROP A DIVISION OF PARATROOPERS ON THE COMPLEX, HITLER ORDERED IT TO BE PROTECTED BY HUGE MINE-FIELDS AND A SPECIALLY TRAINED ÉLITE DEFENSE UNIT, THE FAMOUS *FÜHRER BEGLEIT* BATTALION.

231

Q Which medal is Britain's highest decoration for "conspicuous bravery or devotion to the country in the presence of the enemy"?

A The Victoria Cross.

Q What is the difference between the British George Cross and the George Medal?

A The George Cross ranks next to the Victoria Cross, and is awarded mainly to civilians, i.e. a civilian Victoria Cross. The George Medal is awarded in circumstances similar to those required for the award of the George Cross, but of lesser merit. It is thus "junior" to the George Cross.

" THE TANKS ARE IN GREAT FORM. THEY WON'T STOP FIRING. THEY ARE SPRAYING EVERYTHING

MAJOR FRED MAJDALANY, MONTE CASSINO, MAY 1944 "

Q What was the main machine gun for all British tanks during the war?

A The 7.92mm Besa.

Q What was the smallest mortar in British Army service during the war?

A The 2in mortar, designated Ordnance ML2.

Q What was the Blacker Bombard?

A A British mortar designed by a Lieutenant Colonel Blacker, hence its name.

Q What was a PIAT?

A Projector Infantry Anti-Tank, a British antitank weapon.

Q What Swedish antiaircraft gun was used by both Allied and Axis armies during the war?

A The 40mm Bofors.

Q What was the name of the British A22 infantry tank?

A The Churchill.

Q In British service, what was a FANY?

A A member of the First Aid Nursing Yeomanry, a voluntary women's service.

Q Which British division had as its insignia a blue shield edged with red with a white eye in its center?

A The Guards Armoured Division.

DID YOU KNOW

233

THE NUMBER OF GENERALS IN HITLER'S ARMY HAD REACHED 2,242 BY 1944, NOT INCLUDING 150 LUFTWAFFE GENERALS AND THE SENIOR COMMANDERS OF THE WAFFEN-SS. SOME 40 ARMY AND 10 AIR FORCE GENERALS WERE PROMOTED TO COLONEL-GENERAL, OR FOUR-STAR RANK. HIGH RANK IN THE WEHRMACHT MEANT GOOD SALARIES. THE EQUIVALENT OF $100,000 WENT WITH THE RANK OF MAJOR GENERAL. LARGE HOUSES AND ESTATES WERE ALSO SHOWERED ON THE FÜHRER'S FAVORITES. HEINZ GUDERIAN, THE FAMOUS FATHER OF THE PANZER FORCE, WAS PROMISED AN ESTATE FOR HIS SERVICES TO THE REICH BY THE FÜHRER. IN SPITE OF SACKING HIM DURING THE RETREAT FROM MOSCOW, HITLER KEPT HIS WORD, AND IN JANUARY 1943 THE GENERAL WAS INSTALLED IN A 947-HECTARE ESTATE IN EASTERN GERMANY (NOW PART OF WESTERN POLAND). A GRATEFUL FÜHRER EVEN PAID FOR ALL THE GENERAL'S FURNITURE AND FARM MACHINERY. NOT SURPRISINGLY, GUDERIAN WAS EAGER TO RETURN TO HITLER'S SERVICE IN 1943 AS INSPECTOR GENERAL OF PANZER TROOPS. IN THE WAKE OF THE JULY 1944 BOMB PLOT HE SERVED HITLER AS OKH CHIEF OF STAFF. HE THEN CALLED ON HIS FELLOW GENERALS TO STAY LOYAL TO THE FÜHRER.

Q The insignia denoting Bellerophon astride Pegasus in pale blue on a maroon background was worn by which units?

A The British 1st and 6th Airborne Divisions.

Q What was the motto of the British Navy, Army, and Air Force Institute (NAAFI)?

A "Service to the Services."

Q In the Pacific theater, what was Operation Flintlock in January 1944?

A The U.S. invasion of the Marshall Islands.

" WHEREVER WE WENT WE CAME UPON
DEAD HORSES, SMASHED-UP VEHICLES, AND CORPSES
LEON DEGRELLE, CHERKASSY POCKET,
FEBRUARY 1944 "

Q What was the first phase of Operation Flintlock?

A Landings on Majuro Atoll and Kwajalein Atoll by U.S. Army and Marine Corps troops. The attack was supported by large numbers of U.S. land-based and carrier-based aircraft.

Q What were the next two islands invaded by U.S. forces during Flintlock, at the beginning of February 1944?

A Roi and Namur Islands. The two islands took two days to occupy and cost U.S. forces 737 casualties.

DID YOU KNOW

ARMORED VEHICLE PRODUCTION IN GERMANY REACHED ITS PEAK IN 1944, AT JUST THE TIME WHEN BATTLEFIELD LOSSES WERE REACHING THEIR HEIGHT. PANZER IV PRODUCTION ROSE ONLY MARGINALLY TO SOME 3,800, BUT PANTHER PRODUCTION SURGED AHEAD TO 3,584, PRODUCTION OF 623 TIGER IS WAS AUGMENTED BY THE BUILDING OF 376 TIGER IIS, STUG III AND IV PRODUCTION REACHED NEARLY 6,000, AND SOME 2,357 OF THE NEW PANZERJÄGER IV WITH THE L70 CANNON WERE BUILT ALONG WITH 226 OF THE 88MM-ARMED JAGDPANTHER. THESE FIGURES NEED TO BE CONSIDERED AGAINST TOTAL LOSSES IN 1943 OF NEARLY 8,000 TANKS AND ASSAULT GUNS, AND MORE THAN 9,000 IN 1944. THIS PRODUCTION SURGE ALLOWED THE FRONTLINE UNITS JUST TO KEEP THEIR HEADS ABOVE WATER AND GAVE ROMMEL A FIGHTING CHANCE OF DEFEATING THE D-DAY LANDINGS IN JUNE 1944.

Q Following the successful conclusion of Operation Flintlock, U.S. forces began preparing for Operation Forager. What was this?

235

A The capture of the Mariana Islands, which included the islands of Saipan, Tinian, Rota, and Guam.

Q What was the codename of the U.S. 5307th Provisional Regiment?

A Galahad.

Q This regiment had a more famous nickname. What was it?

A Merrill's Marauders. It was the U.S. equivalent of the Chindits, and had actually trained with Chindit units. Its nickname came from the name of its commander, Brigadier General Frank D. Merrill.

Q Which British units conducted Operation Thursday in Burma in March 1943?

A The Chindits.

Q What was the aim of the operation?

A About 9,000 men were deployed by glider in an area between Indaw and Myitkyina. The purpose of Operation Thursday was to harass Japanese forces to the south of Chinese and U.S. operations against Myitkyina, and cut the flow of Japanese supplies and communications heading north.

Q The Japanese launched an offensive in Burma and India which began on March 7, 1944. What was its codename?

A Operation U-Go.

Q Who led the offensive?

A Lieutenant General Renya Mutaguchi.

Q Which army did he command during the offensive?

A The Fifteenth Army.

" A JAPANESE MACHINE GUN CHATTERS HYSTERICALLY, AND BULLETS CLACK AND CLAP OVERHEAD
JOHN MASTERS, CHINDIT, BURMA, MARCH 1944 **"**

DID YOU KNOW

THE WAFFEN-SS FOUGHT IN EVERY THEATER ON MAINLAND EUROPE, AND
BECAME INDISPENSABLE TO HITLER'S WAR EFFORT FROM 1943 ONWARD.
THE SEVEN ELITE WAFFEN-SS PANZER DIVISIONS BECAME KNOWN AS THE
"FÜHRER'S FIRE BRIGADE" BECAUSE HE RUSHED THEM FROM ONE CRISIS
FRONT TO ANOTHER TO "EXTINGUISH" ENEMY BREAKTHROUGHS. TO EQUIP
THEM FOR THIS ROLE, THEY RECEIVED THE BEST EQUIPMENT THE REICH'S
WEAPONS FACTORIES COULD TURN OUT. THEY WERE ALSO TOP OF THE LIST
FOR THE REPLACEMENT OF DESTROYED OR DAMAGED TANKS, FIELD GUNS,
AND ARMORED VEHICLES. IN ADDITION, EVERY EFFORT WAS MADE TO KEEP
THEM UP TO STRENGTH WITH TRAINED MANPOWER. THE MAJORITY OF THE
OTHER WAFFEN-SS DIVISIONS WERE EMPLOYED ON LESS CRUCIAL FRONTS,
IN LARGELY STATIC DEFENSE ROLES OR ON COUNTER-PARTISAN DUTIES. THE
REPUTATION OF THESE UNITS WAS MIXED, TO SAY THE LEAST. THE DIVISIONS
THAT FOUGHT WITH ARMY GROUP NORTH BESIEGING LENINGRAD AND
LATER DEFENDING THE BALTIC STATES, SUCH AS THE *NORDLAND*
PANZERGRENADIER DIVISION, ACQUITTED THEMSELVES WELL. THIS
DIVISION PLAYED A KEY ROLE IN SAVING THE EIGHTEENTH ARMY FROM
ENCIRCLEMENT AT RIGA IN SEPTEMBER 1944. THE SS *NORD* MOUNTAIN
DIVISION FOUGHT FOR THREE YEARS IN THE ARCTIC AS PART OF THE
GERMAN THRUST TO CAPTURE THE RUSSIAN PORT OF MURMANSK,
ESTABLISHING AN EXCELLENT REPUTATION ALONGSIDE THE ARMY'S ELITE
MOUNTAIN UNITS.

Q What was the objective of Operation U-Go?

A To spoil any Allied offensive moves in central Burma by crossing into India, pushing Allied forces out of Burma in the process, cutting the Assam–Burma railway used for supplying Stilwell's Myitkyina offensive, and also occupying Imphal and Kohima and the flat territory between (which was an ideal launch point for an Allied offensive). The first part of the offensive involved the Japanese 33rd Division advancing out and cutting the Tiddim-Imphal Road, a major Allied supply route to Imphal, and trapping the 17th Indian Division.

Q Which British commander was killed in an air crash over Burma in March 1944?

A Major General Orde Wingate.

Q In April and May 1944, Japanese and British forces fought a bitter two-week battle at Kohima, at which location?

A The Tennis Court.

Q Which Japanese admiral was killed in an air crash at the end of March 1944?

A Vice Admiral Mineichi Koga.

" WE WERE TWELVE HOURS A DAY ON THE TRAIL, AS A RULE—WHETHER THERE WAS A TRAIL OR NOT "
CHARLTON OGBURN, MERRILL'S MARAUDERS, JULY 1944

Q Which fleet had he been commanding at the time of his death?

A The Combined Fleet.

Q On the Eastern Front, the capture of Kamenets Podolsk by the Soviet Fourth Tank Army at the end of March 1944 resulted in the encirclement of which German army?

A The First Panzer Army.

DID YOU KNOW

THE RAPID ADVANCE OF GERMAN ARMIES INTO THE SOVIET UNION IN
MID-1941 RESULTED IN THOUSANDS OF RED ARMY SOLDIERS BEING CUT
OFF BEHIND GERMAN LINES IN THE UKRAINE, BELORUSSIA, AND THE
BALTIC STATES. MANY TOOK REFUGE IN THE FORESTS OF THE WESTERN
USSR AND IN THE PRIPET MARSHES, THUS FORMING THE NUCLEUS OF A
PARTISAN MOVEMENT. THE FIRST PARTISAN ACTIVITIES WERE SPONTANEOUS
AND UNCOORDINATED, WITHOUT ANY ASSISTANCE FROM MOSCOW (BOTH
STALIN AND HIS SECRET POLICE CHIEF, BERIA, WERE SUSPICIOUS OF ARMED
BANDS OUTSIDE THEIR SPHERE OF CONTROL). HOWEVER, RECOGNIZING
THAT PARTISAN DETACHMENTS COULD BE USEFUL, STALIN IN LATE 1941
BEGAN TO SEND CADRES BEHIND GERMAN LINES TO COORDINATE
RESISTANCE. THE FIRST COORDINATED PARTISAN ATTACKS TOOK PLACE
DURING THE WINTER OF 1941–1942, AND IN MAY 1942 THE SOVIETS
ESTABLISHED THE CENTRAL PARTISAN STAFF TO DIRECT THE OPERATIONS
OF AN ESTIMATED 142,000 PARTISANS OPERATING BEHIND GERMAN LINES.
PRIOR TO THE BATTLE OF KURSK IN JULY 1943, THE CENTRAL PARTISAN
STAFF ORDERED THAT ALL PARTISAN ACTIVITY BE DIRECTED AGAINST
GERMAN COMMUNICATIONS IN THE CENTRAL SECTOR. THIS RESULTED IN
2,500 PARTISAN ATTACKS AGAINST GERMAN RAILROADS IN JUNE AND JULY
1943. SUCH LARGE-SCALE PARTISAN ACTIVITY MEANT THE GERMANS HAD
TO DEPLOY SUBSTANTIAL FORCES IN THEIR REAR AREAS. IN 1942, 25
SPECIAL SECURITY DIVISIONS, 30 REGIMENTS, AND MORE THAN 100 POLICE
BATTALIONS WERE INVOLVED IN ANTI-PARTISAN DUTIES. THERE IS LITTLE
DOUBT THAT THE GERMANS AIDED PARTISAN RECRUITMENT. TREATING THE
LOCALS AS SUB-HUMANS, RANDOM REPRISALS IN RESPONSE TO PARTISAN
ATTACKS, AND LAYING WASTE WHOLE AREAS TO DENY PARTISANS SUPPLIES
DID LITTLE TO ENDEAR THE GERMANS TO THE POPULACE. BY 1943, FOR
EXAMPLE, TYPICAL ANTI-PARTISAN SWEEPS INVOLVED 10,000 TROOPS.
ALTHOUGH SOVIET CLAIMS THAT PARTISANS KILLED 300,000 GERMANS
DURING THE FIRST TWO YEARS OF THE WAR ARE EXAGGERATED, IT IS
CERTAINLY TRUE THAT THE PARTISAN MOVEMENT MADE A SIGNIFICANT
CONTRIBUTION TO THE SOVIET WAR EFFORT.

Q Why did the Germans occupy Hungary in March 1944?

A Ever since the Hungarian Army suffered huge losses around Stalingrad in early 1943, Hungary had been a lukewarm member of the Axis. Indeed, from April 1943 Premier Miklos Kallay had committed only a small number of poorly armed troops to the Axis war effort. Hitler received reports proving that Hungary had been clandestinely dealing with the enemy and, in mid-March, Himmler learnt from agents in Budapest that Kallay was advocating the sabotage of German military trains running through Hungary to German army groups on the Eastern Front. In view of all these things, and fearing that Hungary might conclude a separate peace, Hitler ordered the occupation of Hungary.

Q Which two field marshals did Hitler relieve of their commands on the Eastern Front in the spring of 1944?

A Erich von Manstein and Ewald von Kleist.

Q Why?

A He was irritated by the continual retreats in the Ukraine.

DID YOU KNOW

ABOUT 1,000 WOMEN AVIATORS WERE TRAINED AS FIGHTER AND MILITARY TRANSPORT PILOTS BY THE USSR IN THE WAR, 30 OF THEM BEING DECORATED FOR THEIR HEROISM IN COMBAT. THREE AVIATION REGIMENTS, THE 586TH WOMEN'S FIGHTER REGIMENT, THE 587TH WOMEN'S BOMBER REGIMENT, AND THE 588TH WOMEN'S NIGHT BOMBER REGIMENT (THE SO-CALLED "NIGHT WITCHES," LATER ELEVATED TO THE 46TH GUARDS BOMBER AVIATION REGIMENT) WERE STAFFED BY WOMEN PILOTS, ENGINEERS, AND MECHANICS.

" MANY BOYS NEAR ME WERE HIT BY
SNIPER FIRE OR SHRAPNEL
FROM THE JAP MORTARS
RICHARD KENNARD, 1ST MARINE DIVISION, PELELIU,
SEPTEMBER 1944 "

Q The Packard V-1650 engine powered which single-seat U.S. fighter?

A The P-51 Mustang.

Q What type of aircraft was the Soviet Lavochkin La-5?

A A fighter and fighter-bomber.

Q Artem Mikoyan and Mikhail Gurevich were designers of what?

A These two Russians were famous aircraft designers.

Q What type of vehicle was the German Wespe?

A A self-propelled gun.

Q What was its main armament?

A A 105mm leFH 18M L/28 howitzer.

Q Who was the Allied general who requested the bombing of the monastery at Monte Cassino in February 1944?

A Lieutenant General Sir Bernard Freyberg.

Q Why?

A German troops had been sighted within the monastery walls, and there were enemy emplacements and strongpoints nearby.

Q Did the bombing kill the German defenders?

A No. Though much of the monastery was destroyed, the bombing did not destroy the subterranean chambers where the defenders were sheltering.

Q What was Operation Strangle, launched by the Allies in Italy in March 1944?

A An air campaign designed to disrupt German supply routes by bombing bridges, roads, and railways.

Q Who were nicknamed the "Green Devils of Cassino"?

A The German paratroopers who defended Monte Cassino.

❝ IT WAS MOST THOUGHTFUL OF YOU
AS AN OLD HARROVIAN TO CAPTURE
ROME ON THE
FOURTH OF JUNE
HAROLD MACMILLAN TO GENERAL ALEXANDER, JUNE 4, 1944 **❞**

DID YOU KNOW

TO SENIOR GERMAN ARMY COMMANDERS, THE WAFFEN-SS WAS A MIXED BLESSING. THERE WAS RESENTMENT THAT HITLER'S PRIVATE ARMY WAS SIPHONING OFF ITS BEST RECRUITS AND HAD THE PICK OF THE PRODUCTION FROM THE REICH'S ARMAMENT FACTORIES. HOWEVER, FIELD COMMANDERS GREW TO VALUE THE FIGHTING QUALITIES OF THE MAINSTREAM WAFFEN-SS DIVISIONS, IN PARTICULAR THE PANZER UNITS. WAFFEN-SS UNITS USUALLY CAME WITH SUPERB EQUIPMENT AND LAVISH SUPPLIES OF AMMUNITION, MAKING THEM A POWERFUL ADDITION TO THE FIGHTING POWER OF ANY ARMY HEADQUARTERS THAT HAD THEM ASSIGNED TO IT. FOR THEIR PART, WAFFEN-SS COMMANDERS WERE KEEN TO WIN THEIR SPURS IN BATTLE AND REGULARLY OFFERED UP THEIR UNITS FOR TASKS THAT ARMY OFFICERS HAD REFUSED. THIS RIVALRY BECAME LEGENDARY, AND NO WAFFEN-SS OFFICER WANTED TO BE SEEN TO FAIL ANY BATTLEFIELD MISSION. THE MORE GLORY THE WAFFEN-SS COULD GAIN AT THE EXPENSE OF THE ARMY, THE BETTER.

243

Q What was the purpose of the British 79th Armoured Division?

A To create specialist armored vehicles to defeat German fixed defenses, i.e. the Atlantic Wall defenses in France.

Q Who was the division's commander?

A Major General Sir Percy Hobart.

Q What was the task of the British Royal Navy's 30th Advanced Unit (30 AU)?

A To capture enemy prisoners, documents, and equipment.

Q What was a German S-boat?

A A fast torpedo boat.

Q At the beginning of May 1944 the Germans formed a new army group in France. What was it?

A Army Group G.

244

Q Which armies did it control?

A The First and Nineteenth Armies.

Q Who was the army group's commander?

A General Johannes von Blaskowitz.

Q In May 1944, the U.S. 82d and 101st Airborne Divisions carried out an exercise in Berkshire, England, as a rehearsal for their D-Day drops. What was the codename of this exercise?

A Exercise Eagle.

Q Which German battleship was damaged by aircraft at the beginning of April 1944?

A The *Tirpitz*.

Q The attacking aircraft flew from which British aircraft carriers?

A HMS *Victorious* and *Furious*.

Q Where did the attack take place?

A Altenfiord, Norway.

DID YOU KNOW

WITHIN THOSE COUNTRIES AND REGIONS OVERRUN BY THE GERMANS AND JAPANESE IN WORD WAR II THERE WERE THOSE AMONG THE VARIOUS POPULATIONS WHO WERE DETERMINED TO OPPOSE THE OCCUPIERS IN SOME WAY, OFTEN AT GREAT RISK TO THEMSELVES AND THEIR FAMILIES. THIS RESISTANCE COULD BE ACTIVE OR PASSIVE. PASSIVE RESISTANCE INVOLVED DEMONSTRATIONS, INDUSTRIAL STRIKES, AND SLOWDOWNS, THE PRODUCTION OF UNDERGROUND NEWSPAPERS AND LEAFLETS, AND WALL SLOGANS. ACTIVE RESISTANCE INVOLVED GATHERING INTELLIGENCE, ASSISTING ESCAPED ALLIED PRISONERS OF WAR AND SHOT-DOWN AIRCREWS, SABOTAGE, AND ARMED ACTION AGAINST OCCUPATION FORCES. THE DANGERS OF FIGHTING BACK AGAINST OCCUPIERS WERE EVER PRESENT, AND RESISTANCE MOVEMENTS WERE UNDER CONSTANT THREAT FROM ENEMY INTELLIGENCE, COLLABORATORS, AND INFORMERS, WITH TORTURE AND DEATH THE USUAL PRICE OF BEING CAUGHT. OWNERSHIP OF A CARRIER PIGEON, FOR EXAMPLE, WARRANTED DEATH BY FIRING SQUAD IN EUROPE.

Q Who was appointed to be commander of the Japanese Combined Fleet in May 1944?

A Admiral Soemu Toyoda.

Q A mass breakout of Allied prisoners of war took place at which German prison camp in May 1944?

A Stalag Luft III near Sagan, Silesia.

Q Was the escape attempt successful?

A No. After capture, 50 Allied airmen were shot by the Gestapo. Only three of the escaped prisoners—two Norwegians and a Dutchman—reached England.

Q What was the first Axis capital city to be captured by Allied forces in the war?

A Rome, by the U.S. Fifth Army on June 5, 1944.

Q What was the codename for the naval and amphibious element of the Allied invasion of France in June 1944?

A Operation Neptune.

❝ WE'RE GETTING KILLED ON THE BEACHES.
LET'S GO INSHORE AND
GET KILLED
U.S. OFFICER ON OMAHA BEACH, JUNE 6, 1944 **❞**

DID YOU KNOW

As Allied aerial photographic interpreters pored over images of the French coastline during the spring of 1944, they became increasingly alarmed at the scale of the construction work under way on the Third Reich's western rampart. They were observing the results of Field Marshal Erwin Rommel's crash program to turn the coastal defenses along the Atlantic coast and English Channel into a real obstacle for any Allied amphibious invasion. After a tour of the dilapidated German defenses from the Bay of Biscay to Holland in December 1943, Rommel wrote a report calling for the fortifications to be revamped. For his efforts, the hero of North Africa was appointed commander of the coastal region of France. He immediately ordered a huge construction effort to strengthen what soon became known as the Atlantic Wall. All major coastal towns and ports were turned into veritable fortresses, with huge concrete pillboxes and gun emplacements positioned to protect them. The monster gun positions in the Pas de Calais symbolized this effort to create "concrete battleships" at key parts along the Atlantic Wall to prevent the Allies seizing a port intact. These efforts were complemented by extensive engineering work to turn likely invasion beaches into a death trap for any Allied amphibious or airborne assault. Explosive-tipped steel and concrete traps were placed out at sea, below the waterline, to penetrate the hulls of approaching landing craft.

247

Q Who was commander-in-chief of Allied Expeditionary Air Forces during the D-Day landings?

A Air Chief Marshal Trafford Leigh-Mallory.

Q Who was commander-in-chief of Allied Expeditionary Naval Forces during the D-Day landings?

A Admiral Bertram Ramsay.

Q Operation Bagration was a Soviet offensive designed to destroy which German formation?

A Army Group Center in Belorussia.

Q Name the Allied D-Day invasion beaches.

A Utah, Omaha, Gold, Juno, and Sword.

DID YOU KNOW

IN JULY 1944, U.S. MILITARY LEADERS, THE JOINT CHIEFS OF STAFF, AND THE U.S. PRESIDENT MET TO DEBATE STRATEGIC OPTIONS FOR COMPLETE VICTORY IN THE PACIFIC. THOSE PRESENT DIVIDED THEMSELVES ROUGHLY INTO TWO CAMPS. GENERAL MACARTHUR ADVOCATED THE PHILIPPINES AS THE PRINCIPAL OBJECTIVE FOLLOWING THE CAMPAIGN IN NEW GUINEA, WHEREAS ADMIRAL KING (CHIEF OF THE U.S. NAVY) WANTED TO BYPASS THE PHILIPPINES AND CUT STRAIGHT TO THE ISLAND OF FORMOSA, SOUTH OF THE JAPANESE MAINLAND. BY TAKING FORMOSA, KING CONTENDED, JAPAN WOULD BE ISOLATED FROM HER RESOURCES IN THE DUTCH EAST INDIES. ALSO, FORMOSA WOULD BE AN EXCELLENT JUMPING-OFF POINT IN THE FINAL INVASION OF JAPAN, AND WOULD AVOID ANY WASTEFUL SLAUGHTER IN THE PHILIPPINE JUNGLES. MACARTHUR'S PLAN HAD A STRONG ETHICAL DIMENSION TO IT; HE BELIEVED THAT THE U.S. WAS UNDER A "MORAL OBLIGATION" TO RETURN TO THE PHILIPPINES AND LIBERATE ITS INHABITANTS. MILITARILY, HE ARGUED THAT IT WOULD NOT BE ADVISABLE TO LEAVE A LARGE JAPANESE PRESENCE IN THE REAR FOR A STRIKE TOWARD FORMOSA. THE OTHER KEY FIGURE IN THE DEBATE WAS ADMIRAL HALSEY. HE WANTED TO DEVELOP THE CENTRAL PACIFIC CAMPAIGN BY CAPTURING OKINAWA IN THE RYUKYU CHAIN, PART OF JAPANESE TERRITORY ITSELF, AND USE THIS AS THE LAUNCH PAD FOR THE INVASION OF THE MAINLAND. THE MOMENTUM WAS TOWARD MACARTHUR AND HALSEY'S PLAN, AND THE PRESIDENT AND THE JOINT CHIEFS OF STAFF GAVE THEIR ASSENT. FORMOSA WOULD BE BYPASSED.

WE SURE LIBERATED THE HELL
OUT OF THIS PLACE
Anonymous U.S. soldier in a Normandy village,
June 1944

Q American troops landed on which beaches?

A Utah and Omaha.

Q List the reasons why American troops landing on Omaha Beach suffered heavy casualties.

A Allied bombers missed their target and dropped their bombs inland; the heavy seas meant all but five of the 32 first-wave tanks were lost before they reached the shore; the naval bombardment did not destroy the German defenses; and many landing craft stopped too far from the shore, which meant that when the troops jumped into the water many drowned.

Q Which U.S. unit stormed the Pointe-du-Hoc on D-Day?

A The 2d Rangers, commanded by Colonel James E. Rudder.

Q Who was the commander of Japanese forces on the island of Saipan when the Americans invaded in June 1944?

A Lieutenant General Saito Yoshitsugo.

Q Which U.S. divisions spearheaded the invasion of Saipan?

A The 2d and 4th Marine Divisions.

249

Q What was "The Great Marianas Turkey Shoot"?

A The Battle of the Philippine Sea, June 19, 1944?

Q Why was it called this?

A The Japanese lost two aircraft carriers and 346 aircraft to U.S. air and naval attacks.

Q The German Pistole 08 was more famously known as what?

A The Luger.

DID YOU KNOW

GERMAN ANTI-PARTISAN OPERATIONS IN RUSSIA WERE A MIX OF STATIC DEFENSE AND MOBILE OFFENSIVE SWEEPS. KEY BRIDGES AND MAJOR STRETCHES OF RAILROADS COULD BE SECURED ONLY BY THE PHYSICAL BUILDING OF FORTIFIED SUPPORT POINTS, MANNED BY A PLATOON OF 20 TO 30 MEN. BATTALION-SIZED REACTION FORCES WERE THEN BASED AT REGULAR INTERVALS TO PATROL THE MAIN ROADS AND RAILROADS, READY TO TAKE THE OFFENSIVE AGAINST ANY PARTISAN RAIDS. ARMORED TRAINS AND SMALL TANK DETACHMENTS WERE USED TO GIVE SECURITY UNITS OVERWHELMING FIREPOWER. AIR RECONNAISSANCE WAS USED REGULARLY TO CHECK RAILROAD LINES AND ROADS FOR MINES AND OTHER ACTS OF SABOTAGE. AREAS OF KNOWN PARTISAN ACTIVITY WERE RINGED WITH SUPPORT POINTS TO TRY TO CONTAIN AND STOP THE SPREAD OF HOSTILE ACTIONS. SMALL PATROLS OF *JAGDKOMMANDO*, OR HUNTER, UNITS WERE USED TO PENETRATE INTO PARTISAN TERRITORY TO GATHER INTELLIGENCE AND RAID THEIR BASES. THE SERVICES OF THE GESTAPO WERE EMPLOYED ON CAPTURED PARTISANS OR THEIR RELATIVES TO MAKE THEM BETRAY THEIR COMRADES BY LEADING GERMAN TROOPS TO THEIR BASES.

Q What was its magazine capacity?

A Eight rounds.

Q The Walther PP handgun was manufactured for German military service in two calibres. What were they?

A 7.65mm and 9mm.

Q When fighting stopped on the island of Saipan in July 1944, more than 30 percent of Japanese casualties had been suicides. True or false?

A True. The final death toll was high on both sides: 3,126 U.S. soldiers killed and 27,000 Japanese (including 8,000 suicides).

251

Q What was the next objective for the U.S. forces in the Mariana Islands after the fall of Saipan?

A The island of Guam.

Q When did U.S. forces invade Guam?

A July 21, 1944.

❝ YOU COULD READ CONCERN ON THE GRIM, SET FACES AS THEY TURNED TO **PEER OUT OF THE WINDOWS**
GENERAL MATTHEW RIDGWAY,
U.S. 82D AIRBORNE DIVISION, D-DAY **❞**

Q U.S. Lieutenant General Holland Smith classed the conquest of which island as being the finest amphibious operation of the Pacific war?

A Tinian.

Q What happened at the Coworra prisoner-of-war camp, Sydney, in early August 1944?

A Japanese prisoners of war attempted a mass breakout. Three Australian guards were killed and 334 Japanese managed to escape, but Australian machine-gun fire killed 234 inmates and wounded 108 others.

Q Who commanded British and Canadian forces during the Allied invasion of France in June 1944?

A General Bernard Montgomery.

Q What was their immediate objective after landing in Normandy?

A The city of Caen.

Q What was the British Operation Goodwood in July 1944?

A General Montgomery's attempt to outflank Caen and open a route to Falaise.

" COUNTERATTACK BY JERRY FROM WOODS.
MORTAR FIRE. 13 OF MY PLATOON
KILLED OR MISSING
CORPORAL G.E. HUGHES, ROYAL HAMPSHIRES,
JUNE 14, 1944
"

DID YOU KNOW

FRANCE'S ROLLING AND WOODED COUNTRYSIDE PROVED TO BE THE GERMAN ARMY'S ONLY ALLY DURING THE BITTER FIGHTING AFTER THE D-DAY LANDINGS IN JUNE 1944. GERMAN DIVISIONS BECAME EXPERT AT DISPERSING THEMSELVES IN WOODS, FARM BUILDINGS, TUNNELS, MINES, AND INDUSTRIAL SITES. ALL VEHICLES WOULD BE ADORNED WITH HUGE AMOUNTS OF FOLIAGE TO BREAK UP THEIR SHAPES AND MAKE THEM MERGE WITH LOCAL VEGETATION. THE GERMANS, HOWEVER, WERE DETERMINED TO AVOID BEING PARALYZED BY ALLIED AIR SUPREMACY AND DEVELOPED TECHNIQUES TO ALLOW THEM TO REMAIN HIDDEN AND STILL FIGHT. A SYSTEM OF CAMOUFLAGE HIDES WAS DEVELOPED, UNDER WHICH GERMAN UNITS WOULD OPERATE FROM CAMOUFLAGED BASES IN WOODS OR INDUSTRIAL BUILDINGS, JUST BEHIND THE FRONTLINE. UNITS WOULD EMERGE AT NIGHT TO REINFORCE AND RESUPPLY FRONTLINE POSITIONS. STRICT TRACK DISCIPLINE WOULD BE IMPOSED, SO ARMORED VEHICLES WOULD USE ONLY PREPARED ROUTES IN AND OUT OF THE HIDE, ON METALED ROADS SO AIRCRAFT COULD NOT SPOT TANK TRACKS ACROSS FIELDS.

Q In Normandy in 1944, U.S. forces fought the Germans in the so-called *bocage*. What was this?

A Normandy's distinctive terrain is known as the *bocage*. Modern intensive farming had yet to arrive in Normandy, with agriculture following much the same pattern as it had for hundreds of years before. Small farm holdings predominated, and this produced an interlinked network of small fields separated by ancient hedgerows. Crucially, these hedgerows had grown into thick barriers, reinforced by very high and thick earth banks.

Q Why was the *bocage* ideal for defensive warfare?

A Even the biggest German or Allied tank found these hedgerows almost impossible to pass through or over without specialist engineering or demolition equipment. Tank movement was effectively channeled along the few roads, making it easy for enemy antitank gunners to delay and hold up advances for hours or days at a time.

Q Which SS division was under constant French Resistance attack as it moved north from Toulouse to take part in the fighting in Normandy in mid-1944?

A The 2nd SS Panzer Division *Das Reich*.

Q Which French town was chosen by this SS division to be the target of a brutal anti-partisan reprisal action?

A Oradour-sur-Glane.

Q What happened at the town?

A The men were herded into barns, the women and children into the church, and the whole town was set on fire. Those who fled were machine-gunned. In total 642 people were killed, with only 10 managing to feign death and escape.

Q Which Waffen-SS tank ace stopped the British 7th Armoured Division at Villers-Bocage in June 1944?

A Michael Wittmann.

" I THEN THREW TWO GRENADES,
WHICH WERE SUCCESSFUL IN
ELIMINATING THE ENEMY
CAPTAIN JOSEPH DAWSON,
U.S. 1ST INFANTRY DIVISION, D-DAY
"

DID YOU KNOW

FOR THE MAJORITY OF ALLIED TROOPS WHO ENGAGED THE GERMAN ARMY IN BATTLE IN NORMANDY, THE EXPERIENCE WAS THEIR FIRST TASTE OF COMBAT. THEY MIGHT HAVE ENDURED MONTHS OF INTENSIVE TRAINING IN ENGLAND BEFORE THEY WERE SHIPPED TO FRANCE, BUT NOTHING COULD HAVE PREPARED THEM FOR WHAT THEY WERE TO FACE. BRITISH, AMERICAN, AND CANADIAN DIVISIONAL, BRIGADE, AND BATTALION COMMANDERS WERE ALL LESS EXPERIENCED IN ALL-ARMS MECHANIZED WARFARE THAN THEIR GERMAN COUNTERPARTS. AT FIRST THEY ALL EMPLOYED RIGID TACTICS, WHICH LED TO THOUSANDS OF ALLIED CASUALTIES IN FRUITLESS FRONTAL ASSAULTS. THEY BELIEVED THEIR FIREPOWER WOULD OVERCOME THE GERMANS, AND THAT THERE WAS NO NEED TO USE THE TERRAIN TO COVER THEIR MOVEMENT OR TO TRY TO INFILTRATE BEHIND CENTERS OF RESISTANCE. THE ALLIES ALSO RELIED ON TOP-DOWN COMMAND PROCEDURES THAT MEANT THEIR INABILITY TO REACT TO SURPRISE GERMAN MOVES WAS A WEAKNESS. WHEN KEY OFFICERS WERE KILLED OR COMMUNICATIONS WITH HIGHER HEADQUARTERS DID NOT WORK, ALLIED ATTACKS OFTEN BROKE DOWN BECAUSE THERE WAS NO ONE TO TAKE THE INITIATIVE AND LEAD THE REMAINING TROOPS FORWARD.

Q What was the codename of the U.S. operation that broke through German lines in Normandy in July 1944?

A Cobra.

Q Which general led the U.S. Third Army in France in 1944?

A George Patton.

Q Why had this general been publicly censured by his superiors the year before?

A For striking a shell-shocked soldier in a field hospital in Sicily.

> ❝ EVERY MILE WE ADVANCE THERE ARE
> DOZENS OF SNIPERS LEFT BEHIND US.
> ## THEY PICK OFF
> ## OUR SOLDIERS
> ERNIE PYLE, NORMANDY, JUNE 26, 1944 ❞

Q What was Operation Bagration in June 1944?

A The Red Army's offensive against Army Group Center.

Q Which German panzer army was destroyed during the first six days of Bagration?

A The Third Panzer Army.

Q At the beginning of July 1944, which German army, deployed east of Minsk, was destroyed following the Soviet capture of the city?

A The Fourth Army.

Q What was Operation Valkyrie, which took place on July 20, 1944?

A The assassination attempt on Hitler's life.

Q Where was it carried out?

A At Hitler's East Prussia headquarters at Rastenburg.

Q Who led the operation?

A Colonel Claus Schenk von Stauffenberg. He fled Hitler's head-quarters after planting the bomb (which failed to kill Hitler) but was shot later that day.

Q What was the Polish Committee of Nation Liberation?

A A Soviet organization formed from the NKVD-controlled Union of Polish Patriots. It was later known as the Lublin Committee and became the official legal authority, according to the Soviets, in liberated Polish territory.

DID YOU KNOW

THE SOVIET LEADER, STALIN, VIEWED THE WESTERN ALLIES WITH SUSPICION, OFTEN ACCUSING THEM OF POSTPONING THE SECOND FRONT BECAUSE THEY WANTED TO SEE THE USSR BLED WHITE. ALWAYS PUTTING HIS OWN INTERESTS FIRST, HE MADE EXORBITANT DEMANDS WHEN IT CAME TO LEND-LEASE SUPPLIES, AND PLANNED THE FINAL OFFENSIVES OF THE WAR WITH A RUSSIAN-DOMINATED POSTWAR EUROPE IN MIND. AFTER THE WAR HE QUICKLY MOVED TO CONSOLIDATE HIS POSITION BY REMOVING FAMOUS WARTIME COMMANDERS, AND SO FIGURES SUCH AS ZHUKOV, ROKOSSOVSKY, MERETSKOV, VATUTIN, AND KONEV DISAPPEARED FROM PUBLIC VIEW. HE ALSO DID NOT FORGET THOSE RUSSIAN NATIONALS WHO, IN HIS VIEW, HAD COLLABORATED WITH THE ENEMY. HE INSISTED THAT THE BRITISH AND AMERICANS ADHERE STRICTLY TO THE TERMS OF THE YALTA AGREEMENT, WHICH THEY DID, EVEN THOUGH THEY KNEW THAT REPATRIATION WOULD MEAN DEATH OR IMPRISONMENT FOR THOSE RETURNED. THUS, BETWEEN 1945 AND 1947, 2,272,000 SOVIET CITIZENS WERE RETURNED BY THE WESTERN ALLIES TO THE USSR. ONE-FIFTH OF THESE WERE EITHER SHOT OR GIVEN 25-YEAR SENTENCES IN THE GULAG.

Q The weapon designers R.V. Shepperd and H.J. Turpin created which famous submachine gun?

A The Sten Gun.

Q What was its caliber?

A 9mm.

Q What was its magazine capacity?

A 32 rounds.

Q The Japanese Rifle Type 38 was also known as what?

A The Arisaka Rifle.

258

Q Which organization rose in revolt against the Germans in Warsaw on August 1, 1944?

A The Home Army.

Q Who was its commander?

A General Tadeusz Komorowski, who commanded 38,000 insurgents in the city.

Q Which German commander was given the task of suppressing the revolt?

A SS General Erich von dem Bach-Zelewski.

Q Who was the fascist leader of Romania?

A Ion Antonescu.

" UP AND DOWN THE BEACH AND
OUT ON THE REEF, A NUMBER OF AMTRACS
AND DUKWS WERE BURNING
EUGENE B. SLEDGE, 1ST MARINE DIVISION,
PELELIU, SEPTEMBER 15, 1944 "

Q In August 1944 the German Army in Normandy was encircled near which French town?

A Falaise.

Q What was the objective of Montgomery's Operation Market Garden in September 1944?

A An ambitious airborne operation to seize a series of strategic bridges in Holland, to allow the Allies to gain a foothold over the Rhine at Arnhem, and open a route for Allied tanks into the heart of Germany's Ruhr industrial region.

Q U.S. armored divisions were usually divided into three units, in which armor and infantry battalions were combined. What were these units called?

A Combat commands.

Q What type of artillery piece was the German 75mm GebG 36?

A A mountain gun.

> **" I REMEMBER IT AS A CLAP OF THUNDER
> COUPLED WITH A BRIGHT
> YELLOW FLASH**
> HEINRICH BUCHOLZ, DESCRIBING THE BOMB
> ATTEMPT ON HITLER'S LIFE **"**

DID YOU KNOW

THE SIEGFRIED LINE HAD BEEN BUILT IN THE 1930S IN RESPONSE TO THE FRENCH BUILDING THEIR FAMOUS MAGINOT LINE. THE GERMAN LINE STRETCHED FROM THE SWISS BORDER NORTHWARD TO NEAR THE DUTCH BORDER. IN THE "PHONEY WAR" PERIOD OF THE LATE 1930S, THE SIEGFRIED LINE HAD TAKEN ON ALMOST MYTHICAL PROPORTIONS, AS BOTH THE FRENCH AND GERMANS ATTEMPTED TO OUT-DO EACH OTHER IN THE PROPAGANDA WAR, CLAIMING THEIR RESPECTIVE LINES WERE STRONGER, BIGGER, AND MORE IMPREGNABLE THAN THOSE OF THEIR OPPONENTS. IN REALITY, THE GERMAN LINE WAS NEVER AS STRONG AS ITS FRENCH COUNTERPART, BEING MORE A SERIES OF FIELD FORTIFICATIONS FOR ARMY UNITS RATHER THAN A "CONCRETE BATTLESHIP" IN THE STYLE OF THE MAGINOT LINE. THE SIEGFRIED LINE BOASTED LONG LINES OF CONCRETE DRAGON'S TEETH ANTITANK OBSTACLES, PILLBOXES, AND HUGE BARBED-WIRE ENTANGLEMENTS.

Q In the U.S. Army, what were "tank-hunting teams"?

A Usually a tank battalion with an infantry company attached.

Q In the U.S. Army, what were "infantry-heavy teams" used for?

A Usually a group of infantry companies, they were used for attacks against towns and woods and for river crossings.

Q In Red Army service, what were Aerosans?

A A type of ski vehicle propelled by an aircraft engine. An armored version, the NKL-26, was produced for raiding operations in Arctic regions.

Q In the Pacific, the U.S. Navy's submarines experienced two main problems with their Mark XIV torpedoes. What were they?

A The depth-control mechanism of the torpedo was malfunctioning and directed the torpedo too far beneath its target (it ran at about 10–12 ft/3–4 m below set depth). Also, the torpedoes were equipped with the Mk VI magnetic influence exploder mechanism, an unreliable proximity detonator designed to explode the torpedo underneath a ship rather than on contact.

Q In the Pacific theater, where was "Bloody Nose Ridge"?

A On the island of Peleliu.

> " BY MIDDAY THE ENTIRE AREA
> RESEMBLED A MOON LANDSCAPE,
> ## WITH THE BOMB CRATERS
> ## TOUCHING RIM TO RIM
> GENERAL FRITZ BAYERLAIN, PANZER LEHR DIVISION,
> NORMANDY, JULY 1944 "

Q What were the three cornerstones of Lord Louis Mountbatten's Burma policy?

A Morale, monsoon, and malaria. Mountbatten raised Allied morale in Burma mainly through capitalizing on the victories at Imphal and Kohima, and promoting the idea that Japanese invincibility was a myth. "Monsoon" refers to his policy of maintaining the Allied campaign through the five-month monsoon season to enforce the Japanese collapse. As a corollary, he created the Medical Advisory Division to tackle tropical diseases such as malaria, which cost the Allies 120 men for every single battle casualty.

Q In October 1944 the Japanese launched Operation Sho. What was its objective?

A To crush the Allied landings in the southern Philippines using the whole Japanese Combined Fleet.

Q The operation led to which decisive naval engagement?

A The Battle of Leyte Gulf.

Q At that engagement how many aircraft carriers did the Japanese lose?

A Four: *Zuikaku, Zuiho, Chitose,* and *Chiyoda.*

263

DID YOU KNOW

IN SPITE OF BEING FIVE YEARS INTO A LONG AND BLOODY WAR, THE WEHRMACHT PUT UP AN AMAZING FIGHT IN NORMANDY IN 1944. WHILE SOME OF THE GERMAN ARMY'S GENERALS WERE DISAFFECTED WITH THE FÜHRER AND WERE ACTIVELY PLOTTING TO KILL HIM, THE RANK AND FILE OF THE FIGHTING TROOPS STILL BELIEVED IN GERMANY'S CAUSE. ROMMEL'S INFECTIOUS ENTHUSIASM RUBBED OFF ON THE TROOPS BEING TRAINED TO REPEL THE INVASION. HE WAS FAMOUS FOR HIS VICTORIES AGAINST THE BRITISH AND AMERICANS IN NORTH AFRICA; AND MANY OF HIS TROOPS, ALONG WITH THE DIVISIONAL OFFICERS, WERE CONVINCED OF THE LOGIC OF HITLER'S CLAIM THAT IF THE ALLIED INVASION COULD BE THROWN BACK INTO THE SEA, THEN GERMANY WOULD BE ABLE TO TURN ITS ATTENTION EAST TO FINISH OFF THE SOVIETS. "WHEN THE ENEMY INVADES IN THE WEST IT WILL BE THE MOMENT OF DECISION IN THIS WAR," SAID ROMMEL. "AND THE MOMENT MUST TURN FOR GERMANY'S ADVANTAGE."

Q
Why was the Battle of Leyte Gulf in October 1944 so decisive?

A
The final tally of Japanese shipping sunk was four aircraft carriers, three battleships, ten cruisers, eleven destroyers, and one submarine, with most other Japanese ships severely damaged. In addition, 10,000 sailors and 500 aircraft were also lost. The Battle of Leyte Gulf marked the undeniable collapse of Japanese naval power in the Pacific. From that point on, the suicide air strikes that had their inauguration over Leyte Gulf became an increasing feature of a desperate Japanese military that could no longer oppose the mighty U.S. Navy.

Q
What does the Japanese term kamikaze mean?

A
"Divine wind."

DID YOU KNOW

TIME AFTER TIME ON THE EASTERN FRONT DURING 1944, HITLER ORDERED CUT-OFF GERMAN FORCES TO FORM WHAT HE TERMED "FORTRESS TOWNS." HE BELIEVED THEY WOULD TIE DOWN SCORES OF SOVIET DIVISIONS THAT WOULD OTHERWISE BE FREE TO RAMPAGE WESTWARD. IN REALITY, WITH NO PANZER RESERVES AVAILABLE TO RIDE TO THE RESCUE, THE FORTRESS TOWNS BECAME DEATH TRAPS FOR THEIR GARRISONS. THE SOVIETS SIMPLY SURROUNDED THE FORTRESS TOWNS AND WAITED FOR THE GERMANS TO RUN OUT OF FOOD AND AMMUNITION. THE SOVIET OFFENSIVE THAT DESTROYED THE GERMAN ARMY GROUP CENTER IN JUNE AND JULY 1944 DEMONSTRATED THE BANKRUPTCY OF THE FÜHRER'S IDEAS. WITHIN A FEW WEEKS THE RUSSIANS HAD SURROUNDED SEVERAL GERMAN ARMY CORPS IN ISOLATED POCKETS AT VITEBSK, ORSHA, MOGILEV, AND BOBRUISK. HITLER ORDERED THEM TO FIGHT TO THE LAST MAN. WHEN HE AT LAST ALLOWED THEM TO BREAK OUT IT WAS TOO LATE. ONLY A FEW THOUSAND MANAGED TO ESCAPE. MORE THAN 150,000 GERMANS WERE KILLED AND SOME 100,000 WERE CAPTURED. THE PRISONERS WERE LATER PARADED THROUGH THE STREETS OF MOSCOW BY THE VICTORIOUS SOVIETS.

❝ EACH SPINNY AND COPSE CONTAINED ITS
DREADFUL QUOTA OF
DEAD GERMANS
JOHNNIE JOHNSON, RAF PILOT, THE FALAISE POCKET,
AUGUST 1944 **❞**

Q What was it applied to in World War II?

A Volunteer Japanese pilots who crashed their aircraft into Allied
ships. In the same way that typhoons destroyed Kublai Khan's
fleets in 1274 and 1281, saving Japan from a Mongol invasion, it was
hoped that the kamikaze would prevent the Allies from launching an
invasion of Japan.

Q When were the kamikaze first used?

A The first mass attack of 55 kamikaze aircraft came on October
23–26, 1944, around Leyte, sinking five ships (including the carrier
USS *St Lo*) and damaging 40 others, 23 severely.

Q What was the rank of the officer who commanded a U.S. armored division?

A Major general.

Q In U.S. Army offensive doctrine, explain the difference between "Rat Race" and "Slugging Match."

A The "Rat Race" was an advance to contact over open terrain,
using tanks and infantry, in the face of minimal enemy resistance.
The "Slugging Match" was a more deliberate operation against a
known enemy position, in which combat commands attacked in close
cooperation to provide mutual support.

Q What was the Slovak national uprising of August 1944?

A Since the summer of 1944 Slovak partisans of the Czechoslovak Army in Slovakia (18,000 in number) had been engaged in guerrilla activity against German targets, mainly in the central mountains. In response, the Germans moved 48,000 troops into Slovakia, prompting the outbreak of the Slovak national uprising in August.

Q On September 5, 1944, the USSR declared war on Bulgaria. What was the Bulgarian response?

A They surrendered at once.

> **"** SPLATTERED EVERYWHERE WAS BLOOD:
> IT LAY IN POOLS IN THE ROOMS,
> ## IT COVERED THE SMOCKS
> ## OF THE DEFENDERS
> LIEUTENANT MACKAY, 1ST AIRBORNE DIVISION,
> ARNHEM, SEPTEMBER 1944 **"**

Q Who attended the Second Moscow Conference in October 1944?

A Winston Churchill, Joseph Stalin, and U.S. Ambassador Averell Harriman.

Q What was discussed at the conference?

A The USSR's entry into the war against Japan, postwar division of the Balkans, and the future of Poland. The main focus of the conference was Soviet influence in a postwar Eastern Europe.

DID YOU KNOW

THE JULY 1944 BOMB PLOT ONLY SERVED TO FUEL HITLER'S PARANOIA AND DISTRUST OF HIS GENERALS. INCREASINGLY, HE TURNED TO THE NAZI PARTY AND THE WAFFEN-SS TO RUN THINGS FOR HIM. THIS WAS BEST ILLUSTRATED BY THE APPOINTMENT OF THE HEAD OF THE SS, HEINRICH HIMMLER, TO RUN THE REPLACEMENT ARMY IN THE DAYS AFTER THE BOMB PLOT WAS FOILED. HIMMLER PROVED TOTALLY INEPT AT RUNNING THE SYSTEM OF TRAINING MANPOWER FOR THE FIELD ARMY AND MADE AN EVEN GREATER MESS OF THINGS WHEN HE WAS APPOINTED HEAD OF ARMY GROUP VISTULA IN JANUARY 1945.

Q In August 1944 the Allies began the assault on which German defense line in Italy?

A The Gothic Line.

Q Which German commander refused to carry out Hitler's orders to burn Paris to the ground in the fall of 1944?

A General Dietrich von Choltitz.

Q Why did British troops land at Patrai in the Peloponnese at the beginning of October 1944?

A Winston Churchill was determined to prevent a communist takeover in Greece.

Q Who fulfilled his promise "I shall return" by wading ashore in the Philippines in October 1944?

A General Douglas MacArthur.

DID YOU KNOW

268

Q Which Soviet spy was hanged in Tokyo in November 1944?

A Richard Sorge.

Q U.S. B-29 Superfortress bombers mounted their first raid against which Japanese city on November 24, 1944?

A Tokyo.

Q What was the name of the forest, south of Aachen, in which German and American forces fought a series of attritional battles in late 1944?

A The Hurtgen Forest.

Q What was the codename of the German offensive in the Ardennes in December 1944?

A Operation Watch on the Rhine.

Q What was the aim of the offensive?

A To punch through the Ardennes to capture the Belgian port of Antwerp, thereby splitting the British in Holland from the Americans in France.

Q Why was Watch on the Rhine initially successful?

A Because the attack had been planned in great secrecy it took the Allies totally by surprise, and initially swept away the weak American forces holding the frontline in the Ardennes. In addition, for almost a week the bad weather kept Allied air units on the ground and the German panzers were able to race westward. Finally, German commandos wearing Allied uniforms added to the panic among the green GIs trying to hold back the surprise Blitzkrieg.

Q Why did the offensive ultimately fail?

A Once the Allies recovered and brought their airpower and armored reserves to bear, Watch on the Rhine was doomed.

❝ OUR SHIPS HAVE BEEN SALVAGED
AND ARE RETIRING AT
HIGH SPEED TOWARD
THE JAPANESE FLEET
WILLIAM F. HALSEY, ON REPORTS THAT THE THIRD FLEET
HAD BEEN DEFEATED, OCTOBER 26, 1944 **❞**

Q In the U.S. Army, what was a TALO?

A A tactical air liaison officer. TALOs were attached to ground units and were used to call down air strikes on enemy units.

Q Which Waffen-SS division was raised from Croatian Muslims, and which had its own Mullahs and Imans?

A The 13th Waffen-Gebirgs Division *Handschar.*

Q What was General Eisenhower's "Broad Front" strategy in northwest Europe in 1944?

A British and American armies would receive equal shares of supplies and advance in line abreast across France to the German border. This would keep up the pressure on the Germans along the whole of the Western Front and prevent them regrouping and launching a flanking counterattack against any exposed Allied spearheads.

Q What was the "Red Ball Express" that operated in France in 1944?

A 6,000 trucks moving along dedicated one-way roads from the Normandy bridgehead to speed supplies to the front to maintain the Allied advance.

> " EVERYONE IS BUSY SCRAPING
> THE BOTTOM OF HIS BOWL
> WITH HIS SPOON SO AS
> NOT TO WASTE A DROP "
> PRIMO LEVI, INMATE OF AUSCHWITZ, OCTOBER 1944

1945

Imperial Japan and Nazi Germany were finally overwhelmed by a combination of Allied military and industrial might. Allied bombers roamed at will over enemy territory, reducing dozens of towns and cities to rubble, culminating in the dropping of atomic bombs on Japan in August 1945.

Q Which extermination camp in Poland did the Germans evacuate in January 1945?

A Auschwitz. In sub-zero temperatures the Nazis evacuated more than 50,000 prisoners west toward Germany. Many thousands died from starvation or hypothermia in the march to other camps; others were shot when they failed to keep up. Most of the survivors ended up in other concentration camps: Bergen-Belsen, Buchenwald, and Dachau.

Q In late January 1945, the Germans created Army Group Vistula made up of the Second and Eleventh Armies. Who was its commander?

A SS chief Heinrich Himmler.

> " IF ONLY WE MIGHT FALL LIKE CHERRY
> BLOSSOMS IN THE SPRING—
> SO PURE AND RADIANT! "
> ANONYMOUS KAMIKAZE PILOT, FEBRUARY 1945

Q What was the fate of the German cruise liner *Wilhelm Gustav* at the end of January 1945?

A Filled with civilian refugees from East Prussia, she was sunk by the Soviet submarine *S13* off the Hela Peninsula. More than 7,000 people drowned.

Q Which army invaded the Japanese-occupied island of Luzon in January 1945?

A The U.S. Sixth Army under General Walter Krueger.

DID YOU KNOW

GERMANY'S STRATEGIC POSITION IN JANUARY 1945 WAS HOPELESS: IN THE WEST THE ALLIES WERE APPROACHING THE RHINE, IN THE EAST THE RED ARMY MUSTERED OVER 400 DIVISIONS FOR THE DRIVE ON BERLIN, AND IN THE SOUTH SOVIET FORCES WERE BESIEGING THE HUNGARIAN CAPITAL, BUDAPEST. ONLY IN ITALY WAS THE FRONT STABLE.

Q The Allied advance to the River Rhine involved three operations —Veritable, Grenade, and Lumberjack—what did each involve?

A Operation Veritable was designed to move Allied forces close to the Rhine opposite Wesel. Operation Grenade would involve Allied forces sweeping northeast from the River Roer to link up with the Veritable formations, while the U.S. First and Third Armies taking part in Lumberjack would move forward to reach the Rhine between Cologne and Koblenz.

Q What was the German Operation Bodenplatte in January 1945?

A A Luftwaffe offensive in support of the Ardennes Offensive, with 1,035 fighters and bombers attacking Allied airfields in Belgium and southern Holland. The Germans destroyed 150 Allied aircraft but lost 277 of their own.

Q Give at least two reasons why the fight for the island of Iwo Jima in February 1945 was so costly for assaulting U.S. forces.

A Japanese troops were pulled back into the interior where they sat out the coastal bombardments and allowed U.S. forces to land before engaging them from preprepared defensive positions. Around the island were more than 800 pillboxes, bunkers, dug-in armored vehicles, and 3 miles (4.8 km) of tunnels. The bunkers had an extremely low-profile sloping face resistant to artillery fire. All pillboxes were situated to have overlapping fields of fire; all beaches, and the slopes leading off them, were zeroed in advance by Japanese machine guns, artillery, and mortars.

Q How did the terrain of Iwo Jima assist the Japanese defenders?

A Iwo Jima is a volcanic island, its convoluted rocky landscape full of caves, ravines, ridges, and other natural defensive positions. In one 1,312 ft x 1,968 ft (400 m x 600 m) area, U.S. Marines had to neutralize 100 individual defensive caves. The slope of the beaches was extremely steep with crumbly volcanic ash (the Japanese embedded antitank mines in the slopes), and U.S. Marines struggled simply to walk across such terrain carrying their 100 lb (45 kg) packs. Also, U.S. soldiers found in many places that the volcanic landscape was too hot to dig foxholes.

Q Which U.S. photographer immortalized the moment when U.S. Marines raised the Stars and Stripes on the summit of Mount Suribachi on Iwo Jima?

A Joe Rosenthal.

Q What was the main Soviet demand at the Yalta Conference held in the Crimea in February 1945?

A Stalin demanded a strong, pro-communist government in Poland to guarantee the future security of the USSR. As the Red Army controlled most of Eastern Europe, the British and Americans had little choice but to agree.

DID YOU KNOW

BY MID-1943, THE RED ARMY FIELDED SO-CALLED TANK ARMIES TO COMBAT THE GERMAN PANZER CORPS. THE CREATION OF THE FIRST TWO ARMIES— THE THIRD AND FIFTH—WAS ORDERED ON MAY 25, 1942. IN THEORY EACH TANK ARMY WAS MADE UP OF TWO TANK CORPS, ONE MECHANIZED CORPS, AND SUPPORTING UNITS—A STRENGTH OF 560 TANKS AND 45,000 MEN, THOUGH SOME WERE LARGER. IN JANUARY 1945, FOR EXAMPLE, THE THIRD GUARDS TANK ARMY HAD 670 TANKS, 43,400 TROOPS, 254 ASSAULT GUNS, 24 BM-13 ROCKET LAUNCHERS, AND 368 ARTILLERY PIECES.

❝ THE RAISING OF THAT FLAG ON SURIBACHI
MEANS A MARINE CORPS FOR
THE NEXT 500 YEARS **❞**
JAMES FORRESTAL, FEBRUARY 23, 1945

Q Why did the Allies bomb the city of Dresden in February 1945?

A In response to a specific Soviet request for bombing German communications, and in particular with regard to the Berlin-Leipzig-Dresden railway complex.

Q Why did Syria and Saudi Arabia declare war on Germany in late February 1945?

A The rush to join the Allies stemmed from the announcement that only those states that declared war before March 1 would be invited to a conference in San Francisco on the proposed postwar "United Nations" organization.

Q Which bridge over the River Rhine was captured by American troops in early March 1945?

A The Ludendorff Bridge at Remagen.

Q Was it of use to the Allied war effort against Germany?

A No. The bridge had been weakened by demolition charges and it collapsed into the river 10 days after its capture.

Q The Soviet SU-152 assault gun was armed with which main gun?

A The ML-20 152mm gun howitzer.

Q Why did the U.S. wish to conquer the island of Iwo Jima?

A The island had to be taken for four reasons: the unescorted U.S. bombers flying from the Marianas to Japan were suffering heavy losses, and, therefore, airfields closer to Japan were needed for fighter escorts; Iwo Jima had two air bases and was only three hours' flying time from Tokyo; Iwo Jima was prewar Japanese territory, whose loss would be a severe psychological blow to the homeland; and the island was a necessary link in the air defenses of the Marianas.

Q What was the Burmese National Army?

A An independence movement fighting on the side of the Japanese.

❝ AMONG THE MEN WHO FOUGHT ON IWO JIMA, UNCOMMON VALOR WAS A COMMON VIRTUE ❞
ADMIRAL CHESTER NIMITZ, MARCH 16, 1945

Q What was Operation Iceberg?

A The codename for the U.S. invasion of Okinawa.

Q Which were the two main elements of the Operation Iceberg U.S. invasion force?

A U.S. III Marine Amphibious Corps (6th Marine Division and 1st Marine Division) was on the left flank, with the objective of advancing to the west and up into the north of the island; while, beneath it, U.S. Army XXIV Corps (7th Infantry Division and 96th Infantry Division) began operations to clear southern Okinawa.

DID YOU KNOW

THE JAPANESE OHKA ("CHERRY BLOSSOM") WAS A ROCKET-POWERED PILOTED BOMB DESIGNED BY NAVAL ENSIGN MITSUO OHKA IN LATE 1944. EFFECTIVELY, THE AIRCRAFT WAS NOTHING MORE THAN A 2,646 LB (1,200 KG) WARHEAD WITH WINGS AND POWERED BY THREE SOLID-FUEL TYPE 4 MARK 1 MODEL 20 ROCKETS. TO DEPLOY THE WEAPON, IT WAS FIRST ATTACHED TO THE MODIFIED BOMB BAY OF A MITSUBISHI G4M BOMBER AND FLOWN TO WITHIN 25 MILES (40 KM) OF THE TARGET. ONCE RELEASED, THE OHKA'S ROCKETS WOULD IGNITE AND THE PILOT WOULD THEN FLY THE BOMB INTO HIS INTENDED TARGET. TO ENSURE THE UNSWERVING COMMITMENT OF THE PILOT, HE WAS SEALED INTO THE COCKPIT FOR HIS ONE-WAY TRIP.

Q What was Nazi Germany's last offensive of the war?

A Operation Spring Awakening at the beginning of March 1945.

Q What was the objective of the offensive?

A The German plan was to recapture Budapest by breaking through the junction of the Soviet Fourth Guards and Twenty-Sixth Armies, thereafter annihilating the 2nd and 3rd Ukrainian Fronts trapped on the west bank of the River Danube. The offensive was also designed to seize Hungary's oil supplies.

Q Why was chief of staff Heinz Guderian against the offensive?

A He wanted the divisions to be used for the defense of Berlin.

Q Which German forces were involved in Operation Spring Awakening?

A The Sixth SS Panzer Army (I and II SS Panzer Corps and III Panzer Corps), Sixth Army (IV SS Panzer Corps and Hungarian VIII Corps), and Second Panzer Army (XXXXIV and LXVII Corps).

Q Why was the plan totally unrealistic?

A The Germans had 430,000 troops, 5,600 artillery pieces, and 880 tanks and assault guns, supported by 850 fuel-starved aircraft, whereas the Soviets had 407,000 troops, 7,000 artillery pieces, 400 tanks and assault guns, and 960 aircraft. In the Stavka reserve was the Ninth Guards Army, while the 2nd Ukrainian Front lay to the south.

"
I STARED CURIOUSLY AT MY FIRST
GERMAN CIVILIAN. HE WAS AN
OLD MAN DRESSED
IN SHABBY SERGE
JOHN FOLEY, BRITISH TANK OFFICER,
FEBRUARY 28, 1945
"

Q The commander of the U.S. 4th Armored Division, Major General John S. Wood, had two nicknames. What were they?

A "Tiger Jack" and the "Rommel of the American forces."

Q The modern American Abrams main battle tank was named after which World War II commander?

A Lieutenant General Creighton Abrams, a tank commander in World War II and later chief of staff of the U.S. Army.

Q Major General Philippe Leclerc was the commander of which armored division?

A The 2nd Free French Armored Division.

Q Leclerc was a *nom de guerre*. What was his real name?

A Vicomte Jacques-Philippe de Hautecloque.

Q Why did he conceal his true identity?

A To protect his family in France, who lived in German-occupied territory.

DID YOU KNOW

WHEN IT ENTERED SERVICE IN JULY 1943, THE BOEING B-29 SUPERFORTRESS 10-CREW BOMBER HAD A RANGE OF 4,100 MILES (6598 KM) AND A BOMB LOAD OF 20,000 LB (9,072 KG). IT WAS AN ADVANCED AIRCRAFT—THE GUN TURRETS DOTTED AROUND THE FUSELAGE WERE CONTROLLED REMOTELY BY GUNNERS SITTING INSIDE THE FUSELAGE WHO AIMED THE WEAPONS VIA PERISCOPES. THE B-29 WAS IDEAL FOR THE VAST DISTANCES OF THE PACIFIC THEATER. FROM MARCH 1945, B-29S BEGAN OPERATIONS FROM FIVE BASES IN THE MARIANAS ISLANDS, CAUSING DEVA-STATION ON THE JAPANESE MAINLAND. ATTACKING AT NIGHT (PREVIOUSLY, THE B-29S HAD MAINLY CONDUCTED HIGH-LEVEL DAYLIGHT RAIDS), THE B-29S SCATTERED MILLIONS OF INCENDIARIES OVER JAPANESE CITIES—THE WOOD AND PLASTER CONSTRUCTION OF JAPANESE HOUSING MADE THE BUILDINGS INTENSELY VULNERABLE TO FIRE ATTACKS. THE FIRST SUCH FIRE ATTACK ON TOKYO CAUSED 80,000 DEATHS, A SIMILAR DEATH TOLL TO THAT CAUSED BY THE HIROSHIMA BOMB. SOME 3,970 B-29S WERE PRODUCED DURING THE WAR, SOME LATER SERVING IN THE KOREAN WAR.

Q The Soviet SU-152 assault gun used the chassis of which tank?

A The KV-1S heavy tank.

Q One of the Lend-Lease tanks supplied by the Americans to the Russians was referred to by Red Army personnel as the "grave for seven brothers." Which tank?

A The M3 Lee medium tank, because of its thin armor.

Q What was the only Soviet armored car manufactured during the war?

A The BA-64, which was based on the GAZ-67 jeep.

280

DID YOU KNOW

LEND-LEASE AID AS PROVIDED TO THE USSR BY BRITAIN AND THE UNITED STATES DID NOT INFLUENCE THE OUTCOME OF THE WAR ON THE EASTERN FRONT—WITHOUT IT, THE RED ARMY WOULD STILL HAVE BEEN VICTORIOUS. THIS WAS BECAUSE THE SOVIET UNION WAS ALSO ABLE TO GALVANIZE ITS VAST INDUSTRIAL RESOURCES TO PRODUCE TANKS, ARTILLERY, AND SMALL ARMS ON A SCALE THAT GERMANY COULD NOT MATCH. BUT WITHOUT ANY AID FROM THE WEST, THE SOVIET UNION WOULD HAVE TAKEN LONGER TO DEFEAT NAZI GERMANY, AND WOULD HAVE SUFFERED MANY MORE CASUALTIES DOING SO. BETWEEN 1943 AND 1945, WESTERN AID, SPECIFICALLY TRUCKS, RAIL ENGINES, AND RAIL WAGONS, ALLOWED THE RED ARMY TO MAINTAIN THE MOMENTUM OF ITS OFFENSIVES BY TRANSPORTING TROOPS AND SUPPLIES TO REINFORCE BREAK-THROUGH ARMIES, THUS DENYING THE GERMANS TIME TO ORGANIZE FRESH DEFENSE LINES AND ESCAPE ENCIRCLEMENTS.

WORLD WAR II TRIVIA BOOK

THIS EVENING'S MOSQUITO RAID WAS
PARTICULARLY DISASTROUS
FOR ME BECAUSE OUR
MINISTRY WAS HIT
JOSEF GOEBBELS, 13 MARCH 1945 **"**

Q Which Nazi military award was intended to replace Imperial awards such as the Pour le Mérite?

A The Knight's Cross.

Q What type of weapon was the Soviet PTRS?

A A semiautomatic antitank rifle.

Q Lend-Lease aid to the Soviets included locomotives, boots, and field telephones. True or false?

A True. The Soviets received 1,860 locomotives, 11,181 rail cars, 15 million pairs of boots, and 422,000 field telephones.

Q What type of fighting vehicle was the German Panzer IV/70(V)?

A A tank destroyer.

Q What was the name of the U.S. M26 tank?

A The Pershing.

Q What was the main gun on the American M26 heavy tank?

A The 90mm Tank Gun M3.

Q What type of weapons were "Tallboy" and "Grand Slam"?

A Deep-penetration aircraft bombs.

Q What type of aircraft was the German Focke Wulf Fw 190?

A A single-seat fighter.

" THE BABY'S RIGHT THIGH
HAD BEEN TORN OFF, AND THE
LITTLE STUMP WAS
WRAPPED IN RAGS
HANS GLIEWE, GERMAN SCHOOLBOY, DANZIG,
MARCH 9, 1945 "

Q What was Britain's first operational jet combat aircraft?

A The Gloster Meteor.

Q Who was its designer?

A George Carter.

DID YOU KNOW

THE HEAVIEST TANK PRODUCED BY THE GERMANS, AND POSSIBLY THE HEAVIEST TANK EVER PRODUCED, WAS THE MAUS, WHICH WEIGHED IN AT A MASSIVE 186 TONS (189 TONNES). DESCRIBED BY THE FATHER OF THE GERMAN PANZERS, COLONEL GENERAL HEINZ GUDERIAN, AS A "GIGANTIC OFFSPRING OF THE FANTASY OF HITLER AND HIS ADVISORS," THE MAUS NEVER SAW COMBAT. DR. FERDINAND PORSCHE PERSUADED HITLER TO ALLOW HIM TO START WORK ON THE MAUS IN THE SUMMER OF 1942. EVERYTHING ABOUT THE TANK WAS BIG. IT WAS TO HAVE THE BIGGEST GUN EVER MOUNTED IN A GERMAN TANK TURRET, A 128MM CANNON, ALONG WITH A 75MM SECONDARY ARMAMENT. THE FIRST FIELD TRIALS OF THE TWO PROTOTYPES GOT UNDER WAY IN LATE 1944, BUT THEY WERE NEVER ANYWHERE NEAR BEING READY FOR SERVICE BY THE TIME THE SOVIETS OVERRAN THE TANK TESTING RANGE AT KUMMERSDORF IN 1945. THE PROTOTYPES WERE ORDERED TO BE DESTROYED, BUT RUMORS PERSIST THAT AT LEAST ONE MAUS WAS CAPTURED BY THE SOVIETS.

283

Q The aircraft initially had a different name. What was it?

A The Thunderbolt.

Q The Meteor was a single-seat fighter, but what was the aircraft's first mission when it entered service?

A Chasing German V-1 flying bombs over southern England.

Q What was the wing armament of the Hawker Typhoon ground-attack aircraft?

A Four 20mm cannon.

> ❝ THE MUZZLES WERE TRAINED ON BERLIN.
> ON THE FORTIFICATIONS OF
> FASCIST BERLIN—"FIRE!"
> GENERAL CHUIKOV, SOVIET EIGHTH GUARDS ARMY,
> APRIL 20, 1945 ❞

Q Which German battlecruiser was towed to Gdynia and sunk as a blockship there in March 1945?

A The *Gneisenau*.

Q Which German light cruiser evacuated the coffin of Field Marshal von Hindenburg, which had been interred at the Tannenburg Memorial, in January 1945?

A The *Emden*.

Q Which two Japanese warships were the largest and most powerful battleships ever built?

A The *Mushashi* and *Yamato*.

Q Four such battleships were planned. What happened to the other two?

A The third, *Shinano*, was completed as an aircraft carrier, and the fourth was never built.

Q Which U.S. heavy cruiser transported components of the atomic bombs from San Francisco to Tinian in July 1945?

A USS *Indianapolis*.

Q Which Allied leader died of a cerebral hemorrhage in April 1945?

A U.S. President Franklin Delano Roosevelt.

Q Which Japanese army defended the island of Okinawa in April 1945?

A The Thirty-Second Army.

Q Why did the Japanese government cancel all education for schoolchildren above the age of six in April 1945?

A So that the young could be redirected into war industries to provide a boost to the Japanese labor force.

Q From which illness did President Roosevelt suffer all his life?

A Polio.

DID YOU KNOW

A MAJOR CONTRIBUTING FACTOR TO THE BATTLEFIELD SUCCESS OF THE GERMAN ARMY IN WORLD WAR II WAS THE FACT THAT ITS OFFICER CORPS WAS TRAINED IN WHAT IS NOW KNOWN AS MISSION ANALYSIS, OR *AUFTRAGSTAKTIK*. GERMAN OFFICERS OF ALL RANKS WERE TRAINED TO BE ABLE TO FIGHT WITHOUT DETAILED ORDERS, TO MAKE DO WITH JUST A BRIEF STATEMENT OF THEIR COMMANDER'S INTENTIONS. THE COMMANDER TOLD HIS SUBORDINATES WHAT HE WANTED ACHIEVED, NOT HOW TO DO IT. SUBORDINATE OFFICERS WERE EXPECTED TO BE ABLE TO THINK ON THEIR FEET AND ADAPT THEIR BRIEF ORDERS TO MEET THE REQUIREMENTS OF THE SITUATION ON THE GROUND.

DID YOU KNOW

THE JAPANESE BATTLESHIP *YAMATO* HAD A TOTAL OF 145 25MM ANTI-AIRCRAFT GUNS FOR HER FINAL OPERATION, A SUICIDE MISSION AGAINST U.S. INVASION FORCES AROUND OKINAWA IN APRIL 1945. WITH ENOUGH FUEL FOR ONLY A ONE-WAY TRIP, *YAMATO* WAS SPOTTED BY U.S. AIRCRAFT WELL BEFORE SHE REACHED HER DESTINATION. AN ATTACK BY MORE THAN 400 U.S. CARRIER AIRCRAFT LED TO MORE THAN 20 BOMB AND TORPEDO HITS. AT 14:20 HOURS ON APRIL 7, HER MAGAZINE EXPLODED, RIPPING THE SHIP APART AND SENDING HER TO THE BOTTOM OF THE PACIFIC. A TOTAL OF 2,475 CREW WENT DOWN WITH HER.

Q **Was the British Royal Navy involved in the Okinawa operation?**

A Yes. A large British carrier force under Vice Admiral Sir Bernard Rawlings operated against enemy positions in the Sakishima group.

Q **Which British aircraft carrier was damaged by kamikaze aircraft off the coast of Okinawa in April 1945?**

A HMS *Indefatigable*.

Q **Who resigned as prime minister of Japan on April 5, 1945?**

A Koiso Kuniaki.

Q **Who replaced him?**

A The 78-year-old Admiral Suzuki Kantaro.

Q In early April 1945, the USSR informed Japan that it would not renew its five-year neutrality pact with Japan. Why?

A Moscow stated the change in policy was a consequence of the Japanese alliance with Germany.

Q In early April 1945, the U.S. First and Third Armies linked up at Lippstadt to complete the encirclement of which economically important German region?

A The Ruhr.

Q What were the gradations of the German Wound Badge?

A Black—for one or two wounds; Silver—for three or four wounds; and Gold—for five or more wounds.

Q Which German award consisted of a vertical oval wreath of oak-leaves with a skull and crossbones at its base, and in its center a hydra with a broad-bladed sword plunging through its center?

A The Anti-Partisan Badge.

Q What was Germany's equivalent of the U.S. Jeep?

A The Volkswagen Kübelwagen.

MY FÜHRER, I CONGRATULATE YOU!
ROOSEVELT IS DEAD
GOEBBELS TO HITLER, APRIL 1945

I'D GET UP EACH DAY AND
START DRINKING.
HOW ELSE COULD I
FIGHT THE WAR?
JOHN GARCIA, 7TH U.S. INFANTRY DIVISION,
APRIL 1945

Q What did the Soviet Tokarev 4M Model 1931 quadruple antiaircraft machine-gun mounting consist of?

A Four Maxim Model 1910 machine guns on a heavy pedestal mount with associated ammunition and water-cooling tank.

Q What type of vehicle was the Volkswagen Schwimmwagen?

A An amphibious jeep.

Q What was the German SdKfz 234/2 Puma?

A An eight-wheeled heavy armored car.

Q Which two Allied armies took part in the final campaign in Italy in the spring of 1945?

A The U.S. Fifth Army and the British Eighth Army.

Q Who was the Allied commander-in-chief in Italy in 1945?

A Field Marshal Harold Alexander.

Q Why did Hitler issue the decree on Demolitions on Reich Territory in March 1945?

A In response to the Soviets and Western Allies entering German territory.

Q What did this decree authorize?

A The destruction of "all military transport and communication facilities, industrial establishments, and supply depots, as well as anything else of value within Reich territory, which could in any way be used by the enemy immediately or within the foreseeable future for the prosecution of the war."

Q By what other name was the decree known?

A The Nero Order.

289

DID YOU KNOW

THE SCIENCE BEHIND THE ATOMIC BOMB IS RELATIVELY SIMPLE. A NEUTRAL NEUTRON PARTICLE HITS THE NUCLEUS OF A URANIUM ATOM, WHICH SPLITS INTO TWO FRAGMENTS: A KRYPTON ATOM AND A BARIUM ATOM. THE REACTION ALSO RELEASES AN ENORMOUS BURST OF ENERGY. ONE OR TWO FRESH NEUTRONS ARE RELEASED, SOME OF WHICH FIND OTHER NUCLEAR TARGETS AND REPEAT THE PROCESS. EACH SPLITTING OR "FISSION" CAUSES MORE—THE CHAIN REACTION. A RAPID CHAIN REACTION BECOMES A NUCLEAR EXPLOSION. HOWEVER, URANIUM HAS SEVERAL ISOTOPES, AND THE TRICK IS TO FIND A WAY OF ISOLATING THE URANIUM ISOTOPE U-235, WHICH HAS THE HIGHEST ENERGY FACTOR FOR THE DEVELOPMENT OF NUCLEAR POWER.

Q The final campaign in Italy centered on control of which valley?

A The Po Valley.

Q How did the Allies plan to defeat the Germans in Italy in the spring of 1945?

A The Eighth Army would attack westward through the Argenta Gap, while the Fifth Army would strike north, west of Bologna, thereby trapping the forces of the German Army Group C between the two.

Q Who commanded the British Fourteenth Army in Burma in 1945?

"IT SEEMS TO BE THE MOST TERRIBLE THING EVER DISCOVERED, BUT IT CAN BE THE MOST USEFUL
PRESIDENT HARRY S. TRUMAN ON THE ATOMIC BOMB, JULY 1945**"**

A General William Slim.

Q In Waffen-SS service, who were *SS-Helferinnen*?

A Female auxiliaries. They undertook clerical and administrative tasks.

Q What was the purpose of the SS-Kriegsberichter?

A This unit provided positive propaganda for Waffen-SS troops. Its members were in effect war correspondents.

DID YOU KNOW

BY LATE 1944, THE U.S. HAD MADE AMPHIBIOUS LANDINGS A FINE ART, HAVING LEARNT PAINFUL LESSONS ABOUT ISSUES SUCH AS BEACH RECONNAISSANCE AND THE EFFECTIVENESS OF NAVAL BOMBARDMENTS AT TARAWA AND SAIPAN. GENERAL MACARTHUR EMPLOYED AMPHIBIOUS WARFARE NIMBLY AT A TACTICAL LEVEL, USING SIMULTANEOUS MULTIPLE LANDINGS TO TRAP JAPANESE TROOPS OR BYPASSING HEAVILY DEFENDED JAPANESE POSITIONS BY LEAPFROGGING DOWN A COASTLINE. THE JAPANESE LEARNT EQUALLY PAINFUL LESSONS ABOUT U.S. AMPHIBIOUS SUPERIORITY, AND AT OKINAWA IN APRIL 1945 THEY DID NOT MAKE A COSTLY DEFENSE OF THE BEACHES BUT WITHDREW INTO THE INTERIOR WHERE THEY INFLICTED MASSIVE CASUALTIES ON THE AMERICANS. THE LESSON CAME TOO LATE, HOWEVER, AND U.S. AMPHIBIOUS TACTICS TOOK THE ALLIES TO THE VERY DOORSTEP OF THE JAPANESE HOMELANDS.

Q The German SdKfz 7 halftrack was used to tow which artillery pieces?

A The 105mm and 150mm howitzers and the 88mm Flak gun.

Q What were the "Shuri Line" defenses?

A A string of heavy Japanese defensive positions on Okinawa. These positions stretched across the island for roughly 24,000 ft (7,315 m) and included interlocking trench and pillbox systems, blockhouses, fortified caves, and strongly constructed bunkers.

Q Who took over when President Roosevelt died in April 1945?

A Vice President Harry S. Truman.

DID YOU KNOW

WHEN THE SOVIETS REACHED BERLIN, THEY EMBARKED ON AN ORGY OF LOOTING AND RAPE. WHY? FIRST, THE GERMAN ARMY HAD COMMITTED ENORMOUS ATROCITIES IN THE SOVIET UNION, INCLUDING THE DELIBERATE MASSACRE OF CIVILIANS. MANY SOVIET TROOPS HAD SEEN AT FIRST HAND THE RESULTS OF GERMAN POLICIES WHEN THEY LIBERATED CONCENTRATION CAMPS. SOVIET PROPAGANDA AND POLITICAL COMMISSARS STRESSED CONTINUALLY THAT THE RED ARMY WAS FIGHTING "FASCIST BEASTS," WHO DESERVED NO MERCY FOR THE CRIMES THEY HAD COMMITTED ON SOVIET SOIL. THIS HAD THE EFFECT OF FURTHER INFURIATING SOLDIERS WHO WERE ALREADY THIRSTING FOR VENGEANCE. ALTHOUGH THE FRONTLINE SOVIET TROOPS WERE GENERALLY WELL DISCIPLINED, MANY RED ARMY SOLDIERS, ESPECIALLY IN SUPPORT UNITS, CAME FROM AREAS OF CRUSHING POVERTY, PARTICULARLY THOSE FROM SIBERIA AND THE ASIATIC REPUBLICS. WHEN THEY GOT TO GERMANY, THEY WERE DETERMINED TO TAKE WHAT THEY COULD. FINALLY, THE SEARING EXPERIENCE OF COMBAT ON THE EASTERN FRONT MADE MANY RED ARMY SOLDIERS "LIVE FOR THE MOMENT," INDULGING THEMSELVES WHENEVER THEY HAD THE OPPORTUNITY (PRIVATES, NCOs, AND JUNIOR OFFICERS WERE, MOSTLY, YOUNG MEN IN THEIR PHYSICAL AND SEXUAL PRIME).

Q Which famous U.S. war correspondent was killed in the Pacific theater in mid-April 1945?

A Ernie Pyle.

Q How was he killed?

A He was shot by a Japanese sniper.

Q Which capital city fell to the Red Army in mid-April 1945?

A Vienna.

Q Which Soviet fronts took part in the Berlin Offensive that began on April 16, 1945?

A The 1st Belorussian, 2nd Belorussian, and 1st Ukrainian Fronts. Their combined strength was 2.5 million troops, 41,000 artillery pieces, 6,200 tanks and assault guns, 100,000 motor vehicles, and 7,200 aircraft.

Q What were the German formations that defended Berlin against the offensive?

A Army Group Vistula (Third Panzer and Ninth Armies with LVI Panzer Corps in reserve—200,000 troops, 750 tanks and assault guns, and 1,500 artillery pieces) and the northern flank of Army Group Center (Fourth Panzer Army—100,000 troops and 200 tanks and assault guns).

Q Who commanded the Soviet 2nd Belorussian Front in 1945?

A Konstantin Rokossovsky.

Q Who commanded the Soviet 1st Belorussian Front during the Berlin Offensive?

A Georgi Zhukov.

" NO ONE KNEW WHAT HAD
HAPPENED. A HUGE FORCE
HAD BEEN RELEASED
ABOVE OUR HEADS
TATSUICHIRO AKIZUKI, RESIDENT OF NAGASAKI,
AUGUST 9, 1945 "

Q Why did Hitler order the arrest of SS chief Heinrich Himmler at the end of April 1945?

A He had been attempting to broker a peace deal with the Allies.

Q Who were the two key individuals who brought an end to the fighting in Italy at the end of April 1945?

A Karl Wolff, senior commander of the SS and Police in Italy, and Allen Dulles, head of the American Office of Strategic Services (OSS) in Switzerland. As a result of dealings between the two, Wolff and General Heinrich von Vietinghoff, German commander-in-chief in Italy, signed the instrument of unconditional surrender in northern Italy. The Swiss, the Allies, and many Germans and Italians in Italy had been concerned about a drawn-out campaign in Hitler's "Alpine Fortress," and the probable destruction of north Italy's industry.

" YOU MAY SAFELY CALL
ME FRAU HITLER
EVA BRAUN TO A MAID, APRIL 1945 "

Q On what date did Adolf Hitler commit suicide?

A April 30, 1945.

Q How did he end his life?

A He shot himself. His wife, Eva Braun, also killed herself at the same time by taking poison. Their bodies were then taken outside and cremated by the SS.

DID YOU KNOW

ON JULY 16, 1945, THE FIRST ATOMIC BOMB WAS EXPLODED AT ALAMOGORDO, NEW MEXICO, PRODUCING A BLAST THE EQUIVALENT OF 20,000 TONS (20,320 TONNES) OF TNT, SENDING A MUSHROOM CLOUD 40,000 FT (12,200 M) INTO THE AIR AND FUSING THE DESERT SAND INTO GLASS. THE U.S., HAVING ULTIMATELY INVESTED TWO BILLION DOLLARS IN THE MANHATTAN PROJECT, NOW HAD ITS ATOMIC BOMB.

Q **Why did Allied and German representatives meet in western Holland on April 28, 1945?**

A The Reichskommissar for the Netherlands, Arthur Seyss Inquart, had offered the Allies the freedom to import food and coal into German-occupied western Holland to alleviate the plight of the civilian population if they would halt their forces. This led to a cessation of hostilities and saved the country from the ravages of further fighting.

Q **Who captured Italian dictator Benito Mussolini as he attempted to flee to Austria at the end of April 1945?**

A Italian partisans.

Q **Who was captured with him?**

A His mistress, Claretta Petacci.

Q **What happened to them after their capture?**

A On the orders of the Committee of National Liberation, Walter Audisio, a communist member of the Volunteer Freedom Corps, shot them both. Their mutilated bodies were later hung up in the Piazzale Loreto, Milan.

Q Which German general surrendered Berlin to the Red Army on May 2, 1945?

A General Weidling, commander of the Berlin garrison.

Q Josef Goebbels and his wife Magda killed themselves rather than be taken prisoner by the Soviets. But who did they kill first?

A Their six children.

Q Who did Hitler nominate as his immediate successor?

A Admiral Karl Dönitz.

DID YOU KNOW

WITH THE ALLIES ON THE RHINE AND SOVIETS AT THE GATES OF BERLIN IN THE SPRING OF 1945, HITLER ORDERED THE GERMAN POPULATION TO BE MOBILIZED EN MASSE FOR A FINAL *GÖTTERDÄMMERUNG*. THE GERMAN PEOPLE WOULD EMERGE VICTORIOUS OR DIE FIGHTING, DECLARED THE FÜHRER. DESPAIRING OF THE WEHRMACHT AND EVEN THE WAFFEN-SS, HE TURNED TO THE NAZI PARTY TO RAISE, ORGANIZE, EQUIP, AND LEAD THE NEW *VOLKSSTURM* MILITIA. OFTEN COMPARED TO THE BRITISH HOME GUARD, THE *VOLKSSTURM* WAS A SIMILAR DESPERATE MEASURE. OLD MEN, BOYS, AND FOREIGN REFUGEES WERE THROWN TOGETHER WITH FEW WEAPONS AND LITTLE IDEA HOW TO USE THEM, WHILE MANY OF THE LOCAL NAZI LEADERS OF THE *VOLKSSTURM* HAD LITTLE MILITARY EXPERIENCE. ACCORDING TO COLONEL GENERAL HEINZ GUDERIAN: "THE BRAVE MEN OF THE *VOLKSSTURM*, PREPARED TO MAKE ANY SACRIFICE, WERE IN MANY CASES DRILLED BUSILY IN THE PROPER WAY OF GIVING THE HITLER SALUTE, INSTEAD OF BEING TRAINED IN THE USE OF WEAPONS OF WHICH THEY HAD NO PREVIOUS EXPERIENCE."

" IT IS UNTRUE THAT I, OR ANYBODY ELSE IN
GERMANY, WANTED WAR
IN 1939
HITLER'S "POLITICAL TESTAMENT," APRIL 1945 **"**

Q **What was the Nazi Werewolf organization?**

A A stay-behind resistance organization formed to continue the fight even after the Allies and Soviets had occupied Germany.

Q **Who were its members?**

A Only fanatical Nazis were allowed to join.

Q **What was the German E-100 vehicle?**

A A super-heavy tank.

Q **Which vehicle was it intended to replace?**

A The Tiger II (King Tiger).

Q **What was its main armament?**

A A 128mm cannon. Work on this vehicle was at a very early stage when the war ended.

Q In the Pacific theater, what was Operation Dracula in May 1945?

A The capture of Rangoon, Burma. On May 1, soldiers of the Gurkha Parachute Battalion were dropped south of the city, with a landing of the 26th Indian Division in the Gulf of Martaban on May 2. Rangoon was caught in a pincer movement between the southern advance and the 17th Indian Division advancing down from the north, which reached Pegu —40 miles (64 km) from Rangoon—on May 2. The Japanese in Rangoon realized their position was untenable and abandoned the city.

Q In one day—May 5—17 U.S. ships were sunk off Okinawa by mass kamikaze attacks. True or false?

A True.

> ETERNAL GLORY TO THE HEROES WHO FELL
> IN THE FIGHTING FOR THE
> ## FREEDOM AND INDEPENDENCE
> ## OF THE MOTHERLAND
> JOSEPH STALIN, MAY 9, 1945

Q On the same day the U.S. suffered its first civilian fatalities of the Pacific war. True or false?

A True. A Japanese bomb balloon, one of the hundreds released in the Pacific weeks earlier, killed six U.S. civilians—a teacher and five children—in Oregon.

Q How did U.S. forces at Okinawa celebrate the end of the war in Europe on May 9, 1945?

A In celebration of the final unconditional surrender of Germany, every U.S. naval gun and artillery piece on and around Okinawa fired a single shell at Japanese positions.

DID YOU KNOW

MICHINOMIYA HIROHITO (1901–1989) WAS THE LONGEST-REIGNING MONARCH IN JAPANESE HISTORY, TAKING THE THRONE IN 1926 AND KEEPING IT UNTIL HIS DEATH IN 1989. ALTHOUGH THE FIGUREHEAD OF JAPANESE POWER, WITH A QUASI-DIVINE STATUS AMONG HIS PEOPLE, HIROHITO'S CONTROL OVER THE EVENTS THAT LED TO WAR WAS LIMITED, DE FACTO POWER RESIDING IN THE CONTROL OF THE JAPANESE STATE BY THE MILITARY ESTABLISHMENT. RECENT RESEARCH HAS SHOWN THAT HIROHITO WAS ACTUALLY OPPOSED BOTH TO AN ALLIANCE WITH GERMANY AND ITALY IN THE TRIPARTITE PACT, AND TO THE JAPANESE WAR WITH THE U.S. HIDEKI TOJO WAS THE TRUE INSTIGATOR OF THE PACIFIC WAR, AND IT WAS HE WHO REJECTED A NOTE FROM PRESIDENT ROOSEVELT ON DECEMBER 6, 1941, THAT ATTEMPTED TO AVERT A CONFLICT. FOLLOWING THE DEVASTATION OF HIROSHIMA AND NAGASAKI BY ATOMIC BOMBS, HIROHITO BROKE WITH IMPERIAL PRECEDENT (TRADITIONALLY, THE EMPEROR IS PUBLICLY SILENT) AND ANNOUNCED ON RADIO ON AUGUST 15, 1945, THAT JAPAN WOULD ACCEPT THE U.S. DEMAND FOR UNCONDITIONAL SURRENDER. IN A FURTHER STEP, ON JANUARY 1, 1946, HE ANNOUNCED TO THE JAPANESE PEOPLE THAT THERE WAS NO DIVINE STATUS IN HIS OFFICE OR PERSON. BY SO DOING, AND FOR HIS ROLE IN CLOSING THE JAPANESE RESISTANCE, HIROHITO MANAGED TO ESCAPE ALLIED WAR CRIME TRIALS.

Q "Conical Hill" and "Sugar Loaf Hill" were fought over on which Pacific Island?

A Okinawa.

Q In May 1945 Chinese Nationalist troops captured the city of Nanning. Why was this so decisive?

A Nanning was only 80 miles (128 km) from the border of Indochina, and its loss meant that the Japanese Army in China was cut off from its forces in Burma, Thailand, Indochina, and Malaya.

> **CEASE FIRING, BUT IF ANY ENEMY PLANES APPEAR, SHOOT THEM DOWN IN A FRIENDLY FASHION**
>
> WILLIAM F. HALSEY, MESSAGE TO THE U.S. THIRD FLEET, JAPAN, AUGUST 15, 1945

Q What caused large-scale damage to the U.S. fleet off Okinawa on June 5, 1945?

A A huge typhoon. Thirty-five ships were damaged, including four battleships and eight carriers.

Q Name the two senior Japanese commanders who committed suicide as the battle for Okinawa drew to a close.

A The commander of the Japanese naval base on Okinawa, Admiral Minoru Ota, and the overall Japanese commander, Lieutenant General Ushijima Mitsuru.

Q The commander of the U.S. Tenth Army was also killed on the island. Who was he?

A Lieutenant General Simon B. Buckner.

Q Estimate Japanese and American losses incurred during the battle for Okinawa.

A The Japanese lost 100,000 dead, and nearly 7,500 Japanese soldiers surrendered. U.S. losses were 7,613 U.S. Marines and U.S. Army infantry killed, and 31,807 wounded. In addition, the U.S. Navy lost 4,900 seamen with 36 vessels sunk and 368 damaged. The air war over Okinawa was equally bitter. Japanese aviation losses numbered 8,000; 4,000 of these shot down in combat. U.S. aviation lost a total of 763 aircraft.

INDEX

303

WORLD WAR II TRIVIA BOOK